CONTEMPORARY SPIRITUALITY
FOR AN
EVOLVING WORLD

"Nicolya Christi writes with the soul of a mystic, the mind of an evolutionary, and the heart of a lover of life itself. She brings forth the agenda for human conscious evolution—social and beyond—to guide us toward the next era of our evolution. . . . This book is magnificent, a labor of love and a gift to us all."

BARBARA MARX HUBBARD, AUTHOR OF *BIRTH 2012 AND BEYOND* AND PRESIDENT OF THE FOUNDATION FOR CONSCIOUS EVOLUTION

"Every now and then a rare book comes along that synthesizes the key trends of an epoch and where we are headed. Such was Marlilyn Fergusons's *The Aquarian Conspiracy* in 1980. Nicolya Christi has achieved a similar tour de force by synthesizing the fields of spirituality, psychology, and personal development. One feels that her understanding of spirituality is something she has lived through, experienced, and felt in a manner we have rarely encountered in the contemporary literature."

PIERRE PRADERVAND, AUTHOR OF *THE GENTLE ART OF BLESSING* AND *MESSAGES OF LIFE FROM DEATH ROW*

"Nicolya Christi's new book is a roadmap that speaks to the authentic self within each of us. This rich and compelling book is a psychological tour de force for finding our way back to the wisdom of the Self. Nicolya Christi speaks from the intelligence of the heart in offering a crystal-clear vision of psycho-spiritual integration, the 'new human,' and the significance of Higher Love. This book is indispensable for anyone wishing to connect with a contemporary spirituality for an evolving world."

KINGSLEY L. DENNIS, AUTHOR OF *NEW CONSCIOUSNESS FOR A NEW WORLD* AND *STRUGGLE FOR YOUR MIND* AND COFOUNDER OF WORLDSHIFT INTERNATIONAL

"This book is beautiful. The chapter 'Contemporary Spirituality for an Evolving World' is revolutionary, thank God, and very, very timely. This book is about You. I highly recommend you read it."

REV. PETER OWEN-JONES, AUTHOR OF *BED OF NAILS* AND *LETTERS FROM AN EXTREME PILGRIM*

"Nicolya Christi is a bridge between the old world and the New Earth that is arising, and so is this—her latest book. It connects the reader to deep psychological and spiritual truths explored in simple, accessible concepts and language. It connects the mind and the heart, the inner and the outer life, and shows how we have imprisoned ourselves and how we can liberate ourselves. It will prove a blessing to all who enter its pages and apply the wisdom through their own heart's knowing, thus blessing all life."

WENDY WEBBER, CORE PROCESS PSYCHOTHERAPIST, TRAUMA RESOURCE FACILITATOR, COACH/MENTOR FOR PERSONAL AND ORGANIZATIONAL CHANGE, AND FOUNDING MEMBER OF THE VERMONT PEACE ACADEMY

CONTEMPORARY SPIRITUALITY
FOR AN
EVOLVING WORLD

A Handbook
for Conscious Evolution

NICOLYA CHRISTI

Bear & Company
Rochester, Vermont • Toronto, Canada

Bear & Company
One Park Street
Rochester, Vermont 05767
www.BearandCompanyBooks.com

SUSTAINABLE FORESTRY INITIATIVE   Certified Sourcing
www.sfiprogram.org
SFI-00854

Text stock is SFI certified

Bear & Company is a division of Inner Traditions International

Library of Congress Cataloging-in-Publication Data
Christi, Nicolya.
  Contemporary spirituality for an evolving world : a handbook for conscious
evolution / Nicolya Christi.
      p. cm.
  Summary: "A practical guide to conscious evolution for personal, spiritual, and
global transformation" — Provided by publisher.
  ISBN 978-1-59143-166-4 (pbk.) — ISBN 978-1-59143-843-4 (e-book)
  1. Spirituality—Miscellanea. 2. Spiritual life—Miscellanea. 3. Evolution—
Miscellanea. 4. Consciousness—Miscellanea. I. Title.
  BF1999.C5555 2013
  204—dc23
                                                          2013009987

Printed and bound in the United States by Lake Book Manufacturing, Inc.
The text stock is SFI certified. The Sustainable Forestry Initiative® program
promotes sustainable forest management.

10   9   8   7   6   5   4   3   2   1

Text design and layout by Virginia Scott Bowman
This book was typeset in Garamond Premier Pro, Gill Sans, and Legacy Sans with
Granjon and Helvetica used as display typefaces

To send correspondence to the author of this book, mail a first-class letter to the
author c/o Inner Traditions • Bear & Company, One Park Street, Rochester, VT
05767, and we will forward the communication, or contact the author directly at
www.nicolyachristi.com.

This book is dedicated to Mahatma Gandhi,
Omraam Mikhael Aivanhov,
and Thich Nhat Hanh.

Contents

The Gentle Art of Blessing

By Pierre Pradervand

On awakening, bless this day, for it is already full of unseen good, which your blessings will call forth: for to bless is to acknowledge the unlimited good that is embedded in the very texture of the universe and awaiting each and all.

On passing people in the street, on the bus, in places of work and play, bless them. The peace of your blessing will accompany them on their way and the aura of its gentle fragrance will be a light to their path.

On meeting and talking to people, bless them in their health, their work, their joy, their relationships to God, themselves, and others. Bless them in their abundance, their finances . . . bless them in every conceivable way, for such blessings not only sow seeds of healing but one day will spring forth as flowers of joy in the waste places of your own life.

As you walk, bless the city in which you live, its government and teachers, its nurses and street sweepers, its children and bankers, its priests and prostitutes. The minute anyone expresses the least aggression or unkindness to you, respond with a blessing: bless them totally, sincerely, joyfully, for such blessings are a shield that protects them from the ignorance of their misdeed and deflects the arrow that was aimed at you.

To bless means to wish, unconditionally, total, unrestricted good for others and events from the deepest wellspring in the innermost chamber of your heart: it means to hallow, to hold in reverence, to behold with utter awe that which is always a gift from the Creator. He who is hallowed by your blessing is set aside, consecrated, holy, whole. To bless is yet to invoke divine care upon, to think or speak gratefully for, to confer happiness upon—although we ourselves are never the one who bestows, but simply the joyful witnesses of Life's abundance.

To bless all without discrimination of any sort is the ultimate form of giving, because those you bless will never know from whence came the sudden ray of sun that burst through the clouds of their skies, and you will rarely be a witness to the sunlight in their lives.

When something goes completely askew in your day, some unexpected event knocks down your plans and you, too, also burst into blessing: for life is teaching you a lesson, and the very event you believe to be unwanted, you yourself called forth so as to learn the lesson you might balk against were you not to bless it. Trials are blessings in disguise and hosts of angels follow in their path.

To bless is to acknowledge the omnipresent, universal beauty hidden to material eyes; it is to activate that law of attraction, which, from the furthest reaches of the universe, will bring into your life exactly what you need to experience and enjoy.

When you pass a prison, mentally bless its inmates in their innocence and freedom, their gentleness, pure essence, and unconditional forgiveness: for one can only be prisoner of one's self-image, and a free man can walk unshackled in the courtyard of a jail, just as citizens of countries where freedom reigns can be prisoners when fear lurks in their thoughts.

When you pass a hospital, bless its patients in their present wholeness, for even in their suffering this wholeness awaits in them to be discovered. When your eyes behold a man in tears, or seemingly broken by life, bless him in his vitality and joy: for the material senses present but the inverted image of the ultimate splendor and perfection, which only the inner eye beholds.

It is impossible to bless and to judge at the same time. So hold constantly as a deep, hallowed, intoned thought that desire to bless, for truly then shall you become a peacemaker, and one day you shall, everywhere, behold the very face of God.

P. S. And of course, above all, don't forget to bless the utterly beautiful person *you* are!

PIERRE PRADERVAND has worked for decades in personal development and social justice. His impressive career includes work on nearly every continent. As a speaker and workshop facilitator, Pierre often gives talks on how to live a more enriched and centered life. This opening blessing is from his book *The Gentle Art of Blessing: A Simple Practice That Will Transform You and Your World.*

Foreword

By Ervin Laszlo

We are approaching a critical tipping point of human life on this planet, and we need guidance. Our future is at stake: the destiny of the biosphere's grand experiment with a species capable of consciousness. Such a species not only experiences the world, it also experiences itself in the world. And it can make a fateful mistake: it can conceive of itself as separate from the world.

This mistake puts the entire experiment with a conscious species at risk. It can put at risk not only the species that embodies the experiment, but the whole web of life in which the experiment takes place.

A conscious species can make the fateful mistake of separateness, the mistake known as duality. But it can also rectify that mistake and recover—more exactly, rediscover—its fundamental unity. Herein lies the crux of the problem, and the crux of its solution. Humankind has lost the instinctive, intuitive oneness in which other species are embedded. It cannot go back to its instinctive, intuitive oneness because a higher level of consciousness, once evolved, cannot be put on hold; it colors everything that is experienced. The way forward is not a return to the previous intuitive state of oneness, but the conscious rediscovery of that oneness. This rediscovery is not uniquely prompted by reasoning but does include the realization that it is objectively, factually needed.

There are two ways to move toward rediscovering our oneness with the world rather than just one. One way is offered by science: the way of careful observation and logical reasoning. This is the way that highlights the objective need for a higher level of oneness. When we look at our condition in the biosphere in the framework of science's observations and discoveries, we see that the web of life constitutes a vast, organically interconnected, and basically coherent system. However, on a closer look we find that this system has become partially incoherent. It harbors an incoherent element that disturbs and partially destroys its basic harmony: it is a species that evolved a higher form of consciousness thirty or perhaps even fifty thousand years ago.

The species itself is much older, its origins reaching back five million years or more. But the kind of consciousness that can make the mistake of separateness is of far more recent origin. The mistake rendered possible by a more highly evolved, but apparently not sufficiently highly evolved, consciousness is that of thinking of itself as the sole distinctly conscious species in the biosphere, surrounded by other species that have a lesser consciousness, or possibly no consciousness at all. The others merely serve the needs and obey the dictates of this species. Acting on this belief gives rise to behaviors that damage the integrity of the system of life: it suboptimizes it by favoring one of its elements over the rest.

If behavior prompted by the mistaken belief of separateness is not corrected, it could damage and ultimately destroy the delicate balances that alone can ensure the persistence of higher forms of life on the planet. These balances are of critical importance because the system of life, and all its elements, persists in the physically improbable state far from thermal and chemical equilibrium—a state that requires constant replenishment of the energy degraded by its use with fresh free energy, thereby maintaining the high level of negative entropy that is the precondition of life.

Maintaining a species in the living state calls for both the cooperation and coherence of all its elements, and the coherence of all its elements with the rest of the biosphere's suprasystem. It calls for the condition known as *supercoherence*—the coherence of systems that are already coherent within themselves.

The mistaken perception of duality introduces incoherence into the system. The species that commits this mistake is a threat to itself and it is a threat to the entire web of life on the planet. Hence there is an urgent and objective need for the species to reestablish its coherence within the supercoherent web of life. If it fails to do so, it becomes a cancer that only multiplies itself without regard for the persistence and development of the rest of the system. In the end it destroys its host, and so destroys itself.

The realization of the objective requirement for coherence is one path toward regaining our lost coherence: the path of science-based rediscovery. There is also another path: the path of direct, lived experience. This is to experience oneness as a fundamental aspect of our life experience—a basic correlate of human existence. This kind of experience is branded extrascientific in the modern world and is relegated to the shadowy world of spirituality, religion, and esotericism.

Yet it is a real experience, one that has accompanied the human species throughout its cultural history. It leads to the same insight as the scientific approach: the insight of fundamental interconnection between our species and the web of life on this planet. This insight is expressed as coherence in science and as oneness in the spiritual domain. When it comes to inspiring and informing behavior, the two approaches are of equal relevance, and in regard to rediscovery of our coherence and oneness with the world, they are of equal importance.

Nicolya Christi is endowed with the precious ability to experience oneness as a lived element of conscious experience. She describes the nature of this experience and offers guidance to others for achieving it. Or, if they have already achieved it, she offers guidance for communicating it so that still others can experience it as well.

The information offered in her book is a precious guide for everyone concerned with our chances of meeting the challenge of surviving and thriving on this planet. It could prove to be as effective in changing and inspiring people's behavior as the information conveyed through the method of science. Nicolya Christi's way conveys the direct experience of oneness: the experience of connection, communication, and even communion with the cosmos.

In my own research, lecturing, and writings, I have attempted to convey the argument for coherence provided by the application of the method of science. Now it gives me great pleasure to write a foreword to a book that highlights the power of spiritual experience for achieving basically the same end. Science and spirituality, far from being mutually distrustful and often warring opponents, are partners in the great search for finding the way that brings our aberrant species back into the embrace of oneness and coherence. Achieving this supreme goal calls for a further evolution of human consciousness: the evolution of a holistic, planetary consciousness. If a half-evolved consciousness led modern civilization astray, a further evolved planetary consciousness can lead postmodern civilization back to the path—the same path that is highlighted by scientific reason and evidenced by genuine spiritual experience.

ERVIN LASZLO, twice nominated for the Nobel Peace Prize, is editor of the international periodical *World Futures: The Journal of General Evolution* and Chancellor-Designate of the newly formed Global*Shift* University. He is the founder and president of the international think tanks the Club of Budapest and the General Evolution Research Group and the author of eighty-three books translated into twenty-one languages.

Acknowledgments

I begin by offering a heartfelt thank you to Ervin Laszlo for writing the foreword of this book. I would also like to offer my deep appreciation and gratitude to my good friend Pierre Pradervand for his beautiful "Gentle Art of Blessing," which I have chosen as the opening blessing for this book.

I would also like to thank Barbara Marx Hubbard, Pierre Pradervand, Rev. Peter Owen-Jones, Kingsley Dennis, and Wendy Webber for their endorsements of this book.

I would like to offer my gratitude to Cherry Williams for the editing of this book. I offer my deep appreciation to Kingsley Dennis for his written contribution in chapter 9. My deep heartfelt gratitude goes to Wendy Webber for her written contributions included in chapter 9 and the appendices. I extend my gratitude to Matteo Baronti for his rendering of the Psycho-Spiritual Pyramids of Humanity in chapter 2. I offer gratitude to Padma Aon for his permission to publish the discourses between us, which can be found in the appendices. I offer my deep gratitude to David Woolfson, whose unconditional support has made it possible for me to continue with this work.

I also wish to offer my gratitude and love to all those, too numerous to mention, who have been a part of my own journey of psychological, conscious, and spiritual awakening and evolution.

Finally, I would like to thank my publishers, Inner Traditions (Bear & Company), for choosing to publish this, my second mainstream book. I was blessed enough that they published my first, *2012: A Clarion Call.*

I am very comfortable in the Inner Traditions stable for they seek to be truly aligned with new paradigm consciousness and so serve as torch bearers for this in the world of publishing.

Love in Light Waves.

NICOLYA CHRISTI

Introduction

What then is most truly transformative? Is it merely a matter of changing one's clothes or hairstyle, or joining up with some group that hopes its message will change the world? Could it be simply a matter of receiving the ultimate mantra or initiation; learning to perform the proper rite or ritual; finding out how to meditate; doing yoga, praying, breathing, chanting; having cosmic sex; going to the Himalayas, Jerusalem, Mecca, Machu Picchu, Mount Kailash, Mount Shasta; or meeting the right guru? I don't think so.

Or, is it not most transformative, most earthshaking, to pierce the veils of self-deception and illusion, and crack the eggshell of ignorance to most intimately encounter oneself? Through honest self-inquiry and no-holds-barred meditative introspection over a sustained period of time, one can take apart and deconstruct the hut that ego built, thus entering the mansion of Authentic Being.

LAMA SURYA DAS, *AWAKENING THE BUDDHA WITHIN*

Today is a new day. Here you stand holding this book that has been written to support and facilitate your psychological, conscious, and spiritual evolution. This in turn will automatically serve to support the psychological, conscious, and spiritual evolution of the collective.

Today is a good day for awakening, for opening, and for evolving.

Today offers a wonderful opportunity to acquaint yourself more intimately with who you truly are. Opening the pages of this book could prove to make this day the first day of the rest of your life.

The following quote, by someone who wished to remain anonymous, is a wonderful thought to ponder on: "If you are looking for a happy ending and cannot find one, find a new beginning instead." This book is that new beginning for those who have outgrown waiting for the happy ending that never seems to arrive. It is for all those who are now ready to reach out and seek a new beginning for themselves.

Many teachings and words of great wisdom from visionaries, including Jesus, Buddha, Thich Nhat Hanh, and Gandhi, are to be found scattered throughout this book. There are core teachings from a cross section of established spiritual practices and religions, including great wisdom from Jung, Abraham Maslow, Carl Rogers, Lama Surya Das, Pema Chodron, and Wendy Webber.

You will find in chapter 3 the first-ever written account, by me, of a self-development model originated by the First Nations Peoples, which they termed the "Seven Dark, Seven Light, and Seven Rainbow Arrows." I have added the subtitle, "A Map for Evolving Consciousness."

This book also contains a fairytale I wrote in chapter 6 about Ego and Self titled aptly, "Ego/Self: A Fairytale." It calls into question everything that religion and most spiritual practices have stated about the ego and introduces a pioneering approach that encourages the type of relationship with the ego that is more fitting for the twenty-first-century human being and a contemporary spirituality. Spiritual and psychological institutions, practices, and practitioners across the board, including psychotherapists, psychologists, psychiatrists, Buddhists, Christians, Hindus, and the layperson, have contacted me to state how the approach illustrated by the Ego/Self fairytale is a groundbreaking, exciting, and liberating one. It is unlike anything they have been taught or discovered and is an approach that makes more sense to them than anything they have previously learned or read.

You will find in the appendices a profoundly important piece written by Wendy Webber, which proposes that all trauma is the result of empathic disconnection. In my opinion this is one of the most important insights ever to have arisen from the field of psychotherapy. When I first read this paper a few years ago, I deeply resonated with all that it shares—the simple, direct, and yet profound understanding it brings to the psychological arena. It is an essential read and simply had to be included in this book to complete the psychological support and understanding that is contained here. In the appendices you will also find further specific and important models and teachings for psychological, conscious, and spiritual evolution.

Be assured, this book will facilitate an evolutionary shift within your consciousness. Read it with an open heart and mind as well as a sincere desire to evolve, find deep and lasting peace, free yourself from the past, and become the incredible being that you truly are.

So, dear friends, take a deep breath and have pens and writing pads at the ready.

Let us begin.

ONE

Consciousness

For self-actualization to become possible it requires just one thing—a conscious desire to evolve.

Conscious awakening stimulates an evolutionary trajectory from ego to I—I to I Am—I Am to I AM—I AM to God/Source/Creator.

NICOLYA CHRISTI

WHAT IS CONSCIOUSNESS AND HOW DO WE DEFINE IT?

The exploration of just what consciousness is dates back for millennia.

The question of what consciousness is has been explored by indigenous peoples, ancient cultures and civilizations, and every mystery school in human history. In modern times, science and religion have also been preoccupied with this existential question. Yet, a definitive universal understanding of what consciousness is still does not exist.

A rational approach explains that consciousness is a function of knowing, a continuous process of thought and awareness. It seems that a division of thought exists between cognitive science, which views consciousness as a neurological phenomenon contained within the brain, and spirituality, which suggests consciousness to be a multidimensional phenomenon that exists both within and beyond the individual.

If we adhere to the spiritual explanation of what constitutes consciousness, we can ascertain that the degree to which our consciousness is awakened determines the evolution of the soul. It is said that to some extent consciousness is influenced by our social environment and conditioning, which has its role in supporting us to awaken and evolve. The conscious mind is an aspect of consciousness but not consciousness itself. However, inner and outer experiences shape, influence, and evolve an individual's consciousness.

Consciousness can also be described as an experience of gnosis—a deep and certain inner knowing that arises from the depths of our Being. Gnosis means to know, but without knowing how we know, since this level of knowing is unlearned.

An expanded view of consciousness acknowledges the presence of the *I* within that experiences multidimensionally. Consciousness includes altered states, paranormal occurrences, out-of-body experiences, and heightened states of awareness created by meditation and prayer or psychotropic substances, channeling, visions, and ESP (extrasensory perception). Indeed the whole range of esoteric, metaphysical, and spiritual experiences can awaken, raise, and expand consciousness.

Rational thought is incapable of defining consciousness and even our basic capacity of perception makes the definition of consciousness elusive. Consciousness is a paradox. It is both the expression of many levels of existence of being yet, at the same time, it is all one expression.

Following unending explorations and experiments in the quest to define consciousness, quantum physicists have scientifically proven that it can and does affect matter existing beyond the boundaries of the physical body. H. W. Percival, author of *Thinking and Destiny* (1946), wrote of his own experiences when in an altered state of consciousness. Percival perceived himself to be conscious on another level known as the *Buddhic plane*. It was while in this heightened state of consciousness that a book was "dictated" to him. Percival went on to explain:

> Consciousness is the ultimate, the final Reality. Consciousness is that by the presence of which all things are conscious. Mystery of

all mysteries, it is beyond comprehension. Without it nothing can be conscious; no one could think; no being, no entity, no force, no unit, could perform any function. Yet Consciousness itself performs no function: it does not act in any way; it is a presence, everywhere. Although there are countless degrees in being conscious, there are no degrees of Consciousness. Consciousness has no properties, no qualities, no attributes; it does not possess; it cannot be possessed. Consciousness never began; it cannot cease to be.

Consciousness transcends all space and time. It is the source of our Being—it is All of Existence, All that Is, God, Creator, Source, Divinity. It is the true domain of individual, collective, galactic, and universal Truth: our spiritual home and the dimension from which we originate and to which we shall return.

In quantum field theory, consciousness denotes the zero-point field, which contains fleeting electromagnetic waves and particles that pop into and out of existence. Quantum scientists continue to research and make groundbreaking discoveries about the correlation between the consciousness of humanity and its impact on what they term the zero-point field.

Recently, I came to realize that individual human consciousness is also impacting the zero point within the Self. I include my thoughts here as I feel this merits a mention.

ARRIVAL AT ZERO POINT

Many, many conscious individuals have the feeling that the structure of their lives is breaking down. This reflects what is taking place within the collective and the old world paradigm. Many, many of us are immersed in this breaking down of the old at a personal level, and thus we are a reflection of the process that is taking place within the collective. We are fully aligned with and experiencing the shift. We have arrived at zero point in our own evolutionary development.

Having arrived at this point in our own lives, we now need to hold a clear vision of an emerging new world. It is equally important to hold our personal vision for our new life and how this will be expressed in a new world paradigm.

For those of us who feel like we are being stripped to the core and find ourselves standing naked, without possessions, attachments, any practical knowledge of just where we will find ourselves, or whatever else may have occurred to pull the proverbial rug from under our feet, know this—we have arrived at zero point.

The compass of the old paradigm has broken. It is the energy of zero point that we must now use to manifest our dreams. We need to use this time to become very clear as to exactly what it is that we wish to manifest, what life experience we choose for our immediate future— a future that we may more appropriately and accurately term the *Now*. And if that vision shows us an entirely different reality from the life we have been living, the work we have been doing, and how we have been relating to others, then we must now focus our attention on the manifestation of this different reality. Hold the vision you have uncovered or discovered, no matter how it may contradict the experience of your life to date or go against your expectations of yourself or the expectations of other people.

The process of being stripped to the core during these recent years—most especially since 1999 at the time of the total solar eclipse at 11:11 a.m. (GMT) on August 11, 1999—began, according to the Maya, a thirteen-year initiation for humanity, which they termed the *Quickening*. During this window of time leading to December 21, 2012, human conscious evolution would undergo an exponential shift that would bring revelatory insights and an accurate vision of ourselves in a new and higher vibrating paradigm, post-2012.

Humanity is in a time of great transition, and because of this we find that we are also transcending our old selves. All time lines are converging, including those within, and because of this we are no longer a product of our past, nor are we a random outcome of our future. We are—Now.

It is the reality of the Now that we must hold to, a reality that is clearly exposing that the need for *doing* is falling away; replaced instead by the greater need to *be*. It has been said by many, including myself, that 2012 was the final year of the "rescuing" mentality whether this applies to our relationships or our work. Our focus on saving, striving, sacrificing, and suffering, in addition to our being swept along with an all pervading sense of intensity regarding the pace of our lives and experiences, is falling away to be replaced by a deep felt need to reconnect with ourselves and with nature, to embody peace and *be* love by way of our very presence.

We are becoming. We are shifting from doing to being, from words to presence, from talking of the shift to being the shift in all our interactions and exchanges. The time is upon us to no longer talk the talk, but walk the walk. The year 2012 was the bridge between the old and New, past and Future, personality and Soul, head and Heart, doing and Being.

Rejoice and celebrate uncertainty, confusion, disorientation, the breaking down of close relationships, the experience of everything falling away, of shattered belief systems, of concrete plans changing or crumbling at the very last minute, knowing that you have arrived at the most significant crossroads of your evolutionary journey to date—zero point.

You are a reflection of the collective and planetary process that was taking place throughout 2012, as prophesied by ancient wisdomkeepers and foretold by astronomy, astrology, and quantum science. It seems that those who are reaching zero point were not able to move through 2012 without entirely perplexing and unexpected occurrences taking place within their personal experiences. Within 2012 was a crescendo, a peak moment that placed us at zero point within our own evolutionary and transformational journey and as forerunners for the process taking place within the collective field.

So, let us celebrate all that is symptomatic of having arrived at zero point in ourselves: the unknown, the baffling, the contradictory, the confusing, the breaking down of our lives, the sudden and unexpected reorientation of our life vision, the losses, and the stripping away of the final layers to reveal the Authentic Self that we truly are.

WE ARE ALL SPARKS
OF DIVINE CONSCIOUSNESS

Writer Thomas Merton shared: "If I penetrate to the depths of my own existence, to this indefinable Am that is myself in its deepest roots, then through this deep center I pass into the infinite I Am, which is the very name of the Almighty."

We are all sparks of Divine Consciousness. We all hold a deep gnosis that we are part of something vast and unfathomable, so infinitely inexpressible and boundlessly indefinable that may be termed Creator, God, Source, or Divine Consciousness. However we name it, our gnosis reveals to us that we are Consciousness, and that Consciousness can be best defined as existence.

We are in the time of the great awakening—the awakening of Consciousness and of Divine Consciousness. We are awakening to the reality of our own divinity and to the Divine. Consciousness permeates every atom, every molecule, and every cell of our very Being, of every living energy on the Earth, beyond the Earth, and beyond the universe. All that Is, the Am, and the I Am are immersed in the infinite and boundlessness of Divine Consciousness.

There are three primary gateways to self-actualization: psychological evolution, conscious evolution, and spiritual evolution. Psychological awareness leads to consciousness, and consciousness leads to spiritual awakening. Therefore, this book explores, as its main focus, the psychological, conscious, and spiritual evolution of the human being.

TWO

Psychological, Conscious, and Spiritual Evolution

There is no coming to consciousness without pain. People will do anything, no matter how absurd, in order to avoid facing their own soul. One does not become enlightened by imagining figures of light, but by making the darkness conscious.

CARL GUSTAV JUNG

The 1960s saw an unprecedented reactive kick against the Western establishment. The sixties proved to be a decade steeped in rebellion, revolution, experimentation, reaction, liberation, and reevaluation. Even though the foundation stones of mainstream society and established religion withstood the powerful undercurrents of revolutionary change, substantial cracks appeared marking a moment in human history, which revealed how the manipulation and control of the masses, by the few, had entered the earliest stages of breakdown.

At first, evidence of this was subtle. However, fifty years on, those underground rumblings have resurfaced into a world now ready for a new conscious infrastructure within society, politics, media, religion, and spirituality.

PSYCHOLOGICAL EVOLUTION

In the late nineteenth century came the timely arrival of Freud's work, with a message that his twentieth-century protégé, student, and successor Jung evolved and profoundly refined. However, the emerging psychological mind dates back to Plato (ca. 424–348 BCE), Pliny the Elder (23–79 CE), and Paracelsus (1493–1541 CE). Moving forward once again to the twentieth century, further evolutionary contributions to psychological development have hailed from those such as Roberto Assagioli, Abraham Maslow, Carl Rogers, and more.

Many years ago, I sat with an accomplished psychotherapist and supervisor who was well versed in the ways of the First Nations Peoples. I always recall him saying to me that "the psychological is the second gateway, the first being the physical." I have no idea what the other levels of such a model might be composed of as we never discussed it further and yet, this statement really struck a chord within me, ringing true at a more deeply felt level of knowing. What I do know is that psychological exploration is an initiatory gateway to self-actualization. We could say that it stands as a gateway to the Self.

By the mid-1900s Roberto Assagiolo, an Italian psychiatrist, had developed a spiritual psychology known as psychosynthesis, which began to be internationally recognized in the 1950s and '60s. The focus of this psychotherapy is the means by which the psyche can and does synthesize all parts of the personality to work together to reach the highest human potentials. Assagioli drew upon both Eastern and Western philosophies in developing the core concepts of psychosynthesis, and his work has been continued and further developed by others in the field since his death in 1974. My own personal introduction to this psychotherapy has had a profound impact upon my life.

When I first encountered the psychological arena, I had been looking to engage in some psychological self-exploration and had been searching for a psychology with a soul. I was seeking a psychology that was not going to label me or put me in a box and was not going to offer me textbook answers to the questions I was asking about myself. I was looking for a psychology that held a "wholistic" approach and viewed a human being through the lens of body, feelings, mind, heart, soul, and spirit. I spent several weeks of searching and finally discovered the transpersonal psychotherapy known as psychosynthesis. So, aged twenty-nine, I arranged an appointment with a psychosynthesis psychotherapist and began a revelatory and transformational journey of my Self.

By the end of the first session I was hooked. It was one specific insight that resulted in never viewing life again without using the lens of psychological awareness. I had been asked a question by the therapist, "How do you feel about that?" in relation to something I had shared with her about my earliest experience of trauma. My response was to spiritualize and rationalize, which was something I had done for years about this core trauma. She asked me again, "How do you feel about that?" Confused, I continued to recite my well-rehearsed script, which at the time I believed to be my actual true feelings.

Recognizing how out of touch I was with the authentic-feeling level of my experience of this core trauma and myself, she invited me to close my eyes and imagine myself at the age I was when the trauma occurred. She encouraged me to share with her how the "infant" in me was feeling. This was a lightbulb moment! Suddenly and unexpectedly I connected with a level of feeling and realization that I had no idea existed. It was an evolutionary leap in the journey of my Self.

Several months later, experiencing a noticeable personal transformation taking place within me, I signed up for the psychosynthesis psychotherapy training. The first year covered what was termed the Fundamentals of Psychosynthesis. One year later at the end of this process of self-exploration, I found myself wishing that everyone could be given the opportunity to make the one-year journey of the Self. It was truly incredible. The discoveries, the realizations, and the breakdown in order to breakthrough that occurred during this one year alone contained all the possibilities necessary to catalyze a personal shift of consciousness and support peace in the world.

At the close of that year I felt profoundly changed. I was experiencing my life force as being stronger than ever; my skin was warm and full of color, my eyes were shining, and my heart was opening with a sense of wonder because of who I was discovering myself to be. What inspired me even more was the promise of who I could become if I continued on this journey of psychological awakening and healing. I had stumbled upon my Self and there was no turning back.

I embarked upon a further two years of intense training and continued in weekly therapy throughout the three years I was studying psychosynthesis. By year four I decided to leave the psychosynthesis training, having a strong sense that whatever I had needed from it had been completed. However, three intense years of continual training, group work, client work, ongoing supervision, and therapy had set the groundwork for what was to come.

After leaving the training, I still felt there was something core that I had yet to heal and integrate in my psychological healing journey up to that point and so I found myself searching for what I knew I needed in order to become healed and more whole in my Self. My search did not take long, and just weeks after leaving my former training course, I found myself with a leaflet in my hand, intrigued by a title that had really grabbed my attention. The course advertised was titled, The Mustering of the Warrior Angels. This was not a terminology particularly representative of the psychological, yet gnosis told me to follow it through and contact the organizers.

I called the number on the leaflet and a very, very gentle yet strong voice answered. I made inquiries and the woman who answered listened with great patience and sensitivity before responding to my many questions. At the end of the call I had to raise the inevitable subject of the cost of the nine-month course, which I realized I would not be able to afford. This humble woman responded with deep understanding and a willingness to support and enable me to attend the course. I informed her that I would consider it and would get back in touch with her. The course was due to commence within one week.

During that week I battled with myself in terms of my worthiness to merit the kind offer and unconditional support of this woman who was facilitating the course. Her approach was unlike any I had ever encountered in my life. And so, I wrestled with myself, reeling at the new experience of *really* feeling seen, heard, valued, acknowledged, and validated for the first time. Even though the part of me that represented my then unhealed and unintegrated ego resisted the willingness of this woman to meet my need to attend this course, I was able to find my yes and accept the hand that was reaching out to me. That nine-month course transformed my life.

For the first time I experienced what it felt like to be unconditionally loved and at all times be held in unconditional positive regard, deep love, empathy, understanding, and compassion. For the first time, I experienced the kind of love an integrated, psychologically healthy and spiritually balanced mother would bestow upon her child. For the first time, I experienced what it felt like for someone to continually find ways of saying yes to me, when my experience of cultural conditioning and family history repeatedly said no.

Throughout that nine months, in the presence of this woman, I was exposed to a way of being that prioritized the needs of all concerned. This was done in groundbreaking and unconventional ways that entirely respected the morals, values, and ethics of each individual present.

When I look back over the past fifteen years and contemplate the single most profound and transformational experience I have had the blessing and grace to undergo in this lifetime, my thoughts always turn to that woman and that nine-month course I had the courage to say yes to. I am blessed to say that when the course finished, the ongoing unconditional love and support of the woman who facilitated my deepest healing continued. This was a woman whose humble wisdom ways and truly authentic spiritual example proved to be the most powerful healing force and influence in my own self-actualization process. This was a woman who eventually became my mentor, and ultimately one of my dearest, closest, and most cherished friends. Her name is Wendy Webber.

CONSCIOUS EVOLUTION

In essence, conscious evolution represents our capacity to evolve *consciously* and not merely by chance. Humanity is consciously evolving at an exponential rate and it is doing so through the wide-scale spread of expression, connection, love, compassion, innovation, co-creation, and recognition that has been made possible by advances in technology that have initiated a viral awakening of personal and collective consciousness. It was the great futurist and pioneer of free energy, Nikola Tesla, who first introduced the idea of a global brain when he said, "When wireless is fully applied the Earth will be converted into a huge brain, capable of response in every one of its parts." It was indeed Tesla who first introduced the concept of what Jose Arguelles later termed the *noosphere*.

Humanity has evolved a highly sophisticated and vastly upgraded global nervous system and brain known across the world as the Internet. This online phenomenon has given birth to a social media gone viral that has connected people, communities, countries, nations, and the world. Extraordinary advances in technology have enabled the covert and secret governmental agendas regarding interplanetary, off-planet, and extradimensional experiments and research to be made possible. These include the reality of other life-forms within the cosmos, wormholes, time travel, and extraterrestrial contact and communication.

This new global nervous system and brain, also known as the noosphere, has given people choice, a collective voice, and the capacity for empowerment. This is a fact that global agenda authorities have recognized and are now seeking to control, as humanity campaigns for human, animal, and planetary rights, including the replacing of existing power resources, such as oil, electricity, and gas, with free energy. This becomes possible with online "freedom technology."

The consciousness model of human beings is changing from one of dysfunctional instant gratification to that of a more healthy and functional model of instant manifestation. This proves how we can indeed become manifesters and co-creators. It is new technology that has made this potential a reality. It is critical that we campaign and seek to eliminate the government agendas to control the new global nervous system and brain, and protect the rights of the individual and the collective.

Conscious evolution is an aspect of human evolution that has been slowly but surely emerging in this past decade. Those who run the major self-development training institutions and organizations are now studying conscious evolution in order to introduce it as a new training module into their curriculums, training programs, and educational teaching models.

The woman most renowned as the matriarch of conscious evolution is futurist Barbara Marx Hubbard who, at eighty-two years of age, has dedicated her entire adult life to the conscious evolution of humanity and the world. American systems theorist, architect, engineer, author, designer, inventor, and futurist Buckminster Fuller said of her: "There is no doubt in my mind that Barbara Marx Hubbard—who helped introduce the concept of futurism to society—is the best informed human now alive regarding futurism and the foresights it has produced." And her good friend and biographer Neale Donald Walsch refers to her as *The Mother of Invention*.

Barbara Marx Hubbard defines conscious evolution as the following:

> Conscious evolution is the evolution of evolution, from unconscious to conscious choice. While consciousness has been evolving for billions of years, conscious evolution is new. It is part of the trajectory of human evolution, the canvas of choice before us now as we recognize that we have come to possess the powers that we used to attribute to the gods.
>
> We are poised in this critical moment, facing decisions that must be made consciously if we are to avoid destroying the world as we know it, if we are instead to co-create a future of immeasurable possibilities. Our conscious evolution is an invitation to ourselves, to open to that positive future, to see ourselves as one planet, and to learn to use our powers wisely and ethically for the enhancement of all life on Earth.
>
> Conscious evolution can also be seen as an awakening of a memory that resides in the synthesis of human knowing, from spiritual to social to scientific. Indeed, all of our efforts to discover the inherent design of life itself can be seen as the process of one intelligence,

striving to know itself through our many eyes, and to set the stage for a future of immense co-creativity.

This awakening has gained momentum as three new understandings (the 3 Cs) have arisen:

Cosmogenesis: This is the recent discovery that the universe has been and is now evolving. As Brian Swimme puts it, "time is experienced as an evolutionary sequence of irreversible transformations," rather than as ever-renewing cycles.

Our New Crises: We are faced with a complex set of crises, most especially environmental. We are participating in a global system that is far from equilibrium, conditions that are known to favor a macroshift. This kind of dramatic repatterning can be a sudden shift toward devolution and chaos, or it can be an evolution toward a higher more complex order. At this moment in evolution the outcome depends on our choices, and time is running out. We must change, or suffer dire consequences. Our crises are acting as evolutionary drivers pressuring us to innovate and transform.

Our New Capacities: The advent of radical evolutionary technologies such as biotechnology, nanotechnology, quantum computing, space exploration, etc., offer us the possibility of profound change in the physical world. At the same time that we are facing the possible destruction of our life support systems, we can also see that the tools are there to transform ourselves, our bodies, and our world. We can and are actually moving beyond the creature human condition toward a new species, a universal humanity, capable of coevolving with nature.*

SPIRITUAL EVOLUTION

For millennia humans have been engaged in varying forms of spiritual practice, be they sacrificial or reverential. Many have immersed

---

*Barbara Marx Hubbard's official website, accessed March 18, 2013, www.barbaramarx hubbard.com/site/node/10.

themselves, for better or worse, in the aspirational or dogmatic interpretations of world religions, spiritual ideals, and philosophies. Throughout history, religion has been grossly distorted beyond all recognition. Humanity has been exposed to a version of worship and religion that has had the pure heart ripped out of it. However, a true religion is seeking to emerge now, a religion in which the heart remains intact.

For many thousands of years, from the worship of Sun Gods, Mystery religions, Paganism, and more (with Hinduism being the oldest of the existing major religions), humans have been guided (controlled) by external moralistic, authoritative, retributive, punishing, distorted, judgmental, accusative, warring, and misrepresentative unearthly "Gods." Sacred texts have been delivered with misinterpretation and distortion in contradictory sermons paraded as rules and regulations to a vulnerable global congregation.

Mainstream religion and spiritual practice dates back to the Vedas, which predate Hinduism in India. For the Abrahamic religions, Judaism is the mother religion, established around 1500 BCE. Christianity was established in the first century CE and Islam around the eighth century CE. Billions of people have perished throughout human history as a result of ancient "worship," which caused wars and entailed human sacrifice. Untold millions of men, women, children, and animals have lost their lives in the name of religion in the past four to five thousand years.

The most peaceful spiritual practices in modern history appear to be Buddhism and Hinduism, yet even these have ancient roots in battles and war. However, over time, they do seem to have evolved a more authentic expression of their fundamental spiritual teachings based upon love. It is also interesting to note that both encourage and practice vegetarianism, as regard for all life is a fundamental value and ethic.

As the psychological and conscious evolution of the individual and collective begins to establish a firm foothold as a reality, we find ourselves in the midst of a global evolution. Our relationship with our own spirituality is subject to radical questioning as we sense the rumblings of change beneath the surface of the spiritual and religious ground we have stood upon for thousands of years.

As psychologically and consciously evolving individuals, we are seeking and needing a more authentic expression of spirituality that speaks to who we are now in the twenty-first century. As the many layers that hide the heart of the true Self are peeled away through psychological processing and conscious awakening, so too are we now seeking to align with an authentic spiritual and religious practice for the new consciousness and the new world paradigm that is also emerging.

The time is upon us to strip away the many layers that have hidden the heart of religion—layers that were put in place in order to control and manipulate our ancestors who had not attained the degree of conscious evolution that is possible and can become a reality for the twenty-first-century awakened human being. Twenty-first-century humanity seeks a spiritual path that reflects our present time and one in which the heart of religion is laid bare. Our conscious evolution calls for a new spiritual practice—a contemporary spirituality for an evolving world—a religious practice, an authentic teaching of what has lain at the heart of all religion. Just as all rivers lead to the ocean, what takes us to the heart of all religion is love.

Conscious evolution began with spirituality. Yet, owing to the adoption of the widespread distortion and misrepresentation of original religious and spiritual teachings over millennia, the conscious evolution of the human being became buried, along with the pure, peace loving, and peace seeking heart of true religion and spiritual practice.

Following the explosion onto the human evolutionary scene of the psychological Self, some forty or more years ago, we find we have now arrived at the gateway of individual and collective conscious evolution. As the psychologically integrated Self establishes within the personal, cultural, and collective fabric of human reality, so too rises the star of conscious evolution, lighting the way ahead for our ongoing evolutionary development. Psychological evolution is followed by conscious evolution and then spiritual evolution, or more accurately, a spiritual reevolution, which reflects the consciousness of the twenty-first-century human being and a new world paradigm.

Standing upon the bridge of conscious evolution, we remain at the same time connected to both the psychological and spiritual. By simultaneously remaining connected to all three, an unprecedented evolutionary leap becomes possible within the human being. Never before, in the history of humankind, have we stood upon such a threshold that, for the first time, allows us to experience and manifest the greater potential we each hold as consciously evolving human beings. Our full capacity for the expression of this has remained dormant. We use just 8 percent of the human brain. In the words of Roberto Assagioli, just imagine "What we may be." This is the promise of the times we are living in.

The gateways of psychological, conscious, and spiritual evolution are wide open and invite each and every one of us to align with a consciousness and a new world that reflects a twenty-first-century personal and collective shift from an old to a new paradigm. To do so will initiate and activate the vastly unrealized human template we are each born with and, until this century, have barely touched upon.

These three gateways present us with a new human experience and a world that, until this time, has been just a fantasy or a dream. The glimpse we have seen of a utopian world in which all are equal, all are abundant, all are peaceful, and all are well is now within our grasp. We have only to step through these psychological, conscious, and spiritual gateways to realize and manifest a utopian world as a reality.

THE THREE FOUNDATIONAL LEVELS OF HUMAN EVOLUTION

Psychological, Conscious, and Spiritual

The time is upon us now to align and harmonize these three foundational levels of our intrinsic evolutionary nature—a process I often refer to as realigning the personality with the Soul, and not the other way around, which is primarily the case in the unintegrated individual.

The most profound and transformational journey any of us will ever experience is the conscious evolutionary journey of the Self. The journey of true awakening is catalyzed when we turn our attention to our psychological level, which enables us to evolve in a more conscious way. This in turn profoundly influences and accelerates our conscious and spiritual evolution.

Self-awareness and self-realization lead to self-actualization. When we embody and live the Truth of who we really are, this enables global evolution and the attainment of the utopian ideal of a world at peace to become a tangible reality. When enough of us are psychologically, consciously, and spiritually awakened, we can and will coevolve and comanifest a new golden age and a thousand years of peace. This has been prophesied by ancient indigenous wisdomkeepers for millennia, a fact that rare astronomical alignments and momentous Earth changes indicated would unfold post-2012.

The rise of conscious evolution as an intrinsic developmental reality for the twenty-first-century human being marks the arrival of the "new human." This human being is not randomly shaped by circumstances of chance and current themes within society, but one who is conscious and fully engaged in their own evolutionary process as well as working toward the evolution of humanity.

The individual and collective psyche is now ready for a personal and global progressive evolutionary awakening. The twenty-first-century new human seeks a contemporary spirituality that reflects an evolving world. The psychological aspect of human evolution first entered the public domain in the late nineteenth century with Freud and then exploded onto the scene in the 1970s, at which point we entered into the era of psychological evolution. Now as we move further into the twenty-first century, we find we have arrived at a bridge that invites us into a new era of human evolution—a new epoch of conscious evolution. The twenty-first century will catalyze an exponential shift in this in both the individual and the collective and so materialize an aligned spirituality, a twenty-first-century global spiritual evolution—a contemporary spirituality for an evolving world.

THE PSYCHO-SPIRITUAL PYRAMIDS OF HUMANITY

An Evolutionary Trajectory of Conscious Awakening

I have developed the following model to demonstrate twenty-eight levels of human consciousness. I have termed this model "The Psycho-Spiritual Pyramids of Humanity" for it refers to our psychological and spiritual development and evolution. As you can see from the model below, the twenty-eight levels of human consciousness are encapsulated within two overlapping pyramids.

The human quest for self-actualization and spiritual enlightenment is not possible without first having to transcend the various developmental stages of conscious evolution. The Psycho-Spiritual Pyramids of Humanity illustrates the levels that an individual needs to *consciously* transcend to fully self-actualize.

Conscious evolution and spiritual transcendence begin when we recognize the need to transform our physical, emotional, mental, psychological, energetic, and spiritual realities. Once this realization has been experienced at the deepest levels of our being, an extraordinary transformation begins to occur within the Self.

The Psycho-Spiritual Pyramids of Humanity illustrates the specific arenas of consciousness that seek awakening, activation, integration, and transcendence. This model can be utilized as a map to help facilitate us in gauging where we may have arrived, in terms of our own conscious evolution. It is also interesting to observe where on the map our attention is drawn, in terms of where we stand on our own evolutionary journey.

Spiritual (Self-Actualized/Self-Realized and Enlightenment)
Soul (living in alignment with Soul/Seeking and living Truth of Who You Are)
Super-Conscious (imagination is bridge to Higher Dimensions/imagination is Soul in action)
Consciousness (consciously evolved to level of Self-Mastery and Self-Actualization)
Energetic (alignment of all energy bodies/activation of Merkaba and Kundalini)
Psycho-Spiritual (integration and alignment of psychological and spiritual)
Visionary (Seer/Gnostic/Visionary for personal and global evolution)
Psycho-Philosophical (conscious awareness that extends beyond
personal toward global evolution)
Psychological (Self-realizing and Self-actualizing)
Mind (Higher Mind expressed through heart field
wisdom/gnosis/heart intelligence/memory release)
Feelings (integrated higher octave of emotions)
Body (experienced and treated as Temple of the Soul)
Heart (opening and deep healing of the heart)
Conscious (awakening/awareness/evolution)
Intuitive (felt sense/gnosis/brow chakra)
Gnostic (heart based/felt sense inspired)

THE SPIRITUAL PYRAMID OF HUMANITY

*Evolutionary
Leap*

THE PHYSICAL PYRAMID OF HUMANITY

Consciousness (consciously awakening)
Psychological (developing psychological awareness
and a concept of Self)
Mind (lower mind expressed through mental field)
Intellectual (emphasis on mental based learning/information/
academia/memory retention)
Psychic (astral level/predictive/solar plexus)
Personality (living from ego/shadow/wounded inner child/
psychologically unintegrated)
Mental (life lived through lens of mental patterning/information derived knowledge)
Emotional (unintegrated emotions/reaction based)
Physical (body as machine mentality/empathically disconnected)
Unconscious
Instinctual
Primal (fear based/survival level driven)

The Psycho-Spiritual Pyramids of Humanity

As you can see, the model consists of twenty-eight levels of human consciousness. In an ascending sequential order from lower to higher levels of consciousness they are:

primal • instinctual • unconscious • physical • emotional • mental • personality • psychic • intellectual • lower mind • psychological (developing awareness) • consciousness • gnostic • intuitive • conscious • heart • body • feelings • higher mind • psychological (self-realizing) • psycho-philosophical • visionary • psycho-spiritual • energetic • consciousness • super-conscious • soul • spiritual

To assist you in your own journey, examine each of the levels in the pyramids to gain a sense of where you are in terms of your evolutionary journey. Once you have done this, spend some time contemplating the next level so as to open yourself fully to the possibility of attaining self-actualization, self-realization, and enlightenment.

THREE

The Seven Dark, Seven Light, and Seven Rainbow Arrows

A Map for Evolving Consciousness

If you want to awaken all of humanity, then awaken all of yourself, if you want to eliminate the suffering in the world, then eliminate all that is dark and negative in yourself. Truly, the greatest gift you have to give is that of your own self-transformation.

LAO-TZU

Fifteen years ago, when I was deeply engaged in my own psychological process and journey to reclaim my True Self, I came across a First Nations Peoples model called the "Seven Dark, Seven Light, and Seven Rainbow Arrows." I cannot recall how this occurred, for it was not part of my psychological training. It was by pure chance and yet, when I read about them, I felt an immediate and deep connection with each one.

Each arrow penetrated my heart and Soul, and these twenty-one arrows became one of the primary psychological compasses I used to navigate through my shadow self, meaning those aspects of the personality and ego that are not consciously integrated, and my inner psychological wounding. Despite extensive research, I could find no details whatsoever giving an in-depth account of the actual meaning of each arrow. All that existed were the names and my sense is that these originated as a First Nations Peoples teaching, which had been handed down through the oral tradition of sacred ancient ways.

So profound has been the impact of these arrows in terms of my own psychological healing journey, and so influential do they remain in my life to this day, that I felt they merited being written about in some depth and that perhaps I could be the person to do this. And so, I sat with each individual arrow and wrote what I felt *it* wanted to reveal about *itself* at a deeper exploratory level. I transcribed what each arrow had to contribute to the psychological evolution, healing, integration, and liberation of the individual and the collective of the twenty-first century.

As you read through, you will note that all of the Dark Arrows and a number of the Light Arrows can best be understood by asking oneself some searching questions, which I have outlined for you. In those instances, be prepared to consider and respond to the questions with complete honesty. The remaining Light Arrows and the Rainbow Arrows provide insights and truths that are to be integrated in the Self if you are to ultimately achieve Self-actualization, self-transcendence, and enlightenment. I hope you find these Seven Dark, Seven Light, and Seven Rainbow Arrows to be an effective map for your own evolving consciousness and as transformational as I have.

I bow in reverence to these arrows, each one a great teacher for these times.

THE SEVEN DARK ARROWS

The First Dark Arrow Is Attachment

1. To whom or to what are you attached?
2. Can you gain a felt sense of where in your body your attention is most drawn when you feel into the attachment?

3. Staying with your felt sense (not your mind), can you feel what the need is behind the attachment?
4. What do you feel you need in order to no longer be attached?
5. How can you get that need met?

The spiritual lesson of attachment is—nonattachment.

A spiritual mantra for attachment could be: *Even though a part of me feels caught in attachment, I deeply and completely love and accept myself.*

The Second Dark Arrow Is Dependency

1. To whom or to what are you dependent?
2. Can you gain a felt sense of where in your body you experience the feeling of dependency?
3. Staying with your felt sense (not your mind), can you feel what the need is behind the dependency?
4. What do you need in order to no longer feel dependent?
5. How can you get that need met?

The spiritual lessons of dependency are—independence, interdependence, and self-love.

A spiritual mantra for dependency could be: *Even though a part of me feels dependent, I deeply and completely love and accept myself.*

The Third Dark Arrow Is Judgment

1. How aware are you of the energy of judgment in your life?
2. How aware are you of self-judgment? How aware are you of how you judge others?
3. How judged by others do you feel? Recognize that when you experience yourself as being judged, this reveals how you judge yourself. If you were not self-judging, you would not perceive yourself as being judged. Instead, you would perceive another as projecting their own pain onto you and your response would be one of compassion and understanding.

4. On a scale from 1 to 10 (with 10 holding the strongest charge) how often would you say you judge yourself or others? Be honest with yourself.

5. Set an intent to spend a day self-observing and make a note of how often a judgment arises about yourself or another. Write down each time you catch yourself in judgment, and at the end of the day assess how frequently this occurs.

6. Set an intent on the days that follow to catch each moment you find yourself in judgment. Transform those judgments about yourself or another by instead thinking, stating, or feeling something positive and beautiful about yourself or the other.

7. What is it you feel you need in order not to judge?

8. How can you get that need met?

The spiritual lessons of judgment are—unconditional positive regard, self-acceptance, and unconditional love.

A spiritual mantra for judgment could be: *Even though a part of me does not feel good enough, I unconditionally love and accept myself.*

The Fourth Dark Arrow Is Comparison

1. How aware are you of the energy of comparison in your life?

2. How often do you compare yourself with others?

3. How often do you compare people with each other?

4. How often do you feel that other people are comparing you to another? Recognize that when you experience yourself as being compared this reveals how you compare yourself. If you did not compare yourself, you would not perceive yourself as being compared. Instead, you would perceive another as projecting their own hurt onto you and your response would be one of compassion and understanding. When another compares you to someone else, it is because there is a deep need within them that is not being met. Therefore the comparison is not about you.

5. On a scale from 1 to 10 (with 10 holding the strongest charge) how often would you say you compare yourself or others? Be honest with yourself.

6. Set an intent to spend a day self-observing and make a note of how often comparison arises in relation to yourself or another. Write down each time you catch yourself comparing and at the end of the day assess how frequently this occurs.

7. Set an intent on the days that follow to catch each moment you find yourself in the mode of comparison. Transform those comparisons by choosing to think, state, or feel something positive or beautiful about yourself or another.

8. What is it you feel you need in order to not compare?

9. How can you get that need met?

The spiritual lessons of comparison are—unconditional self-love, self-validation, and self-acceptance.

A spiritual mantra for comparison could be: *Even though a part of me is caught in comparison, I deeply and completely love and accept myself.*

The Fifth Dark Arrow Is Expectation

1. How aware are you of the energy of expectation in your life?

2. How often do you expect from yourself, from others, or from life?

3. How often do you feel the expectations others have of you? Recognize that when you experience others as having expectations of you this reveals how you also have expectations of yourself and others. If this were not so, you would not experience others as having expectations of you. Instead, you would perceive them as projecting their own expectations onto you and recognize that the reason for this stems from a deep unmet need within them. Their expectation of you is but a reflection of the expectations they place upon themselves, the weight of the expectations they feel from others, and how they are not yet able to meet the need that is behind their own expectation. Therefore, your response would be one of compassion and understanding. When another has expectations of you, it is because there is a deep need within them that is not being met. Those who aim the dark arrow of expectation toward you also mirror to you how alive the energy of expectation is in your own life.

4. On a scale from 1 to 10 (with 10 holding the strongest charge) how often would you say you have expectations of yourself or others? Be honest with yourself.

5. Set an intent to spend a day self-observing and make a note of how often expectation arises in relation to yourself or others. Write down each time you catch yourself placing an expectation on yourself or others. At the end of the day, assess how frequently this occurs. First we must identify in order to "dis-identify."

6. Set an intent on the days to follow to catch each moment you find yourself experiencing an expectation, be it your own or another's. Transform any expectation you have of yourself or another by practicing nonattachment to any outcome and by being gently okay with whatever transpires. Trust that the outcome is exactly as it is meant to be and if an expectation remains unfulfilled there is a life-serving reason that will support your Soul's evolution.

7. Try to feel the need behind your own expectation.

8. What need is not being met?

9. What is it that you need in order to get that need met?

10. Set an intent to try to meet that need yourself or to consciously reach out to another, stating just what your need is and asking if they would support you to meet it.

The spiritual lessons of expectation are—self-love, self-nurture, self-acceptance, nonattachment, trust, and surrender.

A spiritual mantra for expectation could be: *Even though a part of me can be needy, I deeply and completely love and accept myself.*

The Sixth Dark Arrow Is the Needy Child Syndrome (Wounded Inner Child)

1. How aware are you of the energy of the needy child syndrome in your life?

2. In what way do you experience your needy child?

3. How often are you aware of the presence of your needy child?

4. On a scale from 1 to 10 (with 10 holding the strongest charge) how

often would you say you experience the wounded child within you as needy? Be honest with yourself.

5. Set an intent to spend a day self-observing and make a note of how often you become aware of your inner needy child. Write down each time you become aware of the hurt child within you. At the end of the day, assess how frequently your inner wounded child has been present.

6. Set an intent on the days that follow to catch each moment you experience this need.

7. Try to feel what is behind your inner wounded child's reactions. Is your needy child feeling fear, hurt, sadness, and anger, or does the inner child have a need to feel safe, secure, seen, heard, validated, held, and loved?

8. What need is not being met?

9. How can the adult in you meet that need?

10. What support might you reach out for from others in order to meet the needs of your wounded inner child?

11. Set an intent to try to meet these needs yourself or to consciously reach out to another stating what you need. Ask if they would consciously support you to meet those needs.

12. Recognize that when you experience another as acting like a needy child this reveals how you also have an inner needy child in need of love and healing. The actions and reactions of others often stem from the needy child within them, an inner child who is in fear, is hurting, and is sad, who may not feel safe and may be unable to trust. Be mindful to note that this is not the behavior of the adult but of a fearful wounded inner child and that the reason for their neediness may originate from deep unmet needs in their childhood. In the recognition of this psychological reality, seek to respond with compassion and understanding, remaining mindful that you are addressing a wounded inner child, not an adult. Turn this around for yourself too. Treat your own needy child with compassion and understanding. When you experience yourself reacting like a child (as opposed to responding like a centered adult), recognize how this is

because there is a hurt needy child within who is in pain. Those who react like a needy child toward you also mirror how alive the energy of the needy child may be within yourself. (My book *2012: A Clarion Call* explores this psychological dynamic in greater depth.)

The spiritual lessons of the needy child are—psychological integration and evolution, trust, inner authority, self-love, compassion, empathy, understanding, and forgiveness.

A spiritual mantra for the needy child could be: *Even though I am aware of the needy child within me, I deeply and completely love and accept myself.*

The Seventh Dark Arrow Is Self-Importance

1. To what degree are you aware of the dark arrow of self-importance? How alive is that energy within you?

2. In what way do you experience yourself when you are wielding the arrow of self-importance? Take some time to write down or sketch or paint what you become aware of visually when you see yourself in the act of self-importance.

3. On a scale from 1 to 10 (with 10 holding the strongest charge) how often do you experience yourself caught in self-importance? Be honest with yourself.

4. Set an intent to spend a day self-observing and make a note of how often you become aware of yourself in the behavior of self-importance. Write down each time you become aware of this. At the end of the day, assess how frequently you have experienced conducting yourself from a place of self-importance. Write down how it makes you feel when caught in self-importance and how you appear to yourself in those moments.

5. Try to gain a sense of what the need is behind your need of self-importance.

6. Now try to identify the need in you that is not being met. Where does it originate from? What original need was not met? What do you need in order to meet that need now? Write down whatever

comes to mind. Do not censor your first response, just simply write it down.

7. How can you begin to meet that need?

8. How might another or others meet that need for you?

9. Set an intent to try to meet this need yourself or to consciously reach out to another or others stating what you need. Ask if they would consciously support you to meet your need.

10. Recognize that whenever you experience another in the act of self-importance this reveals that you may also have a propensity toward the same behavior. The act of self-importance stems from traumatic experiences or unmet needs in childhood as well as karmic influences.

The spiritual lessons of self-importance are—humility, the healing dissolution and integration of the ego, moving from power over (ego defense) to empowered (self-integrating), and from ego to I.

A spiritual mantra for self-importance could be: *Even though I am aware of a part of me that acts from self-importance, I deeply and completely love and accept myself.*

THE SEVEN LIGHT ARROWS

The First Light Arrow Is Self-Awareness

From a psycho-spiritual perspective it has long been theorized that there are differing levels of consciousness. This theory entered the mainstream when American psychologist and philosopher William James, who was trained as a physician, postulated in *The Principles of Psychology* (1890) that there existed a physical, mental, and spiritual self and ego. In approximately 1905, the Austrian Sigmund Freud presupposed an unconscious, preconscious, and conscious mind.

Being self-aware requires a greater degree of psychological awareness and understanding of the mechanisms and workings of the unconscious, conscious, and superconscious minds. We are aware of terms such as *ego, shadow, personality, psychologically wounded inner child,* and *child of history*. We are also aware of the Soul, of Spirit, of energy, and of the creative force. We become watchful of our dreams, recognizing that they can convey important information for us to integrate during wakefulness. Our capacity for perception, cognition, intuition, creativity, visioning, and gnosis becomes greatly enhanced. Self-awareness fosters the awakening or deepening of our connection to the spiritual dimensions of our being.

Generally, we might say that self-awareness is a combination of past events, current life experiences, and future hopes. We might also add that self-awareness requires a more conceptual (as opposed to perceptual) self-exploration process, whereupon our capacity to analyze ourselves at a psychological level and understand ourselves more at a spiritual level is dependent upon our ability for self-directed thought.

Self-awareness constitutes our capacity for self-therapy. In other words we become our own therapist. Self-awareness requires that we develop an inner dialogue to begin a conversation between the wise part of ourselves, the Self (note capital *S*), and the part of us that is reactive, referred to as the small self. How successful we are at this is dependent upon the degree to which we are psychologically integrated.

Self-awareness invites us to turn our attention inward. It encourages us to remove our focus from the external and look instead at what is happening within ourselves. To have awareness of Self we need to actively check in with our experiences, thus practicing mindfulness in our word, thought, action, and deed. To a greater extent we can rely upon our capacity for accurate self-assessment when self-knowledge springs from a fountain of perception based upon the cultivation of a highly evolved psychological and spiritual Self.

When self-aware we are familiar with who we are, where our psychological edges are, what causes a reaction within us, and our capacities for an appropriate response. We are aware of our psychological story, the "myths" from our past and our historical, chronological experience. We are able to self-evaluate, self-reflect, self-regulate, and self-guide.

Being self-aware enables us to monitor and observe our thoughts, actions, beliefs, perceptions, intentions, emotions, sensations, and impulses. It allows us to explore ourselves with interested curiosity, to be inspired, and to connect to our aspirations. We are continually assessing our motives, drives, and intentions. We are in touch with the phenomenological Self that is aware of all feelings and sensations. We can listen to, respond, and be guided by our felt sense.

Being self-aware enables us to bring necessary and evolutionary changes into our lives. Our emotional and mental landscapes begin to alter and become more positive. It literally allows us to change our minds and our mental and emotional patterning. We are able to heal at the deepest levels, reprogram the unconscious mind, reinform the conscious mind, and make an essential connection to the superconscious mind. When we are self-aware we are emotionally intelligent and mentally mature.

Self-awareness is supported by our ability to self-observe. The ability to cultivate self-awareness comes from the degree to which we are willing to commit to turning our attention to the inner world and explore just who we are and what makes us tick. Being curious about ourselves, the reasons behind the patterns and themes of our lives, and just what is possible for us, enables us to develop a level of self-awareness that will prove transformational.

A wonderful tool that greatly supports the development of self-awareness is *focusing*. There are also many other beneficial practices, so please refer to the resources directory at the end of this book. A good practitioner will not tell you what you should think, say, or do. Instead, they will share with you practices and techniques that can facilitate your ability to think, speak, and act for yourself with awareness.

Self-awareness when practiced regularly becomes instinctual—a little like driving a car! When you first take a driving lesson you need to become familiar with the practice of driving. Yet, very quickly driving becomes an automatic and natural experience where you no longer need to think, it just flows.

Self-awareness is a heightened experience of one's Self. When you continually live from a place of self-awareness you will truly marvel at how you were able to function before having become self-aware. It is a watershed moment along the evolutionary path when we become self-aware. It is as if a veil has been lifted, a light has been turned on in the dark, or a misty screen has become crystal clear.

Self-awareness is liberating. Those who become Self-aware experience a life-changing and transformational evolutionary shift in their consciousness. Self-awareness is the most significant step we can take toward Self-mastery, which is itself a prerequisite for Self-actualization.

A spiritual mantra for Self-awareness could be: *I choose to manifest my full potential for Self-awareness. I deeply and unconditionally love and accept myself.*

The Second Light Arrow Is Self-Acceptance

The light arrow of self-acceptance invites us to break the dark arrows of comparison and judgment.

1. Find a quiet moment and assess where along the scale of self-acceptance you are—with 1 being least self-accepting and 10 being the most. Where on that scale are you? Trust your initial response.

2. What would it feel like to unconditionally accept yourself, even those parts of you that you don't feel comfortable with? Why not give it a go and see how it feels and how life responds to you when you do this?

3. Set aside some time to identify and write down all the things you do not accept about yourself. When you have done so, try to be open to exploring the parts of yourself you find difficult to accept.

4. Recognize that when you stop judging yourself, you immediately experience a more positive sense of who you are.

5. When we ask the question "Who am I," it is usually the personality (ego) that responds. However, the personality (ego) is not equipped to answer such a question. This is a question for Self. To embody Self we must embody all of the light arrows.

6. True self-acceptance connects you to your true essence—the Authentic (True) Self.

7. Take some moments to contemplate what you feel is authentic

about you. What would you really wish people to realize about you? Write those qualities down and keep them close.

8. Why not set aside some time, make a nice cup of tea, sit down, and write a biography about your True Self? This is a great way of getting to know more about your True Self and anchoring this true you into your unconscious and conscious mind.

9. Each day for the next seven days, ask yourself what you find hard to accept and would like to let go of. Write down your realizations and at the end of the seven days, consciously and ceremoniously burn the piece of paper on which you have written your list and watch the flames transmute your words into light arrows.

10. Believe in your innate goodness.

11. Treat yourself with loving kindness.

12. Love yourself unconditionally.

13. Treat yourself with unconditional positive regard.

14. Trust your loving, wise heart.

A spiritual mantra for Self-acceptance could be: *I choose to fully accept myself. I deeply and unconditionally love and accept myself.*

The Third Light Arrow Is Self-Appreciation

1. Find a quiet moment and assess where along the scale you are in terms of self-appreciation—with 1 being least self-appreciating and 10 being most. Where on that scale are you? Trust your initial response.

2. What would it feel like to unconditionally appreciate yourself?

3. Recognize that by no longer judging and comparing yourself, you immediately experience self-appreciation.

4. Take some moments to contemplate what you appreciate about yourself. Write those qualities down and keep them close to you. Every time you pick up the dark arrows of judgment and comparison, take a look at the qualities you have written down and visualize discarding these dark arrows for the light arrows of self-acceptance and self-appreciation.

5. Each day appreciate something about yourself. State aloud what

this is. Look into a mirror and tell yourself what it is you really appreciate about yourself.

6. Appreciate yourself unconditionally.
7. When you find yourself appreciating something about another, turn that thought around and appreciate that same quality within yourself. If you did not have that quality you would not be able to recognize it in another.

A spiritual mantra for Self-appreciation could be: *I choose to fully appreciate myself. I deeply and unconditionally love and accept myself.*

The Fourth Light Arrow Is Self-Pleasure

The fourth light arrow focuses our awareness on self-pleasure, the significance of self-pleasure, and more especially how self-pleasure can connect us to our Divine Selves. The light arrow of self-pleasure does not merely refer to a sexual relationship with the Self, it also refers to anything the Self experiences as pleasurable. Pure self-pleasure has nothing at all to do with activities that distract the mind, nor does it represent anything that we may refer to as hobbies or pastimes.

Pure self-pleasure is a state of physical and spiritual bliss permeating every atom of the body, mind, and soul—a state that connects us deeply to the inner and outer aspects of ourselves as spiritual beings having a human experience. Pure self-pleasure is a phenomenological experience. When we experience pure self-pleasure we feel fully connected, energized, vital, and awake. Pure self-pleasure is an experience of absolute union with the physical self, a union not dependent on another. Pure self-pleasure is devoid of guilt or shame and is instead an experience of pure heart and soul and one that offers an experience of pure ecstasy and joy.

Throughout human history the experience of self-pleasure has been lost to us because of the fears and misconceptions about pleasure that have imprinted deeply into both the individual and collective consciousness. These include shame and guilt, which, as a result of the misrepresentation of self-pleasure and sexuality in religion, have infiltrated the individual and collective psyche.

The distortion of religion has separated us from experiencing the state of ultimate bliss, denying us pure self-pleasure, and instead has conditioned us to believe that ultimate bliss is a disembodied, religious, spiritual-peak experience reserved only for the pious, virtuous, or saintly (all of whom are mostly celibate). Because of this gross distortion, a split has occurred within the human psyche in terms of self-pleasure (union with Self) and ultimate bliss (union with the Divine). What we need to come to understand is that there is no difference between the state of ultimate spiritual bliss and our individual, earthly human potential for it.

Every human being has a basic need for pleasure. Pleasure represents the difference between feeling *alive* as opposed to merely existing. In fact, the need for self-pleasure is a prerequisite for a healthy, vital, and fulfilled human experience. A person who is blocked from self-pleasure is also blocked from deep communion with their spiritual Self. The two are interactive and interdependent. (Note: Self-pleasure is not the exclusive domain of sacred sexual union with Self, although is generally considered to mean such.) Self-pleasure is the gateway to a deep and direct experience of spiritual bliss.

The physical level of the human being has an innate potential to align in oneness with the energy streams of cosmic consciousness. A highly developed individual in sacred sexual union with Self is capable of experiencing the most sublime forms of self-pleasure due to their subtle bodies permeating their physical body and the bringing in of cosmic energies and consciousness.

During sacred sexual union with Self, we are able to tap into the superconscious mind, Akashic field, and the higher dimensions. Sacred sexuality with Self (and other) opens us to altered states of consciousness, to a connection with realms beyond those we may already feel aware of, raises our frequency, and initiates us into an elevated state of consciousness that can prove transformational.

Everything is energy. When we are inspired by a beautiful tree, a sunset, a waterfall, or an ocean, when we are enraptured by any natural organic phenomenon, in that moment we are connected to Divine energy, to life force, and to sexual energy. The word *sexual* has been debased and degraded. If in the past this term had been placed upon the rightful throne of Self, its majesty and influence over our lives would have proven evolutionary. Had this been the case, all inspiration from any natural phenomena would have been regarded as a sexual experience. We would feel the powerful and empowering life-pulsating force of this energy fulfilling its truest role within the human form and psyche.

Physical and spiritual pleasure are not opposites, but one and the same. Pure self-pleasure is not momentary, but lasting. It is both intensely physical and intensely spiritual. When the Self is integrated there is no division between the physical and spiritual experience of the human being. Ultimate freedom is experienced through the ultimate bliss of self-pleasure. Bliss is the natural state of an individual who is in deep union and harmony with the body, feelings, mind, soul, spirit, and the Divine.

In order to experience true love with another, we must first experience true love with ourselves. Pure self-pleasure is only possible when we can love, for first and foremost it requires love of Self. Without this, sexual pleasure is an empty experience, which always leaves the sense that something is incomplete. Sexuality without love reveals a psychological split and an imbalance between the body, emotions, and mind. When expressing and experiencing ourselves as sexual and spiritual beings we find that ultimate self-pleasure arises only from our capacity for self-love. When the physical, emotional, mental, and psychological levels of Self are integrated, ultimate self-pleasure and union with Self, other, and Spirit occur.

Most people are afraid of pleasure in whatever form it takes. Pleasure brings with it the experiences of shame and guilt and the act of sexual self-pleasure is where these feelings are most strongly experienced. Psychosynthesis speaks of identifying in order to dis-identify. By allowing ourselves to acknowledge how we are afraid of pleasure, especially sexual self-pleasure, by stating out loud to ourselves, "I am afraid of self-pleasure," we can begin the process of dis-identification from this to identify instead with, "I feel deep love for myself and self-pleasure is a pure expression of the love I feel for my Self." It is possible to transcend all fears no matter how unpleasurable. When you no longer perceive yourself as separate from your Self, other, life, the Divine, you will experience pure self-pleasure and ultimate bliss.

The more you are able to dis-identify from historical and cultural misconceptions as well as the self-sabotaging patterns that keep you away from pure self-pleasure and ultimate bliss, the more you will discover what denies you pure self-pleasure and the more you will discover how ultimate bliss is an entirely natural experience. Pure self-pleasure and ultimate bliss are your birthright and destiny. Conscious, connected, loving, pure self-pleasure is a gateway to well-being and true fulfillment.

A spiritual mantra for Self-pleasure could be: *I choose to engage in life-serving, life-enhancing, liberating, and joyful experiences of Self-pleasure. I deeply and unconditionally love and accept myself.*

The Fifth Light Arrow Is Self-Love

1. Where along the scale of self-love are you, with 1 being least self-loving and 10 being the most? Trust your initial response.

2. What would it feel like to unconditionally love yourself?

3. Recognize that by releasing the dark arrows of self-judgment and self-comparison, you immediately pick up the light arrow of self-love.

4. Take some moments to contemplate what it is that you do love about yourself. Write those qualities down and keep them close to you. Every time you pick up the dark arrows of judgment and comparison, take a look at the qualities you have written down and visualize discarding those dark arrows for the light arrows of self-love, self-acceptance, and self-appreciation.

5. Each day love something about yourself. State aloud what this is. Look into a mirror and tell yourself what it is you love about yourself.

6. Love yourself unconditionally.

7. When you find yourself loving something in another, turn that around and love that same quality within yourself. If you did not have that quality within, you would not be able to recognize it in another.

A spiritual mantra for Self-love could be: *I choose to fully love myself. I deeply and unconditionally love and accept myself.*

The Sixth Light Arrow Is Self-Actualization

Abraham Maslow, in his article "A Theory of Human Motivation" (1943), presented a psychological explanation for self-actualization in the following way:

- Self-actualization refers to the desire for self-fulfillment, namely, to the tendency for the individual to become actualized in what he or she is potentially.
- Self-actualization might be described as the desire to become more and more what one is, to become everything that one is capable of becoming.

Maslow identified some of the key characteristics to be found in Self-actualized people.

Acceptance and Realism: Self-actualized people have realistic perceptions of themselves, others, and the world around them.

Problem-centering: Self-actualized individuals are concerned with solving problems outside of themselves, including helping others and finding solutions to problems in the external world. These people are often motivated by a sense of personal responsibility and ethics.

Spontaneity: Self-actualized people are spontaneous in their internal thoughts and outward behavior. While they can conform to rules and social expectations, they also tend to be open and unconventional.

Autonomy and Solitude: A further characteristic of self-actualized people is the need for independence and privacy. While they enjoy the company of others, these individuals need time to focus on developing their own individual potential.

Continued Freshness of Appreciation: Self-actualized people tend to view the world with a continual sense of appreciation, wonder, and awe. Even simple experiences continue to be a source of inspiration and pleasure.

Peak Experiences: Individuals who are self-actualized often have what Maslow termed *peak experiences,* or moments of intense joy, wonder, awe, and ecstasy. After these experiences, people feel inspired, strengthened, renewed, or transformed.*

Maslow's description of self-actualization is a valid model and provides an excellent map for guiding us along the path of our own psychological development. However, Self-actualization has a higher spiritual octave to it. Mystics, masters, and sages have always taught that Self-actualization extends far beyond the psychological and physical realms.

Self-actualization is an ongoing process and one that is rarely achieved and then only by those who have reached the most advanced levels of human evolution, such as Buddha and Jesus. For most who are not at this level of human evolution, the fact remains that we are on an evolutionary path and, therefore, the potential for this will continue. The spiritual evolutionary trajectory of an awakened human being is such that it compels us to strive to achieve the most exalted expression of human perfection. Self-actualization is a transcendental journey in which we aspire to seek to transcend the limitations of the brain, the unconscious and conscious mind, and our psychological programming.

Self-actualization compels us to attain the highest ideals in relation to becoming a perfected expression of a Soul incarnate in human form. When we no longer carry the dark arrows and instead hold only the light, only then will we have attained the Self-actualization in our psychological development that Maslow so beautifully spoke of. At this point we experience an evolutionary leap in the expansion of our

---

*Kendra Cherry, "What Is Self-Actualization?" About.com Psychology, accessed March 22, 2013, http://psychology.about.com/od/theoriesofpersonality/a/hierarchyneeds_2 .htm.

consciousness and thus align with the superconscious mind and begin to explore our potential for greater degrees of Self-actualization at a spiritual level, as we continue along the evolutionary journey of our Soul.

A spiritual mantra for Self-actualization could be: *I choose to dedicate myself to the manifestation of myself as a Self-actualized individual. I deeply and unconditionally love and accept myself.*

The Seventh Light Arrow Is Impeccability

The seventh light arrow requires us to cultivate impeccability in word, thought, action, and deed. In each step—each movement—and each moment—the invitation from the seventh light arrow is to cultivate impeccability. What is impeccability?

Impeccability is when our conduct, our presence, and our actions are expressed in the highest possible way. It constitutes a crystal clarity and purity in the relationship we have with ourselves, with others, and with the world. Self-conduct is the core focus of impeccability. When we are holding the light arrow of impeccability, we experience ourselves and are experienced by others, as highly refined, deeply sincere, responsible, aware, and mindful.

The sole focus of one who holds this seventh light arrow is on the cultivation of impeccability in its truest and most "wholistic" expression. Impeccability differs from perfection in that the quest for the latter more often than not causes the Self (and others) to suffer, whereas impeccability gifts us with an ongoing experience of freedom, joy, and fulfillment in all that we do, while we are doing it and long after completion. We are left with a deep sense of satisfaction when we aspire to impeccability, whereas perfectionism often leaves us with a sense of being unfulfilled and unsatisfied. Perfectionism can be a hard taskmaster, whereas impeccability is a wonderful joy.

An analogy that involves the planets Saturn and Jupiter might help to further illustrate this point. In this context Saturn represents an attitude of *rolling up our sleeves* and *pushing against all odds to succeed,* often resulting in a difficult and challenging experience for Self (and others). Whereas Jupiter skips along with a happy-go-lucky approach, enjoying a wholly satisfying and re-sourcing experience. Simply put, if our quest for impeccability causes suffering to ourselves or others, then we are caught in the shadow of perfectionism. If, however, we are experiencing a joyful flow in our quest to meet the highest, most exalted level of whatever it is that we are engaged in, then we are aligned with impeccability.

An impeccable nature reflects a pure heart, a pure mind, and pure intent. The process of becoming impeccable entails the purification of the body, the emotions, and the mind. It requires us to scrutinize our conduct under a magnifying glass. Impeccability reveals that pure intent is behind everything we do and say.

Impeccability could be described as a virtue of the heart, a visible expression of the Soul. Impeccability requires absolute mindfulness as well as dedication to cultivating the highest achievable state of the physical, emotional, mental, psychological, and psychic levels of the Self. Impeccability is a state of grace. It requires us to live from crystal clarity and pure intent.

Impeccability calls on us to live from transparency in ourselves and in our interactions with others. It invites us to be scrupulously honest in *all* endeavors, to honor commitment, to take responsibility, and to walk our talk when it comes to our intention to live from impeccability without any expectation of or dependency on others doing the same.

One who lives from impeccability has healed, integrated, and transcended the seven dark arrows: attachment, dependency, judgment, comparison, expectation, the needy child syndrome, and self-importance. They have mastered the seven light arrows: self-awareness, self-acceptance, self-appreciation, self-pleasure, self-love, self-actualization, and so hold the seventh light arrow of impeccability, ready to begin the next level of self-mastery—the seven rainbow arrows.

When we carry the seventh light arrow of impeccability we have attained an elevated state of human conduct and this has a profoundly beneficial influence on all we come into contact with. When we live from impeccability we experience ourselves and are experienced by others as conducting ourselves in an impeccable manner, whether we are washing up, taking care of an animal, communicating with another, parenting a child, caring for an elderly relative, or running a multinational organization.

When carrying the seventh light arrow of impeccability we become like a tuning fork. The tone we emit is of the highest and purest frequency and one that supports others who interact with us to realign with higher levels of consciousness. The key notes that constitute the frequency of impeccability are purity, perfection, love, humility, grace, compassion, understanding, and empathy.

Seek to cultivate impeccability in every thought, word, action, and deed. Impeccability places us at the gateway to ultimate self-mastery, which is achieved when we have mastered all seven rainbow arrows.

A spiritual mantra for impeccability could be: *I choose to cultivate the exalted state that is impeccability. I deeply and unconditionally love and accept myself.*

So far, we have explored the seven dark arrows:

- Attachment
- Dependency
- Judgment
- Comparison
- Expectation
- The Needy Child Syndrome
- Self-Importance (un-integrated ego)

And the seven light arrows:

- Self-Awareness
- Self-Acceptance
- Self-Appreciation
- Self-Pleasure
- Self-Love

- Self-Actualization
- Impeccability

The First Nations Peoples taught that for every dark arrow we break, we automatically receive a light one and that for every light arrow integrated, we earn a rainbow arrow.

THE SEVEN RAINBOW ARROWS

Once we have integrated and mastered the seven rainbow arrows we have achieved mastery over the body, emotions, and mind. Mastery of the seven rainbow arrows is mastery of the Self. We shall now begin our exploration of the seven rainbow arrows.

The First Rainbow Arrow Is Illumination

The consciousness of the true mystic is one of illumination. The consciousness has been fully awakened to the knowing of the absolute. The illuminated Self is subject to experiences that are often described as peak or religious.

Illumination is an exalted state of being when one is filled with a sense of rapture, wonder, and intensity. This exalted state is distinguishable from psychic experiences, which tend to originate from the sacral chakra. Illumination involves all chakras, with an emphasis on the crown.

Illumination is a feeling akin to that of being in love with the totality of life and all creation. We perceive everything with an aura of golden light. Light pours from our eyes and our energy fields pulse in light waves.

One who is illumined radiates mystical qualities. The difference between illuminated and illusional is measured by the degree to which humility, purity, integration, and groundedness are expressed by the individual. To be illuminated is to live from an exalted and transcendent place within oneself.

As the phoenix rises from the ashes of awakening, the face is once more turned toward the sun and we begin to experience illumination.

Those who have attained a state of illumination have often been the very ones who have plumbed the depths of the unconscious. Those who are illumined are initiates of deep wisdom and seekers of truth. They are an exalted expression of the evolved human having liberated themselves from the lower nature. The illuminated live in a state between heaven and Earth with one foot in the world and the other in that transcendental place where inspiration and aspiration are to be found.

To attain an illuminated state involves a profound shift of consciousness. Perceiving the absolute requires an illuminated consciousness, which brings with it a vision and desire for a new Earth. An illuminated individual may have attained an elevated state of consciousness, yet this does not suggest they have reached a state of enlightenment. Enlightenment is an evolutionary trajectory and our growth toward this never ceases.

The evolutionary drive toward the attainment of illumination is an ongoing one. The experience of one who has transcended the personality is of an evolved state of consciousness. Conscious evolution catalyzes the next evolutionary stage of the human being.

To attain a state of illuminated consciousness requires an understanding and a reverence for the absolute. Our entire focus is upon the experience of oneness with the Divine Presence and with the creation of heaven on Earth. Illumination is the next level of conscious evolution beyond self-actualization.

To summarize, the first rainbow arrow is described eloquently in the following analogy, which illustrates the required conditions for one seeking illumination. It conveys St. Francis of Assisi's story of the "drinking deeply, devoutly, and in haste, from the chalice of life." It is taken from one of the most beautiful passages in the *Fioretti* and tells how Brother Jacques of la Massa, "unto whom God opened the door of His secrets," was shown in a vision the chalice of life delivered by Christ into the hands of St. Francis "that he might give his brothers to drink thereof."

Then came St. Francis to give the chalice of life to his brothers.

And he gave it first to Brother John of Parma: who, taking it drank it all in haste, devoutly; and straightway he became all shining like the sun. And after him St. Francis gave it to all the other brothers in order: and there were but few among them that took it with due reverence and devotion, and drank it all. Those that took it devoutly and drank it all, became straightway shining like the sun; but those that spilled it all and took it not devoutly, became black, and dark, and misshapen, and horrible to see; but those that drank part and spilled part, became partly shining and partly dark, and more so or less according to the measure of their drinking or spilling thereof. But the aforesaid Brother John was resplendent above all the rest; the which had more completely drunk the chalice of life, whereby he had more deeply gazed into the abyss of the infinite light divine.*

The Second Rainbow Arrow
Is Introspection

Introspection is the golden gateway to self-awareness and self-realization. Those who hold this second rainbow arrow also hold the wish card.

Carl Gustav Jung wrote: "Your vision will become clear only when you look into your heart. . . . Who looks outside, dreams. Who looks inside, awakens."

To look within is to risk the opening of Pandora's box. For as we lift the lid, all that is within us that has been repressed, split off, and denied is sure to erupt to seek acknowledgement, healing, and integration. Many are afraid to look into Pandora's box for fear of finding what has been long buried in the unconscious mind and what may be brought to their awareness, which they would prefer to not be reminded of.

The contents of Pandora's box (the unconscious) can remain hidden for a lifetime. Ultimately, however, to hide from what is buried only

---

*T. W. Arnold, trans. *The Little Flowers of St. Francis of Assisi* (London: Chatto and Windus, 1908), chapter XLVIII.

results in the breakdown of either the body, the emotions, the mind, or of all three. Continuing to keep the lid on these will result in physical illness, repeated relationship problems, emotional and mental trauma, and, at worst, total breakdown.

We could say that Pandora's box is representative of the Self, for it contains not only the human shadow, but also the light of who we are. If we look at the imagery for Pandora's box, we see light pouring from it as well as what is representative of the psychological shadow. However, we also see an angel arising from it. This is the hidden Angel of the Self. So, as we release trauma, so too do we release the Angelic/Authentic Self, which has also been locked away.

There are three levels of mind. These are the unconscious, the conscious, and the superconscious. These three levels of mind can have an enormous influence over the day-to-day experience of our lives, yet it is the unconscious mind that has the greatest influence of all.

I often describe the three levels of mind as being akin to a three-story house with the unconscious sitting beneath the conscious, and the superconscious positioned above the conscious. Imagine entering the basement of this metaphoric house to visit the unconscious mind. Now imagine that this basement contains wall-to-wall recording devices with accompanying visual screens running a continual reel of every memory, experience, and every thought you have ever had throughout your entire life.

Cellular biologist Bruce Lipton, Ph.D., suggests that the unconscious mind is capable of processing one million times more information than the conscious mind, handling up to forty million pieces of data per second. This suggests that 95 percent to 99 percent of our reactions (reactions stem from psychological wounding) or responses (from the Authentic Self) are governed by the unconscious mind.

The unconscious mind forms our patterning and conditioning. The impressions that we receive and the behavior we witness of those around us as we develop into adulthood influence and condition the unconscious mind. Most of the stories held in the unconscious mind belong to others. Our stories are barely formulated due to the stories of other people from our childhood and teens whose own stories have pervaded our unconscious minds. The stories that we act out are not our own but belong to the generations that went before us, who reenacted the stories of the generations that preceded them. And so it continues that we re-create the ancestral story/myth until someone says, "Enough. It ends here."

Unhealed childhood and teenage trauma remains alive within us, so determining our life experiences. For example, if as a child or teen you were told you were not good enough, you will unconsciously create situations and attract people into your life that reflect this unconscious belief back to you. This is the power of the 99 percent active unconscious mind.

A positive sign of these times is that many people are waking up and stating, "Enough. It ends here." However, many of these people may also be asking themselves just how to ensure this occurs. The second rainbow arrow of introspection reveals the answer. As Lama Surya Das says in *Awakening the Buddha Within,* "Through honest self-inquiry and no-holds-barred meditative introspection over a sustained period of time, one can take apart and deconstruct the hut that ego built, thus entering the mansion of Authentic Being."

So, how can we use this rainbow arrow to guide and teach us each day? Introspection requires dedication and time set aside for exploration of the Self. It invites us to work one-to-one with a professional practitioner who is skilled in supporting us to rediscover our Authentic Self, to hear, see, and validate our shadow self, to heal and integrate self-sabotaging behavior and, by so doing, change the prerecorded, self-destructive subliminal messages held deep within our unconscious minds.

The rainbow arrow of introspection encourages us to join groups that seek to heal and integrate the shadow self. It counsels us in our personal meditations and journaling so that we may each rediscover our True Self. Conscious media gives us access to the information that is needed to facilitate our quest for self-healing, self-discovery, and self-realization.

We need only be curious about what is behind our reactions (as opposed to responses), our discontent, or the themes and patterns that repeat in our lives and be willing to examine our thoughts, emotions, motivations, decisions, words, actions, and deeds. By doing so we transform our lives as well as create new and positive self-serving "recordings" in the unconscious mind. These can transform the pre-programmed, self-sabotaging messages to self-affirming ones instead. The possibilities for healing, evolution, transformation, and inner peace are endless when we hold the second rainbow arrow.

For the most part our actions and reactions (including those of others) confuse or surprise us when we remain unaware of the ruling 99 percent of the unconscious mind. This suggests that in any given moment, rather than the more neutral conscious mind experiencing other people and the environment as an invitation for deeper introspection, the conscious mind of those who are not engaged in introspection instead remains dominated by messages, myths, and stories from the past that are stored in the unconscious mind.

The wall-to-wall recording devices and screens of the unconscious mind continually run visuals of unhealed trauma. Thus, there is a continual outpouring of forty million pieces of data per second, all colored by psychological trauma, that keeps us in maintaining cycles of attack and defense, fight or flight, reaction and self-sabotaging behavior. New and self-loving messages need to be downloaded into the grids of the unconscious mind so as to dissolve existing negative imprints.

To evolve spiritually and heal and integrate psychologically we must carry the rainbow arrow of introspection. Take hold of this rainbow arrow and dare to look deeply within and at your life. By doing so you will discover the buried treasure of your Authentic Self and so come to experience transformation, liberation, peace, joy, and love.

The Third Rainbow Arrow
Is Trust and Innocence

Trust is found at the core of all meaningful relationships, including the relationship with ourselves. Without trust we cannot bond, be open to, or experience right relationship with ourselves or other people. The roots of mistrust are to be found as far back as infancy. As babies, we are vulnerable and entirely dependent upon our caregivers. The degree to which we learn to trust originates from the quality of love and care and the dependability of those who were our primary caregivers at that time.

When we learn to successfully develop trust in early childhood we feel secure and safe in the world. However, when we have experienced our primary caregivers as emotionally or physically absent, abusive, unreliable, contradictory, or rejecting, we develop deep feelings of mistrust. Where trust has been broken we experience a deep rupture within our emotional and mental bodies, as well as deep psychological wounds, which result in an inability to trust others. We then perceive the world as a hostile and unpredictable place.

> Here are some signs that may suggest you have trust issues: fear of intimacy, suspicion, anxiety in many forms including during physical intimacy, impotence, inability to orgasm or inability to orgasm when sexually intimate with a partner, panic attacks, irrational fear and terror, agoraphobia, claustrophobia, phobias in general, repeated patterns of relationship breakdown (romance or friends), and attracting dishonesty, betrayal, or deception.

Trust is essential for our overall well-being. In order to function in society and to live fulfilled lives, we need to trust. There is a fundamental difference between the experience of fulfillment and that of security. The need for security has become greater than our ability to trust. When we are unable to trust, our entire life choices revolve around fear and security. We remain locked in the "known," which becomes a prison and yet it is where we feel safest.

Security needs are really safety needs. When we lack trust we view people, places, and opportunities as a threat to our safety. When we trust we embrace the unknown, opportunities, and adventures, recognizing these as potentials for growth. Living in the known equates to safety, security, and merely surviving, whereas engaging in what is unknown can lead to fulfillment and give us a feeling of being alive.

A healthy relationship with trust has parameters. It is important to gauge whom to trust, when to trust, when not to trust, how much to trust, and to ascertain why we can trust. We could refer to this kind of trust as "discerning trust"—where the choices are life-serving and not life-denying.

For those who do not have trust issues, life-serving choices are part of everyday life and bring us little concern or preoccupation. However, for those who do have trust issues, hours, days, and weeks can be lost in confusion and conflicting inner dialogue, imagining worst-case scenarios. We usually manifest these if the shadow side of our consciousness is given free rein to create our reality.

It is important to have a healthy relationship with trust on a day-to-day basis. Total mistrust indicates a need to heal and free ourselves of trust issues. Where there is no trust, there is no inner peace. Nearly every human being longs for world peace. We are beginning now to comprehend that to achieve this requires that each one of us must first find peace within. It is important that those who long for inner peace realize that in order to achieve this they must learn to trust.

You may notice that those who appear at ease with themselves are mostly positive and in love with life, have wonderful relationships and friendships, radiate light and well-being, and also display a childlike innocence. Children who trust convey vulnerability, purity, and transparency. This can also be said to be true of those adults who are able to live in trust. They appear to live from the heart, which is wide open and free of past conditioning. This is not to suggest that there is no past conditioning, only that they have worked to heal, overcome, and transcended it.

What you are called to now is a return to innocence. To go back in time to the very moment before your heart began to close through fear and mistrust. Enter into the pure heart that is to be found buried within your own, and call to this so it will begin to expand and open as you learn to trust once more, as you did so long ago.

If you ever find yourself wondering why it is that the same patterns of broken trust, betrayal, deception, or loss of innocence keep reoccurring, understand this psychological reality—we re-create our history in order to do now what we could not do back then. Every experience we have of broken trust and loss of innocence as adults, has its roots in our earlier lives. We unconsciously attract the same storyline (or myth) in order to say and do now what we were unable to do or say back then. However, attracting the experience of broken trust is deeply unconscious and so most people never recognize that these patterns repeat themselves only because a primary wound is seeking to be healed. Until we recognize this and consciously work with it, we will continually attract people and situations who reenact our primary psychological wounds and so present us with an opportunity for healing and integration. Those with whom we struggle and suffer are often healing angels in disguise.

Where trust is broken, innocence is lost. Yet, no matter how much trust has been broken, know that you have all that you need within you to fully restore both trust and innocence. Integrating the seven dark and the seven light arrows will bring you back home fully to yourself and will locate you, once again, in that heaven that exists within each one of us, which remains whole and unbroken.

You are called to acknowledge the degree to which you feel you can trust or not, as the case may be, to gauge from this an understanding of the extent trust or mistrust permeates your life. If you find that mistrust is tipping the balance of the scales, then now is the time to seek support in order to free yourself from the ties that are binding you to a life lived from mistrust. True love, peace, and joy are to be found in the vulnerability of an open heart, not in a heart that is closed.

When we are fully present in our heart we are empathic and understanding, compassionate and unconditionally loving. Whereas once we may have viewed the unreliable or dishonest conduct of another through the lens of fear, when we live from the heart we view such a person through a lens of love. Live from an open heart and live a life of extraordinary peace, love, joy, wonder, and beauty.

You are reading this for a reason. Listen. Your heart is calling you and inviting you to trust and to return to innocence. By so doing you will hear the greatest symphonies, observe the most exquisite of colors, experience the purest of emotions, sense the profound and sublime, know the greatest love, and touch the heart of the Earth and the spiritual ecstasy of the heavens.

The Fourth Rainbow Arrow Is Wisdom

Let us first begin our exploration of the fourth rainbow arrow of wisdom by defining just what wisdom is. It may help our understanding to begin with an assessment of what wisdom is not. Wisdom is not rationale, it is not information, it is not of the intellect, or found in academia, nor does it have its origins in the left brain.

What then do we mean by wisdom? Wisdom is the expression of the heart's knowing. It is the connection to the felt sense. Wisdom is gnosis, we just *know*. It dwells within the domain of the intuition, the gut feeling, and the inner voice. Wisdom engages the right side of the brain, the feminine aspect of the male and female, the creative impulse, and the intuitive Self. Whereas knowledge is of the mind, wisdom is of the Soul.

From a spiritual perspective we could say that the wisdom that resides in each one of us constitutes the sum total of all that we have learned throughout the many incarnations we have had on Earth. The more self-aware we are, the more we are able to access our inborn wisdom.

Wisdom is the voice that guides us to take a different train, to cancel an appointment, to go to an unusual gathering we would ordinarily not have gone to. Wisdom is a knowing that something is wrong or something significant or special will occur. Wisdom is the wise counsel that directs us through life as harmoniously as possible if we would but listen.

However, the fact is that wisdom has been sidelined in favor of knowledge, information, and intellect. The world is obsessed with these and so wisdom has paid the price. The more that people have hungered after knowledge, information, intellectual prowess, and achievement, the less connected they have become to wisdom. The voice of wisdom has been drowned out, and instead of being the wise sages that each one of us is, we have become slaves to an overdeveloped and stimulated left brain. And on the occasions that wisdom, like the sun, manages to pierce through the blanket cloud of gray matter and the domineering left brain, it is paid no heed, being banished to a lowly position once again only able to penetrate the consciousness of an individual in moments of suffering or pending danger.

What these times call for is the return of hemispheric synchronization of the left and right brain. The left brain, when in balance, is of equal value to the right brain. However, when the left brain is favored to the degree it is in our present world, we find imbalance in our lives and in all our endeavors.

How did we move so far away from the wisdom within ourselves? Wisdom is an experience of feeling, heart, felt sense, and Soul and, therefore, it connects to the emotional Self. As a result of the suppression of the emotional Self, through the lack of value placed on the psychological development of the individual in school curriculums and the family environment as we grow, we come to hide our emotions, our true thoughts, and our feelings and so create a disconnection from wisdom.

Wisdom is Truth. It speaks only the language of truth. As soon as our first lie is uttered or we behave in a dishonest way (ego ensuring survival of Self), we disconnect from wisdom. By the time most have reached adolescence, the disconnect from wisdom is almost total and the preoccupation instead is fully focused upon proving oneself worthy to family, educational authorities, or community. For those who do not feel they have an intellectual predisposition, the ego nevertheless remains firmly implanted in the driver's seat of their lives where it can manifest as a preoccupation with appearance, attraction to the opposite or same sex, and where self-worth becomes dependent upon the approval of peers, friends, and colleagues.

And then there are those who fit into neither of the above categories. Their lives have been simply poverty and struggle and so are dependent upon the welfare state for survival. Often such people who have neither an inclination toward the intellectual or are too poor to impress their peers with fancy clothes and the latest smart phones fall into apathy, suffering, angst, and pain, which disconnects them from their hearts and any concept of Soul is far removed from their reality.

That is not to say that one who has wisdom cannot be wealthy and live an abundant life. People do; however, this is the exception rather than the rule. The point to make here is that whenever there has been an experience in childhood where one has not been seen, heard, acknowledged, or validated for expressing a true and pure feeling, there has been a disconnect with wisdom. The individual reads the messages of the environment and is impacted by the consequences that occurred when they first attempted to express a pure feeling in response to something unjust or discordant that took place. Rather than attempting to once more use wisdom, they rapidly adapt, recognizing that to do this will avoid the experience of physical, emotional, and mental pain.

We need to find our way back to wisdom. It is essential for the health and true happiness of any individual. So, how do we do this? We must begin by addressing the first dark arrow and working our way through the subsequent dark arrows, ideally with someone who is therapeutically trained to a high enough standard to support us. We need to align with whatever reconnects us to wisdom, even though it may not at first feel like a direct connection. Just by our seeking to reconnect with the heart, the emotions, the thoughts, the feelings, and the felt sense, the creative part of ourselves and our imagination (which is the Soul in action) will begin to connect us to wisdom.

When asking ourselves a question or making an important decision, rather than being in a "should" or "ought" mentality (ego-driven reactions), we need to pause, breathe, and check in with our felt sense to ascertain what is it telling us. A simple way to know is noticing if your body expands or contracts, relaxes or tenses, when making a decision. Do you feel like going out for lunch with friends on a Sunday, or do you feel like a long, luxurious day of pottering around your home? Listen out for the "I should" or "I ought" or "they will be expecting" or "I don't want to let them down." Now, turn that around. What expectations are you placing upon yourself? How are you letting yourself down? What do *you* need?

Remember you have had a life of adapting your truth, hiding your true feelings, silencing your true voice, saying or doing what you have to in order to please or placate others. The price you have paid is the highest price of all, the loss of wisdom, which translates to the disconnection from your heart, feelings, your True Self, Soul, and Spirit.

When in balance, knowledge, information, and wisdom stand side by side as great and necessary pillars of support for the Self. When all three are in harmony and have a place in our lives, then we are experiencing ourselves as whole. As Paracelsus said, "Inside each one of us is a piece of heaven whole and unbroken." Seek wisdom today and in that find your own inner heaven, which will support you to create a whole and unbroken life.

Love and wisdom are the prerequisites for a joyful and fulfilled life. A person who has overly developed the intellect and places undue importance on knowledge, at the expense of the heart and wisdom, will never be spiritually wise, as their focus is purely on the material and the worldly. Society has misrepresented knowledge and masqueraded it as wisdom, yet wisdom is found in the true spiritual nature of each human being.

Intelligence that springs from emotion and from the heart is wisdom; most other forms of intelligence reflect an extraordinary gift for memorizing reams of facts and information. One who embodies wisdom has developed many qualities, including unconditional love, unconditional positive regard, a nonjudgmental outlook, humility, compassion, understanding, honesty, and integrity. Throughout history, the good and great and the honest and true have all been recognized by these virtues.

Seek wisdom today and every day and you will never have felt more connected with yourself, with others, and with the world around you.

The Fifth Rainbow Arrow Is Open Heart-to-Heart Communication

This fifth rainbow arrow stirs an immediate response within the heart. It is as if the heart instinctively opens merely by reading the title of this arrow. In the 1950s pioneering psychologist Carl Rogers said this of communication: "Love, genuineness, and empathy are the three essential elements to constructive communication."

We need to find ways to communicate that support ourselves and other people. At the core of all communication has to be love. Love has to be the foundation stone upon which we build a loving and heart-centered communication. The issue that so often arises is that our quest for loving communication can be interrupted by a reaction that is a result of triggering unconscious memories of trauma and these are then projected onto the one with whom we are communicating. We need to learn what lies behind our reactions, be they projections of anger or hurt or a withholding and punishing silence.

Most people are unaware of what mechanisms are at play in the arena of communication. Their bodies may indicate something is occurring as the heartbeat increases, the palms sweat, the cheeks flush, the voice stammers, or in many cases the person is gripped by irrational fear. Such reactions can occur simply by walking into a family dinner or a work-related social night, joining a new group of colleagues or friends, starting a new job, or entering a supermarket. Even making an inquiry on the telephone can result in feelings of panic or rage.

Unless we have been raised by conscious or deeply heart-centered, psychologically balanced parents, it is likely that we have never learned how to effectively and naturally communicate with others. The majority of us have never experienced heart-to-heart communication with our own parents and have been raised under the repressive, dualistic model of an educational system that fails to support functional and healthy communication. This is not an issue of blame, as parents and those involved in our growing process from infancy to adulthood were raised under the same systems that failed to meet their own needs, and so they are merely mimicking and replicating what they were taught themselves.

However, we live in times where our generation has more choice. We can state, "It ends here" and take responsibility to learn now what could not be learned back then and, in that, to do now what could not be done back then. We come to understand that as we do so, we become the voice for the generations that have gone and for the generations to follow.

The fact is that our models for communication have been about defense and attack. We have only to look at the mainstream media, the work place, the community, and the home to see evidence of this. We have been raised in a fear-based, repressive culture where honesty equates to punishment, blame, rejection, judgment, and attack. What we have learned about communication is how dishonesty, disconnection, and repression are the ways in which to survive, and because of this we have developed a highly sophisticated survival mentality, which protects us against any further hurt. It is the fundamental experiences of being hurt that have caused us to adapt ourselves in order to survive.

What we need to feel is *alive* in body, mind, and soul; in our hearts; in our creativity; and in our Spirit. We need to feel engaged, connected, and enraptured with ourselves, other people, and the world. Yet, for the most part, we remain disconnected, lost in a twilight zone of self-preservation, but at what cost to the True and Authentic Self?

In transpersonal psychotherapy, we speak of the *adapted self* and the *Authentic Self,* a subject I delve more deeply into in the writings on the ego in chapter 6. However, in essence, in order to survive, the Authentic or True Self quickly disappears into hiding as a result of the incongruent and confusing messages being received from external sources. This occurs mainly in infancy and as toddlers; and what steps forward to take the place of the Authentic Self, to champion it, is the adapted self (note the small *s*) also known as the personality, the ego, the wounded self, the historical self, the wounded child, the historical child, and so on.

NVC (nonviolent communication) has a four-step process— observing, feeling, needing, and requesting. How these work is that when applying them to either ourselves (What am I noticing/observing?

What am I feeling? What do I need? What is my request?) or to another (What are you noticing/observing? What are you feeling? What do you need? What is your request?) we begin to open the channels to authentic and heart-to-heart communication.

When we have engaged these four steps we can ask ourselves, or another, three further questions: How can I acknowledge what is noticed or observed? How can I respond to the feeling? How can I meet the need/request?

In all cases, when these four basic principles are engaged with, we come to understand not only our own feelings and needs, but also those of others. Practiced regularly these four steps transform us into compassionate communicators. The requirement is to feel seen, heard, validated, and acknowledged and when engaging in these four steps this becomes possible. You may find yourself silently practicing these steps in your everyday communications.

Do not expect others to know what to do, how to do it, or how to respond. In fact, it is likely they will react in the usual way. However, by engaging in a different style of communication you will bring about change within the pattern of dialogue, and perhaps even rouse another's curiosity to question why the communication on your part is supportive and responsive as opposed to reactive and dismissive. At this stage, you can introduce them to this new model of communication and look forward to enjoying heart-to-heart conversation for the first time. Remember, however, that the important point is to be practicing and refining this within yourself.

NVC is a transformational technique that can change the relationship with yourself and others. It will transform your life. Visit the CNVC website (check the resources in the back of this book) where you will find many resources, practice groups, trainings, and practitioners. You can begin to learn to communicate your feelings appropriately and nonviolently and so express your feelings and needs without blame or shame and from an empowered and centered place, which is the heart of heart-to-heart communication.

The Sixth Rainbow Arrow Is
Balancing Male and Female Energies

For millennia, duality has been a powerful and ever-present phenomenon. It has been understood to consist of two opposing states. However, duality does not mean opposites; it merely constitutes two forces that can be complementary when their differences are understood.

Duality is present in all levels of human experience. For example, we are both human and Divine, we are Soul and Spirit, we are heart and mind, and we are woman and man. We live within a physical and spiritual paradigm of heaven and Earth. When observing human emotions we find that where there is fear there is love; where there is sadness there is joy; where there is anger there is peace; where there is pain there is happiness; and so forth.

It is believed that once upon a time, many thousands of years ago, when the Soul first came to the Earth from heaven, we each descended as one androgynous Being, where both masculine and feminine were an integrated whole consciousness within one body. (I write more extensively about this in chapter 8, "Higher Love and Sexuality.") As we descended further into matter from Spirit and became increasingly attached to the physical and sensory pleasures of earthly life, we began to lose our divine connection to Source/God Consciousness. Instead, we began to develop separation consciousness, which resulted in the birth of the ego. It is said that our androgynous body separated into two halves taking the form of a physical man and a physical woman.

Since that time we have remained on the earthly wheel of reincarnation, attempting to once more reunite with our twin soul and so feel complete. Within the male is contained the blueprint of the female and within the female, the blueprint of the male. For each incarnation, whatever gender our form takes—and we have lived as both sexes equally—we have been developing both aspects, so that often in a masculine body we have moved toward the expression of female qualities and vice versa.

The "new man" of the nineties was a domesticated house-husband who wanted to remain at home to nurture his children while his female partner chose to work in the world. Conversely, a Soul may incarnate into a male form and desire to immerse himself in all things masculine, perhaps having just completed a series of feminine lives. The same can apply to females who choose to develop and fully experience their femininity, for they may have just finished a series of masculine lives. However, despite the Soul's agenda for the integration of male and female energies, no matter how much we are polarized into the definitive expression of maleness or femaleness, we still retain the male/female template within and will always be drawn to its expression.

The balance of male and female energies within the individual are a prerequisite, alongside one's capacity for self-actualization, to magnetize a lasting union, and in rare cases reunion with the lost twin from the days of the androgynous Self. Humanity has lived through both matriarchal and patriarchal epochs, but this present day calls for neither and something new entirely. Self-rulership, or in other words self-mastery, will create a new epoch where neither male nor female dominates or sublimates. Instead, male and female will be together, side by side as equals to inspire, co-create, and collaborate for the highest good of humanity in two physically separate forms, yet as one aligned energy.

Throughout the ages man has feared woman, especially in the matriarchal era, and woman has feared the patriarchal man. Now we live in an era that invites self-awareness and self-realization. It is time to put aside fear and replace it with love, to dare to express the soft and loving and those discerning and fully empowered aspects of ourselves. It is time to celebrate and revere our differences and worship the opposite sex as an aspect of our own integrated inner male and female.

The following is a list of some of the male and female traits and qualities that are required for integration and balance.

Positive Qualities for the Masculine to Develop	Negative Traits of the Masculine to Be Overcome
Positive action	Aggression
Empowerment	Domination
Analysis	Power driven
Left-brain activity	Competitiveness
Strength	Impatience
Striving	Distraction
Assertion	Control
Organizing	Head driven
Endurance	Base instincts at sexual level
Rational and logical thinking	Projection of unhealed inner female onto women
Solidity	
Self-control	
Authority	
Autonomy	
Heart driven	
Instinctual	
Protective	
Meeting survival needs	
Initiating	
Mental development	

Positive Qualities for the Feminine to Develop	Negative Traits of the Feminine to Be Overcome
Being	Passivity
Empowerment	Inferiority
Intuition	Overemotional (as opposed to centered in feelings)
Surrender	
Trust	Gossip
Receptivity	Mistrust
Giving	Too abstract
Calmness	Victim mentality
Patience	Preoccupation with security needs
Softness	
Tranquillity	Projecting unhealed inner male onto men
Creativity	
Abstractness	
Right-brain emphasis	
Feeling	
Nurturing	
Nourishing	
Gnosis	
Heart	
Unconditional love	

All these lists can be used by both men and women to cultivate their own masculinity or femininity and, at the same time, be cross-referenced in order to develop the positive qualities of their opposite inner gender. Take particular note of the negative traits and be honest with yourself about those that feel familiar! Women may notice negative male traits in their own behavior; the same applies to men regarding the negative traits on the female lists. Accordingly, both genders may also recognize positive qualities from the list of the opposite sex. Embrace these as a wonderful sign of male/female balance taking place within.

There is an enormous consciousness shift occurring in the world today. The boundaries and defenses between people, authorities, and nations are now ready to be dissolved, and so too is the divide between male and female. Many are experiencing a deep and tangible inner shift and a rebalancing of what has been split within the Self: for example, left/right, male/female, heart/mind, past/present, inner child/empowered adult, adapted self/Authentic Self.

It is time for all to be equal. Both male and female positive qualities can be expressed through each one of us. By both sexes integrating all the positive qualities and releasing all those negative traits found on both lists, not only will the relationship with yourself improve radically, but so too will your relationships with partner, children, mother, father, friends, and colleagues as you become a role model for an integrated, well-rounded, and positive example of a man or woman in today's modern and conscious global society.

The Seventh Rainbow Arrow Is Abundance and Prosperity

The seventh and final rainbow arrow is abundance and prosperity. Everyone longs to live an abundant and prosperous life. However, exactly what is the abundance and prosperity that this seventh rainbow arrow speaks of?

Is it referring to us being rich beyond our wildest dreams, owning several properties around the world, a yacht moored in Cannes, eating out at expensive restaurants most nights, and jetting to exotic locations for holidays whenever it suits our mood? Is it the type of abundance and prosperity that is the result of our working eighteen hours a day in a soulless job, or working for an organization or within an establishment that has no humanitarian values, morals, and ethics?

Is it the type of abundance and prosperity that takes quality time away from ourselves, families, and friends? Is it the type of abundance and prosperity gained through dishonesty, betrayal, and greed? In other words, is it generated through the human shadow, not the human heart?

Or, does the seventh rainbow arrow refer to a type of abundance and prosperity that speaks of the riches to be found living life from the heart and Soul? Could it be referring to the wealth we can enjoy when working at jobs that make our hearts sing, even though that particular line of work may be deemed to lack prestige by those who would judge, rather than be curious as to why we radiate such joy, commitment, and passion.

We can pour ourselves into work that we find deeply rewarding for eighteen hours a day, even though there may be just enough funds to meet the minimum requirements for our basic survival needs. We can still find time for family and friends, for even though we may feel tired, the passion for doing something we love keeps us energized—in contrast to finding ourselves exhausted and depleted by working eighteen hours a day at something that disconnects us from the heart and Soul.

Abraham Maslow was once quoted as stating, "All who have a vocation are well." A vocation is a calling of the Soul and constitutes any work where we feel we are engaging our Soul. This does not necessarily mean we are able to work at what we have always dreamed of doing (for example, performing, acting, singing, working as an artist, writer, author, designer, or becoming the figurehead of a better-world initiative, and so forth), for the work we end up doing is dependent upon our psychological, conscious, and spiritual evolution.

Karma exerts an influence and yet can be addressed more speedily when we become psychologically, consciously, and spiritually aware. So for example, we may dream of being a singer yet we find ourselves cleaning offices and in that feel uninspired. However, if we choose the path of self-development, self-awareness, and self-realization, if we continue to work at cleaning offices it is because we actually enjoy doing so, for it brings us great satisfaction. And if this is not the case, we will move toward manifesting a vocational path that reflects the dreams and aspirations we hold dear. Everything we experience and all that we are is a result of how far along the path of our evolutionary spiritual journey we are at any given time.

There is an enormous divide between poverty and wealth in this world. We ask ourselves how is it that many are extremely rich and yet many are so poor? This is an existential, deep, and multilayered question that requires an existential, deep, and multilayered response and, as such, is too much to address here. However, let us consider the fact that we are spiritual Beings having a human experience and because of this we are here with specific spiritual lessons to learn and karma (redressing of balance) to work through.

Let us consider a person who may be labeled as being poor; someone whose presence on Earth, despite their circumstances, is experienced as a gift to all those who know them; a person who works tirelessly from their heart, shining in all they do, bringing light, love, reassurance, and comfort to all those whose lives they touch. This can be said of the heart-centered postman, nurse, gravedigger, supermarket check-out cashier, builder, teacher, healer, someone physically challenged or of ill health, or someone dependent on state benefits to survive. If you were to ask such a person if they felt poor, they may share with you that although materially things are very tight, they feel rich inside. It will be evident in their demeanor, as others experience them as a golden ray of sunshine.

A spiritually awakened person who lives in material poverty might judge and blame themselves for their situation and feel that they must have done something dreadful in a previous life to be suffering to such a degree on a material level. In some circumstances this could well be the case and, if so, karma must be balanced by acts of goodness and self-development. However, for many who struggle at the material level it may be an indication that they are at an advanced level of their spiritual evolution. For, living in material poverty yet still being able to give of oneself 100 percent for the well-being of others, the community, animals, and the world indicates an advanced consciousness.

Thousands of years of ignorance and cultural conditioning have resulted in the rich regarding the poor as inferior and the poor may think themselves less worthy. This is changing. It is true to say, from a karmic perspective, that if we had wealth and abused it in a previous life, or acted selfishly, not utilizing our privileged position to help those in need, we may be required to experience and understand the condition of poverty in this lifetime.

However, we may have experienced a life of great wealth and been very conscientious in our fortunate circumstances and supported others in need. Yet, we may still incarnate into poverty in the next lifetime. The reason for this is that we learned the lesson of possessing material wealth in that life. In this life, we would be continuing our soul's evolutionary journey and understanding what constitutes true wealth (abundance and prosperity) in order to experience how being materially poor can present an opportunity to enrich the Soul.

When we look at the great spiritual teachers throughout history, they did not work for money and were instead supported by those who most valued their teachings. This practice continues to this day, with small and large sums of money donated to support not only the basic needs of the spiritual teacher, but also their resident communities and their own spiritual work in the world.

Keeping our focus on the true meaning of this seventh rainbow arrow, let us turn our attention now to what constitutes true abundance and prosperity. True abundance and prosperity are primarily experiences of the heart and Soul. The heart and Soul are naturally abundant and prosperous. Whether the former is open to receive and give, or the latter is awakened enough to experience this, is dependent upon the development of the Soul. An open heart gives and receives love unconditionally in abundance, never really feeling poor, for it is sustained by this love even when the life lacks material wealth.

A prosperous Soul sings with joy for the rich inner life it has from day to day, for how inspired it feels, and for how it experiences itself as an inspiration to others. A truly abundant and prosperous person never really feels poor, for the quality of life that they experience at a heart and Soul level makes them feel rich and blessed.

The great divide, the dualistic split between rich and poor, the polarity of success and failure must be healed. The world needs to value all contributions be they material or spiritual. Money and material goods are merely energy. If someone who is poor brings great comfort and joy to one who is rich, then this could be reciprocated with an exchange of energy by offering some material security, be that money for food for that week, gas for the car, that month's rent or mortgage, a new pair of boots, a utility bill paid, or something similar.

All of us, rich and poor, have something important to offer each other. We must understand ourselves to be equals, and the world needs to value the blessings that the poor can bestow upon the wealthy and vice versa. None of us really need to be materially poor or lacking. If all were to share their good fortune, be that material riches or a wealth of love, we would all begin to know what true abundance and prosperity are.

In an ideal world, we would all be able to reach out and ask each other for what we lack, knowing that our needs would be met and our dignity remain intact. Someone of material wealth could reach out to one who is not so fortunate for counsel, healing, guidance, advice, practical support, and to learn about love—about feeling loved for who they really are and not the size of their bank balance. Similarly someone who is poor would welcome the support of one who is in a better position materially, so that they may be able to reduce the crippling and paralyzing stress that is experienced by living below survival level and enjoy what a little money can bring in terms of leisure and relaxation.

It is shocking to note that the average minimum wage paid per hour in the United States is just seven dollars and seventy-five cents. Is this not unbelievable? How can anyone's time per hour be worth so little? At the other end of the spectrum some people earn colossal amounts of money. How can they live in such material wealth and not feel a powerful need to reach out to their human brothers and sisters who are barely surviving? This has to be addressed.

There is a fine line between giving, which results in someone becoming even more lazy or dependent versus offering someone a lifeline to support them to become more self-sufficient and materially stable. We do not live in a utopian paradigm, yet we can live in hope, for we have the power, by the grace of our heart and Soul, to co-create an era of deep peace for humanity for the first time in history.

We must share. We must view each other as equals and worthy of our love, our time, our wisdom, our natural gifts, and material resources. None of us ever need to suffer, be it from lack of love or lack of material abundance and prosperity. For, if we were to reach out our arms, open our hearts, and bare our Souls to each other, we would all be living in true abundance and prosperity.

There is more than enough material wealth to go around. If you are one who has more than most, then count your blessings and then bless another by supporting their needs. Making donations to organizations that seek support for third-world poverty, animal rescue, or environmental causes is a wonderful contribution; however, also look within your local community and see what is needed there. Try not to pass a homeless person on the street without dropping into a café and buying them a meal or hot drink and food for their dog. For the more you live from your heart and allow your heart to rule your head, the more love and appreciation you will bring into your life.

And in turn, those who are poor, what can they do to help make the world a better place that costs nothing? Smile at people, pray for others and the world, be gentle and kind to your fellow humans and to the animals, care about the environment, develop a spiritual practice, and most importantly, tune into your heart and feel what you would really like to do with your life, something with a realistic goal and that with a little effort you could achieve.

When you see someone who is wealthy and yet you know they are lonely, reach out to them with no motivation or hidden agenda other than to ease their loneliness. For the more you live from your heart, the more you will experience true abundance and prosperity, and even though you may have little money you will never feel poor. Whether you are abundant and prosperous in the material sense or live below or just above the poverty line, know that by opening your heart, viewing others and life through the lens of your Soul, wherever you experience lack, you will magically begin to attract true abundance and prosperity.

And for those who are either rich or poor but whose hearts are closed and who remain disconnected from the reality of who they really are, unconditional love and understanding are needed, along with unconditional giving and doing. In every way and all ways the eternal fountain of love, true abundance, and prosperity are to be found within the awakened heart and Soul of an individual, and it never ceases to flow. It is inexhaustible and as it re-sources others, so too does it continue to renew for ourselves.

Whatever the reasons for our material circumstances, the seventh rainbow arrow speaks to the kind of wealth that is found within the heart and Soul. This is the only wealth that is really worth possessing—true abundance and prosperity. When we leave this body we do not take our possessions and bank balances with us. The merit of our Soul is not measured by these as we pass from this realm. No, the only wealth that matters when we meet our Maker is what is to be found within our heart and how freely and unconditionally we gave true abundance and prosperity during our lifetime.

Whether our gifts to each other are material or spiritual, money or love, when given from pure intention and a pure heart, they are what allow a human being to experience true abundance and prosperity, for it is the exchange of love that registers in the records of the Soul. It is not how much material wealth we made available to others or even how much we loved others, but the pure intention, pure motive, and pure unconditional love that was present in every exchange.

What is important is how we lived our lives and how our presence on Earth benefited humanity, all sentient beings, and the Earth herself.

FOUR

Religion and Spirituality

Historical Context

I found I had less and less to say, until finally,
I became silent, and began to listen.
I discovered in the silence, the voice of God.

SØREN KIERKEGAARD

Ordinarily, one might expect a book on contemporary spirituality to contain much historical research and information charting the origins of religion and spirituality to date. Yet, from the perspective of this writer, the subject of religion and spirituality are, by their nature, simplistic and therefore warrant a simple explanation.

Religion has held a vice-like hold over humanity for thousands of years with its 'fire and brimstone' fear-mongering and punishing misinterpretations, which were established to control and manipulate mass consciousness.

People throughout millennia have learned to seek God for salvation, to relieve them of their suffering, to save them, and so forth. The existing model for religion is one of duality with an us-versus-them mentality.

The distorted interpretations of religion, as it has been presented to us, have remained indecipherable and an enigma to the masses who barely understand the complex, multilayered, intellectually falsified language of religious scriptures and doctrines handed down to us by the patriarchy. These have ensured that such information remains in the hands, or should we say left brains, of the privileged few whose minds are trained and able to decipher overintellectualized data.

There remains no doubt that the foundations of any of the leading religious philosophies originated from the finest minds of those who introduced them to humanity, such as Buddha, Krishna, Jesus, and Mohammed. However, following the departure of these great spiritual lights, many of the teachings, for example those of Jesus, were hijacked by those deemed to be the most intelligent, influential, and powerful at that time. This instantly removed these core teachings from the public domain and placed them into the hands of those who had elected themselves to carry the messages given to humanity by the great spiritual teachers.

The torchbearers for these great teachings fell into two categories: those who wished to accurately represent and teach the core messages and those who realized these teachings could be manipulated in order to control people. A good example of this is Christianity.

And so we find ourselves some thousands of years later at the dawn of a new age, one foretold by ancient prophecy to herald the ending of a 26,000-year astronomical cycle. We stand upon a threshold of a new epoch with the need for a true interpretation of the original teachings of the great ones who brought them into this world. What we need is a contemporary spirituality for an evolving world.

So having shared this, I would like to begin this chapter by exploring the origins of Christianity, the main religion that has dominated the Western world for the past two thousand years. The question of religion and spirituality came to the forefront of my awareness some years ago, when I realized there is a profoundly significant astronomical occurrence taking place within the heavens. This awareness coincided with my own gnosis, as we move from an old paradigm and the old ways into a new understanding and vision, that a different approach is needed in regard to religion and spiritual philosophy.

My focus here is on Christianity, yet in truth some of what I share applies to all world religions—although Buddhism, Sufism, and the Krishna faith, for example, already uphold many of these ideas. However, even some of these teachings would benefit from being brought into the twenty-first century. I wish to refer to a number of religious and spiritual teachings, including their approach to the integration of the ego. I have written the Ego/Self fairytale about this, which is also a visionary response to the integration of the ego as opposed to the more reactive approach taught by the majority of the world's religions and spiritual practices. (The fairytale can be found in chapter 6.)

Many people have written to me to state just how revelatory this new way of approaching the ego is and of how they experience it as profound, evolutionary, and appropriate for the times in which we now live. People from all walks of life, versed in all manner of religious or spiritual teachings, have spoken to me of the evolutionary potential and psycho-spiritual transformation that becomes possible when adopting this new approach.

I am sharing this to highlight the fact that it is necessary now for established religious and spiritual traditions to move forward and align with twenty-first-century consciousness. Most religious and spiritual scriptures, doctrines, and teachings were written for the consciousness of humanity many thousands of years ago. We are evolutionary beings. We need a spirituality that is representative of our times. And what is most needed in these auspicious and changing times is a *Contemporary Spirituality for an Evolving World.*

On the winter solstice of 1999 the sun rose to conjunct the intersection of the Milky Way and the plane of the ecliptic to form a cosmic cross. This rare astronomical event, continuing until 2016, occurs just once in a 26,000-year cycle and signifies to the world a return of Christ Consciousness. This configuration could be seen to serve as a catalyst for the activation of Christ, Buddha, Krishna, Allah, or Judaic Consciousness within the human psyche.

Christ Consciousness differs from Christianity in that its focus is spirituality and not the misinterpretations of the teachings of Jesus that form the basis of religion. Spirituality celebrates the equality of the feminine and the masculine, whereas Christianity is a patriarchal system that has distorted the true message of Jesus by disregarding women as teachers and leaders and their equal role in society.

Ancient wisdom, handed to us through the ages by indigenous cultures and great civilizations, offers authentic accounts of our spiritual heritage. Found at the core of all world religions are the seeds of pure teaching. For many, however, spiritual wisdom has been reduced to religious knowledge. Wisdom and knowledge are vastly different: the former is rooted in gnosis, while the latter has its origins in the mind.

Humanity has experienced a spiritual relationship with God/Source/Creator/Goddess/Nature and a Higher Power for thousands of years. However, over millennia our true spiritual heritage has been either misinterpreted or lost to us. The two great tragedies of this have both occurred in the last two thousand years, when a staggering two-thirds of ancient spiritual texts and scrolls were lost to humanity forever.

The first of these occurred in 325 CE when the Emperor Constantine assembled a church counsel, the Council of Nicea, to edit the remaining biblical texts. It is said that Constantine demanded that twenty books be completely removed and a further twenty-five edited. These were rewritten in places and the remaining texts were condensed and rearranged. The purpose of this was to ensure control and manipulation of the masses by the imposition of specific religious rules and codes of conduct.

Then by 391 CE, the Great Library of Alexandria had been burned to the ground destroying more than 536,000 scrolls of ancient wisdom, although the actual number is the subject of much historical debate. The Royal Library of Alexandria was the first known library of its kind to gather a serious collection of books from countries beyond its borders. The library was also a research institute filled with new works in mathematics, astronomy, physics, natural sciences, and other subjects, and its function was to compile knowledge from all over the world. Only with the discovery of the gnostic gospels and Dead Sea Scrolls in the 1940s did we begin to gain a sense of how much of our spiritual heritage we had lost.

THE GNOSTIC GOSPELS

In December 1945 Muhammad Ali, a young Arab peasant, was digging with his brothers for soft soil to fertilize crops in an area of Egypt known as Nag Hammadi. They were collecting this soil at Jabal al-Tarif, a mountain dotted with more than 150 caves, some of which had been used as grave sites for over 4,300 years. While they were digging they hit a red earthenware pot almost one meter in height, which contained thirteen leather-bound papyrus books.

Ali took the books home and placed them next to the oven where his mother proceeded to use many of the papyrus scrolls as kindle for the fire. They remained unaware that these documents were in fact an ancient collection of sacred gospels dating back to the life and times of Jesus. Ali had accidentally discovered the gnostic gospels. These later became known as the Nag Hammadi library, named after the area in which they were first discovered.

Shortly prior to the discovery of these sacred texts, Ali and his brothers had committed a crime of revenge. Because of this the police were due to search his house. Ali asked the local priest to keep the books safe. Unaware of the value of the books, Ali had intended to sell them at the local market for a nominal amount to anyone who would be willing to take them off his hands. Meanwhile, a local history teacher had seen one of the books in the care of the priest and suspected it to be of some value. He sent it to a friend in Cairo to be sold on the black market.

The manuscripts soon began to attract the attention of Egyptian government officials who purchased one book and confiscated ten and a half of the other thirteen bound books. The codices were deposited in the Coptic Museum in Cairo. The thirteenth codex, containing five extraordinary texts, was smuggled out of Egypt to America.

On hearing this, Professor Gilles Quispel, a distinguished religious historian in Utrecht in the Netherlands, urged the Jung Foundation in Zurich to buy it. He succeeded in doing so but some of the pages were missing. Quispel flew to Egypt in the spring of 1955 to search for them at the Coptic Museum. Having photographed the missing pages he returned to his hotel room to decipher them. Quispel began to read the Gospel of Thomas and was startled by the words that confronted him. "These are the secret words which the living Jesus spoke and which the twin Judas Thomas wrote down."

Quispel discovered many statements similar to those in the New Testament. The meaning of some texts, however, was ambiguous and other passages were entirely different from any known Christian teachings. Bound with the Gospel of Thomas was found the Gospel of Philip, who refers to statements and actions attributed to Jesus that are markedly different from those found in the New Testament. He makes reference to the relationship of Jesus to Mary Magdalene with the following words:

> The companion of the [Savior is] Mary Magdalene. [But Christ loved] her more than [all] the disciples, and used to kiss her [often] on her [mouth]. The rest of [the disciples were offended]. . . . They said to him, "Why do you love her more than all of us?" The Savior answered and said to them, "Why do I not love you as [I love] her?"*

Other statements criticize accepted Christian beliefs, such as the Virgin Birth and the bodily Resurrection as naive misunderstandings. Jesus is said to speak of illusion and enlightenment instead of sin and repentance. Instead of coming to save humanity from sin, he came as a guide to help humanity access spiritual understanding. The texts reveal "When the disciple attains enlightenment, Jesus is no longer his Master, the two have become identical." Jesus says to Thomas that they "have both received their being from the same source." The gnostic gospels offer a more authentic understanding of Jesus than can be found in the Bible, for they refer to him and his work in very human terms.

Despite the fact that many of the texts were burned or lost, around fifty-two still remain from the early centuries of the Christian era,

---

*Elaine Pagels, *The Gnostic Gospels* (New York: Vintage Books, 1979).

including a collection of previously unknown early Christian gospels. There is the Gospel of Thomas and the Gospel of Philip, as well as the Gospel of Mary Magdalene, the Gospel of Truth, and the Gospel of the Egyptians, which is described as the sacred book of the great invisible spirit. Other texts consist of writings attributed to followers of Jesus, such as the Secret Book of James, the Apocalypse of Paul, the Letter of Peter to Philip, and the Apocalypse of Peter.

The contents of the texts are diverse and include myths, poems, secret gospels, magic, instructions for mystical practice, and philosophical descriptions of the origin of the universe. These texts remained virtually unknown for nearly two thousand years because orthodox Christians in the mid-second century denounced and banned such documents. Many early followers of Jesus were condemned by other Christians as heretics who described their teachings as blasphemy against Christ.

Some of the texts were so damaging to the Roman Catholic Church that the Vatican paid to suppress them. In the fourth century Christianity became an official religion and possession of books unapproved by the church became a criminal offence. It is said that a monk from St. Pachomius monastery in Upper Egypt hid the banned books in a jar where they remained until their discovery in 1945.*

The return of Christ Consciousness really began when the gnostic gospels were discovered. These thirteen leather-bound books shed a whole new light on the life and death of Yeshua Ben Joseph, otherwise known as Jesus. These thirteen codices are fourth-century copies of second- or third-century scriptures and commentaries on his life and the times he lived in.

There is speculation that some of the texts date back even further. Many of these scriptures challenged the Bible's interpretation of his life and teachings. Questions are raised about the misinterpretation of the role of the feminine, for in the Bible, because of stories from early Christians, Mary Magdalene is referred to as a prostitute. The gnostic gospels returned to us the lost truth about the relationship between

---

*Pagels, *The Gnostic Gospels*.

the masculine and feminine by revealing how Jesus considered Mary Magdalene to be his equal and his closest and most loved disciple and confidant. These sacred texts tell that Mary Magdalene was greatly loved by Jesus and they depict her as a learned and pious woman. The gospels reveal how their relationship would serve as a role model and example of the highest expression of love between a woman and a man.

◆

Reclaiming Sacred Relationship

How different would our own relationships be if we were raised with the knowledge of the truth of the love between Jesus and Mary Magdalene? The gnostic gospels reveal that of all those close to him, he most valued his relationship with her. Had we been raised to understand the truth of the sacred masculine and the sacred feminine, what message would we have received about relationships?

What kind of world would we live in now if that sacred relationship had served as an example of love between two people? Instead, we see around us the results of nearly two thousand years of a distorted view of the relationship between Jesus and Mary Magdalene. By denying the role of the beloved Magdalene as the wife, friend, lover, and partner of Jesus, Christianity has reduced and totally dismissed the value of the feminine in the world.

Religion has played an enormous role in the world in terms of human relationships and politics. We need to reeducate, decondition, and distance ourselves from the misinformed interpretations of the life of Jesus, as well as other religious dogma. We now need to heal the spiritual wounds we have inherited by untangling the distorted messages and indoctrinated information we have received from worldwide religious cultures.

We can heal the loss of our spiritual heritage by reclaiming sacred relationship within ourselves and with others. Reconnecting with nature and Spirit, body and Soul, heart and mind, the Earth and the higher dimensions will help us to heal and restore our balance.

There are many ways to begin this healing process. You may like to try visiting sacred sites, holy wells, crop circles; walking across wide-open moors, in forests, beautiful gardens, or along beaches; listening to the sounds of nature and breathing in her perfumes; sleeping beneath the stars; sitting beneath a full moon; making an outdoor fire; holding ceremonies either alone or with a group; getting in touch with your inner wild man/woman; walking barefoot on the land; feeling the sun and wind on your naked body; bathing in a stream; and swimming in the rivers and oceans. All of these are free and will guide us back to our hearts.

Reclaiming sacred sexuality with our beloved is another way in which we can experience profound healing. There are many excellent courses on tantra and books which help you to remember what your heart and Soul already know about sacred sexual union. A book that I highly recommend is The Magdalene Manuscript, *the first section of which is channeled through Tom Kenyon and transcribed by his partner, Judy Sion.*

It is an account of the relationship between Yeshua and Mary Magdalene. It contains specific sexual, alchemical exercises that originate from thousands of years ago. Tom Kenyon, widely respected in the human consciousness movement and a leading psycho-acoustic researcher, musician, author, channel, and therapist, shares how one night when in Zurich, Switzerland, en route to St Maries de la Mer in the South of France (the place of Mary Magdalene's retreat after the Crucifixion), Mary Magdalene appeared to him and began to dictate a manuscript.

The Magdalene Manuscript *offers a rare insight into true partnership. It is a manual of right relationship and an account of sacred sexual union between man and woman. Mary Magdalene wanted to share the truth of her relationship with Yeshua with the world, to reveal how other people can experience sacred union with their beloved. One of the most powerful experiences Mary shares with us is that for divine union to take place between two people, the man must be 100 percent surrendered and the woman 100 percent in trust.*

When we look at the last two thousand years of distorted religious information regarding male/female relationships, we can see how our conditioning has made absolute trust and absolute surrender virtually impossible. First we must cultivate a relationship of surrender and trust within ourselves. Only then can we surrender our hearts and offer our unconditional trust to others. Let us begin to cultivate this. Let us seek to discover the treasure trove inside of our hearts, the place we find the grail that overflows with the alchemical energy of unconditional love. This is the place of pure wisdom and beauty. This is the seat of the soul.

◆————————————————————————————◆

THE DEAD SEA SCROLLS

The Dead Sea Scrolls have had the greatest biblical impact. They have provided Old Testament manuscripts approximately one thousand years older than our previous oldest manuscript. The Dead Sea Scrolls have demonstrated that the Old Testament was accurately transmitted during this interval. In addition, they provide a wealth of information on the times leading up to, and during, the life of Christ.

DR. BRYANT WOOD, ARCHAEOLOGIST,
ASSOCIATES FOR BIBLICAL RESEARCH

Between 1947 and 1956 over nine hundred documents known as the Dead Sea Scrolls were discovered. These sacred texts are mainly of Hebrew and Aramaic origin and were discovered in the caves of Qumran close to the Dead Sea and Jerusalem. This site is located near to the largest Essene community, where it is speculated that both Jesus and John the Baptist spent time.

These documents date between 150 BCE to 70 CE and are most commonly identified with the ancient Jewish sect known as the Essenes. The scrolls were discovered by Muhammad edh-Dhib, a Bedouin shepherd boy who, when searching for a missing goat, entered a cave and found instead a ceramic pot full of what appeared to be paper. Muhammad gathered the papers, which then remained hanging from a pole in a Bedouin tent for several months. The seven original scrolls were sold to two separate Arab dealers of antiquities in Bethlehem. From there, four were sold (for a small amount) to

St. Mark's Monastery in the Old City of Jerusalem. Scholars at the American School of Oriental Research, who examined them, were the first to realize their age.

These manuscripts are a thousand years older than any previously known Hebrew texts of the Bible and many were written more than one hundred years before the birth of Jesus. Since that first discovery, thousands of other fragments and complete scrolls have been found in eleven other caves at Qumran. The collection includes copies of the Hebrew Scriptures with Essene commentaries and interpretation of these sacred texts.[*]

Considered the most interesting find in terms of insight into the Essene community is the Manual of Discipline, which illustrates their rules, boundaries, and ways of life. It talks about a community that lived in isolation and was totally self-contained. It speaks of the War Scroll, which appears to be a plan for the end of the present age. The Copper Scroll, so named because the letters are inscribed into soft burnished copper, records a list of sixty-four hiding places said to contain treasures from the Temple of Jerusalem. These were hidden for safekeeping and include gold, silver, manuscripts, and aromatics. They are considered to be a possible treasure map for undiscovered riches that once belonged to the Essenes.

In the excellent book *Jesus and the Essenes,* by Dolores Cannon, interesting and thought-provoking information is revealed when the author makes reference to John Marco Allegro, an original member of the international team of eight scholars who began the translation of the Dead Sea Scrolls.

Allegro claims that "At least four hundred documents from the Dead Sea Scrolls had been pieced together and prepared for publication by the end of the 1960s but only four or five have been released to the public." Allegro was the only member of the team of eight who had no religious affiliation. Since Allegro's revelation he is no longer permitted

---

[*]See Will Varner, "Discovery of the Scrolls," accessed March 24, 2013, www.christian answers.net/q-abr/abr-a023.html.

to see the scrolls. Why has this information been withheld? The scrolls are now housed in The Shrine of the Book, in Israel. The building was especially built for their study and translation.

In 1967 Martin A. Larson's *The Essene Heritage* dared to raise the possibility of a cover-up by the church. He suggested that information emerging from the scrolls was unacceptable to the church as there were possible discrepancies between what was written in the scrolls and the modern-day Bible. There were also indications that Christianity had not originated with Jesus, but had begun with the customs and beliefs of the Essenes. These revelations would not be tolerated by the church. The Dead Sea Scrolls highlight obvious historical discrepancies that point to the modern Bible being compiled and edited by powerful men of the time with their own political agendas.

One more manuscript that has come to light in recent years provides a fascinating background to the New Testament. It has been reconstructed from twelve small fragments that contain less than two columns of writing, but provide important information. It is a prediction of "The Birth of a Wonderful Child," possibly drawing on Isaiah 9:6–7.

> For unto us a child is born, unto us a son is given . . . and his name shall be called Wonderful. This child will bear special marks on His body and will be distinguished by wisdom and intelligence. He will be able to probe the secrets of all living creatures and He will inaugurate the new age for which the faithful fervently awaited.

It is interesting to note that even though they are both over two thousand years old, the gnostic gospels and the Dead Sea Scrolls were each discovered by young peasant boys by the name of *Muhammad* within a two-year time span.

JESUS AND THE ESSENES

The Essenes, a religious group that lived between the second century BCE and the first century CE, came to public awareness in 1947 with the discovery of the Dead Sea Scrolls, which are said to represent the Essene library. There were two branches of the Essenes: the Ossaeans and the Nazorean. Jesus was a member of the Nazorean, also known as the B'nai-Amen, which means "children of God."

The Essenes were a community of people who placed emphasis on purity, which ranged from their personal hygiene to their spiritual beliefs and principles. They believed that people were becoming too preoccupied with worldly matters and forgetting their spiritual origins. The Essenes had a sense that the world was moving away from God and used language like *the last days* or *the end*. Could they have been referring to our current time?

The Essenes are thought to have originated as a group who had abandoned Jerusalem as a protest against the way the Temple was being run. They isolated themselves from other Jews, opposing their "less pure" and "increasingly corrupt" ways and moved to the desert to start the first Essene community, many years before the arrival of Jesus. In the scrolls, Jesus is always referred to as Yeshua, his true name.

The Essenes were monastic in their ways and thought of themselves as a sacred community, which became their new temple. No one person owned private property as the community was based on equality and unity. All the principal founders of what was later known as Christianity were Essenes, including Jesus, Mary Magdalene, Mary and Joseph, John the Baptist, John the Evangelist, and Saint Ann.

The earliest mention of the Essenes was by Jewish philosopher, Philo of Alexandria (ca. 20 BCE–54 CE) who wrote of more than four thousand Essenes living throughout Judea. Philo speaks of how the Essenes were thought by their neighbors to have a great love of God and were noted for their holiness, philanthropy, piety, honesty, equality, freedom (possessing no slaves), and how they lived in communal residences sharing property, money, clothing, and food. Most of their time was spent studying mathematics, law, and the mysteries.

The next reference to the Essenes is by a Roman writer, geographer, and explorer, Pliny the Elder (23–79 CE), who mentions in his *Natural History* writings that "the Essenes possess no money and have existed for many generations next to the Dead Sea." Pliny located the Essenes somewhere near the northwestern shore, which is where the Dead Sea Scrolls were discovered in 1947. Around the same time, a writer known as Josephus lists the Essenes as one of three Jewish sects, alongside the Sadducees and the Pharisees, giving the same information about their piety, absence of personal property or money, and belief in community.

Claiming to have had firsthand knowledge, he further adds that the Essenes "prayed, ate, and bathed together, were devoted to charity and benevolence, forbade anger, studied the books of the elders, preserved secrets, and remained very mindful of the names of the angels kept in their sacred writings."

Extensive research undertaken by reputable and professional regressionists Joanna Prentis and Dolores Cannon into the life and times of Yeshua reveals vital facts and details, some of which have been verified by research and cannot be disregarded because of their unconventional source. What has come to light, as a result of hundreds of hours of client case material, is that their findings run parallel to much of the information included in the gnostic gospels and the Dead Sea Scrolls. It also offers further insights into the life of Jesus and the Essenes.

At the time of the passing of Jesus, over four thousand Essenes were gathered together within Essene communities or at other secret locations in the Middle East, including in the areas of Jordan, the Dead Sea, Palestine, and Syria, to pray and to hold a physical, energetic, and spiritual vigil to support him in his passing from this world to the next. These devoted supporters held full knowledge that the Crucifixion marked the fulfillment of his purpose and would change the course of human history.

An intense level of energetic and spiritual support was needed to assist Jesus to fulfill his destiny at the time of his Crucifixion. Through extensive research Stuart Wilson and Joanna Prentis, coauthors of the fascinating book *The Essenes: Children of the Light,* discovered that during, immediately following, and for the decades that followed the devotional vigil held by the entire Essene community and other devoted followers of Jesus to spiritually and energetically assist him in his transition, many either died themselves during the Crucifixion or subsequently suffered long-term illness from which they never recovered.

The Essenes were aware of the Great Plan for the life of Jesus. He was also aware of the critical role of the Essenes (and his other supporters) to ensure the successful fulfillment of his spiritual purpose on Earth.

Ordinarily, death by crucifixion would have taken several agonizing days. However, it was reported that within hours of being on the cross, Jesus left his body. Jesus was assisted in his earthly passing by thousands of dedicated and devoted supporters and left this world at the age of thirty-three.

The Essenes were a spiritually and consciously highly advanced community. They were rooted in an extraordinary capacity to tap into the ancient past and foresee the far distant future. They had access to highly advanced wisdom teachings and were visionaries and seers. As such, they had been preparing for the coming of Jesus for hundreds of years prior to his birth. They understood his spiritual purpose and, for a long time before his Crucifixion, had regularly gathered to pray, meditate, and hold the vision and focus for his earthly purpose.

Ancient prophecies foretold of "A Messiah, born of the house of David, who would come as a great teacher to mankind and whose higher purpose was to prove the existence of an afterlife, a relationship with something beyond earthly existence and who would teach about unconditional love, compassion, and forgiveness and would show humanity that miracles exist." The prophecies spoke of "a highly spiritual being whom, by example, would teach men and women about the divine masculine and feminine, sacred love, unity, and equality."

Humanity now teeters on the threshold of an unparalleled transition. Not since the time of the Crucifixion of Jesus have the combined efforts of so many been necessary to ensure an unprecedented turning point for humanity.

Two thousand years later, millions of people are now required to hold a similar focus and energy, only this time for the ascension of humanity to a higher level of consciousness—one that ensures that the Great Teaching of Jesus for us to "Create Heaven on Earth" comes to pass.

◆

As mentioned earlier, from 1980 until 2016, the winter solstice sun conjuncts the intersection of the Milky Way and the plane of the ecliptic to form a rare cosmic cross. At the time of the solar eclipse in August 1999, the planets aligned to form a grand cross. The purpose of that grand cross was to activate the Earth's "Heart Grid" for the cosmic cross to anchor into.

This cosmic cross is the higher octave expression of the third-dimensional cross that has dominated Christianity for over 2,000 years. Just as the third-dimensional cross was a symbol of religion (distorted by and locked into the Mental Matrix) that spread fear and a belief in suffering throughout the Christian world, this cosmic cross is transmitting and anchoring higher (fifth-dimensional) truth and unconditional love into the Heart Grid, and into all existing Earth grids. This rare cosmic cross is initiating the true expression of Christ Consciousness and heralds the end of two thousand years of spiritual suppression.

Religion and fundamental belief systems will slowly begin to change after 2016 to evolve a more authentic spirituality, as originally taught by the great spiritual masters throughout the ages. After two thousand years, humanity is rising to a level in its evolution that makes possible the conscious expression and establishment within global society of the true values and teachings of those such as Lao-tzu, Buddha, Krishna, Jesus, and Mohammed, as well as so many other great spiritual beings who have walked this Earth.

The "Return of the Christ" is the return of Christ Consciousness, and the cosmic cross that has formed in the heavens is a sign that human consciousness is now sufficiently evolved to embrace the original teachings of Jesus. The awakening of Christ Consciousness within our hearts is the "Second Coming."

The destiny of humanity has led us to this point in our individual and collective evolution to truly awaken the Christ within: to truly embody, embrace, and express unconditional love, compassion, empathy, forgiveness, and understanding, no longer as a mental concept or ideal nor as a spiritual "should" or "ought" but as a felt knowing in our hearts.

Jesus spoke of the four cornerstones of sacred living: harmony, truth, unconditional love, and peace. Now, two thousand years later, (as foreseen and written of in the ancient scriptures of the Essenes), our conscious evolution insists that it must be these very qualities that are the foundation stones upon which to build the new epoch.

Thirty-two percent of the population (including all factions, worldwide) is Christian. There are approximately 2.2 billion Christians, 1.2 billion Islamists, 1 billion Buddhists, and 1 billion Hindus in the world, as well as many other offshoots of established religions.

Twenty-first-century society is seeking a new religious and spiritual experience. The people of today seek an approach to spiritual life that is aligned with the consciousness of the current times.

Complex and complicated doctrines and texts have been written by and for the benefit of the ruling elite of past and present. These complex and multilayered misinterpretations and whole-scale distortions of the true teachings of the great spiritual teachers, including the teachings of Jesus and Mohammed, have been written in indecipherable academic and intellectual terms in order to manipulate and control whole swathes of the world's population.

What is now beginning to emerge in the awareness of the masses is the hypocrisy, dualism, distortion, and politics of those distorted religious systems that seek not to support personal liberation through spiritual evolution to Self-actualization but instead have as a core agenda the suppression, repression, dominance, and manipulation of the masses in order to acquire and maintain power, wealth, and status.

Humanity is consciously awakening and spiritually evolving. We stand on the threshold of realizing just what has really been going on "in the name of religion." We are recognizing that the public face and private agenda of mainstream religion are two contradictory realities. We are living in unprecedented times where anything is possible because of a unique conscious evolutionary trajectory that makes possible an extraordinary opportunity for a Great Shift to occur at every level of human experience.

Jesus has long been associated with the age of Pisces (the fishes), an era that has brought humanity the experience of living in duality, of separation from Spirit, and of suffering. It is an era that has afforded humanity an opportunity to learn forgiveness, compassion, and unconditional love, as well as to determine for ourselves what true spirituality is.

As we approach the age of Aquarius, we will begin to see incredible technological advances that will rapidly accelerate personal and global evolution. We will also begin to experience extraordinary metaphysical phenomena that will eradicate illness and disease and extend the span of human life. The age of Aquarius is the age of humanitarianism, of brotherhood and sisterhood, of the higher heart and higher mind. It is the age of Oneness and Unity Consciousness. And so, as we leave the age of Pisces and enter the age of Aquarius, so too shall we experience an unprecedented spiritual shift from fear to love.

The core message of religion and spirituality is simple and uncomplicated. Its language is universal. What lies at the heart and is the true teaching of religion and spirituality is Love.

In *The Gospel According to Jesus,* Paul Ferrini shares the message of Jesus as follows:

> You know that love is the only answer to your problems. When you give love you cannot help but receive it. Indeed, the more you give, the more you receive. There is no deficiency of love in the world. Love lives in the heart of every human being. If it is trusted, it has the power to uplift consciousness and change the conditions under which you live. Love is ultimate reality. It is the beginning and the end, the alpha and the omega. It emanates from itself, expresses itself and rests in itself. Whether rising or falling, waxing or waning, ebbing or flowing, it never loses touch with what it is.

The time is upon us and we are ready to embrace a new religion, a new spirituality—a contemporary spirituality for an evolving world.

FIVE

Contemporary Spirituality for an Evolving World

We are living in unprecedented times of accelerated change—change that is evident all around us and that we experience in every arena of our lives, from the political, economical, financial, and social to our religious beliefs.

People are asking fundamental questions regarding their basic human rights in relation to their overall well-being and really beginning to question the influence that external powers have over their lives. No longer content with being dismissed or receiving dishonest answers from those in positions of power, people are beginning to recognize that they have the freedom to choose. For many, the balance between disempowered and empowered is beginning to shift.

A global awakening on an unprecedented scale is beginning to occur. Conscious humanity is now ready to release itself from a seemingly powerless versus power-over paradigm. It is poised to begin the process of establishing a unified co-creative, collaborative model that promotes people and authority working together to establish the foundations upon which to build an emerging new epoch.

Humanity stands on a threshold, one that heralds the onset of a new paradigm. We are witnessing the early stages of the birth of this. As this emerges we can be sure that everything is set to change. We are now bearing witness to the collapse of political, economical, and social systems worldwide as people instinctively and intuitively respond to the call of a new epoch. People are reevaluating their lives and asking what has true meaning, true value, and what brings them true peace and happiness.

Humanity has arrived at a choice point and is looking for the basic survival needs of food and shelter to be met with ease and dignity. It seeks to establish a new set of values in which physical, emotional, mental, psychological, and spiritual well-being are prioritized as part of government policy.

People are reclaiming their individual power and, when expressed wisely, this will serve as the catalyst to empower millions across the world. The energy of change is sweeping the globe. People are literally waking up to the reality of their lives and to the current state of the world. Under the spotlight of radical questioning in these times is religion and spirituality.

THE HEART OF RELIGION

At the center of all religion is a spiritual heart. However, this is buried under a multitude of layers of negative conditioning and a distortion of the truth. The heart of religion has remained hidden for millennia because of the manipulation and misrepresentation of what it is that constitutes the original and core teachings.

It is said that all rivers lead to the same ocean, and in that way, we can say that all religious truth leads us to the same fundamental understanding—Love.

WHAT IS CONTEMPORARY SPIRITUALITY?

We could say that contemporary spirituality describes and constitutes the purest essence of all religion. It is what lies at the heart of all religion and at the heart of any spiritual practice or philosophy, no matter how complex the doctrine, how fundamental its scriptures and texts, or how dysfunctional its rules, regulations, and codes of conduct.

Contemporary spirituality is an approach to religion and spirituality that speaks directly to the times we live in and to the consciously evolving human being of the twenty-first century. It offers a way in which to bring the role of religion and spirituality into our present global society.

All religion originated as an immaculate conception, with purity and peace as its basis. The world's varying religions emerged at different points on humanity's time line, when human consciousness reflected those eras. In that respect we understand that religion was written for a bygone age. The rise of religion to prominence occurred at a time when the consciousness of the mass of humanity was in its formative stages of evolution. What constituted the pure heart of religion was adapted and distorted beyond all original meaning by those who held power, who were also in the early stages of their own conscious evolution. Such immature minds used religion to seize power, amass wealth, and to manipulate and control the collective without any remote interest in studying, or aspiring to teach the truth, the heart, and the origins of specific religious practices.

As consciously evolving beings we have come a long way since then. No longer in the infancy stages of our development, we can recognize how alarmingly out of context it is to be following antiquated religious doctrines that have been distorted and rewritten by our less consciously evolved predecessors.

Contemporary spirituality, as a way for the twenty-first-century consciously evolving individual, is at its heart an uncorrupted, uncomplicated, nonfundamental, and simple teaching. It is an expression of spirituality and religion in its purest form. Contemporary spirituality is a true expression of the heart of all religion. The heart of contemporary spirituality is laid wide open for all to see. It is a heart that is sublimely exquisite in its purity and simplicity.

Contemporary spirituality represents an open invitation to *all*, no matter what race, denomination, or creed. Contemporary spirituality invites us to seek and embrace self-mastery: to master our senses, our bodies, our emotions, our thoughts, and the way in which we live our lives. It encourages us to cultivate self-discipline, self-love, self-awareness, self-understanding, self-knowing, self-realization, and self-actualization.

Contemporary spirituality leads us along a clear path, devoid of rules, regulations, judgments, punishments, expectations, dogma, fear or fundamental belief systems. It guides us toward unconditional love of Self and others, leading us toward enlightenment.

Contemporary spirituality does not require an intellectual predisposition, for it is a language of the heart and, as such, is not suited to the mind with its needs for understanding the mechanism of any given subject. Contemporary spirituality calls upon gnosis, intuition, and a deep felt knowing that has no basis in the intellectual or academic.

The joy of contemporary spirituality is to be experienced in its simplicity. Contemporary spirituality gently encourages and guides us to let go of dualistic and separatist religious indoctrination and attitudes, to instead embrace the concepts of unity, equality, and enfolding ourselves and all sentient beings into the true heart of religion. As consciously evolving humans we are ready to embrace a spirituality that is centered around the heart, that speaks and listens from the heart, and that cultivates the heart of each individual and of humanity.

Contemporary Spirituality is a beautifully simple and uncomplicated path. It is a spiritual practice that is stripped to the core to promote unconditional, humanitarian, heart-centered teachings for the contemporary spiritual aspirant.

DEFINING NEW PARAMETERS
FOR A CONTEMPORARY SPIRITUALITY

Let us now begin to look at some of the components that constitute a contemporary spirituality for an evolving world. I have decided to begin with how we interact and communicate with each other. Spiritual visionary Omraam Mikhael Aivanhov was quoted as saying: "True evolution consists in learning to make use of words, either spoken or written, with a divine end in mind, in other words to use elements of the word solely to create what is right, good and beautiful."

Central to and forming the basis of a contemporary spirituality for an evolving world are conscious communication, mindfulness, mastering the emotions, embracing the shadow, the cultivation of presence, transparency, and alignment with the essence of who we truly are. Let us now explore these elements that help to further define contemporary spirituality for an evolving world.

CONSCIOUS COMMUNICATION

As human beings, the greatest gift we have at our disposal can also be the greatest weapon—words. We can heal ourselves, others, and the world with words; yet they can also be used in a destructive manner. Because of the pressure of living in the world cultures that we have been raised in, we have mimicked and learned dysfunctional and entirely inappropriate ways of relating, not only with others but also with ourselves. Most of us are unaware that the ways in which we relate are entirely distorted and unnatural.

We have been conditioned from birth, by the environment and its dysfunctional systems, to hook into a fear-based mentality and *react*. Generally, most cultures of the world exist in survival mode, in a pattern of fight or flight, which is a react and defend mentality. A healthy way of relating is when we are free to express our true feelings without fear, when we speak from the heart and communicate honestly, are emotionally stable, and are able to *respond* instead of react.

Conscious communication requires that we trust in ourselves, in our truth, and in our ability to express this to others. Reacting is a defense mechanism and responding is an expression of the felt sense. To react is to attack and defend. Response is a balanced, calm, and stable communication, speaking directly to the emotions with feelings being expressed consciously and mindfully. Reacting uses language that disconnects, finger points, blames, and shames. The language of response is connected, centered, empathic, and compassionate.

Trust has been broken over and over again, and so we have become numb with the pain of our experiences, creating a hard outer shell to defend the soft and vulnerable core of our Being. This shell keeps others out, yet our true loving nature locked away. We have become prisoners of ourselves. Fundamentally we are Love; even though this may sound a cliché, it is the truth. We are Love. However, this natural and organic core foundation of our Being may feel lost to us. It is not lost but deeply buried under layers of conditioning that have taught us to *survive* at all costs. We are in fight-or-flight mode the majority of the time, surviving in a hostile environment where it appears that every man and woman is looking out for themselves.

However, if we bring ourselves right into the present moment we can ask this: "Do we have to remain in survival mode or can we dare to explore how it would feel to trust, to be open, transparent, and most importantly, to risk sharing from the heart, communicating from the foundation of Love, which forms the core of each one of us?"

To make this shift requires courage and a yearning to know and experience *true peace* at the deepest level of our Being. Courage and yearning lead to an inner-shift—one that can and will transform our lives if we dare to risk all for Love. What is there to lose? Only that which imprisons us. Self-love and a loving relationship with ourselves is the key to our freedom.

To embark upon such a noble quest will require a radical reevaluation of our relationships, a conscious encounter with our wounding, an exploration and clearing of our psychological history, and a period of deconditioning from the ingrained patterns of fear, defense, attack, and survival that have accumulated throughout our lives. We are blessed to live in times when freedom is offered to most of us on a plate. It is ours for the choosing. Never before in modern history have so many of us been free to make life-serving choices.

We are no longer obliged by religion, culture, or any other external pressures to exist in life-denying regimes that are not even our own. We have inherited our reactive, defended, survival mentality from our ancestors. The script that forms the imprint of our relating belongs to generations that have gone before us and the times they lived in. We are literally living in the past, no matter how modern we believe ourselves and our lives to be, or how liberated we feel our relationships are. As we free ourselves from dysfunctional relating, we also free the generations to come.

Choice is the great gift bestowed upon us by the age we live in. You have the choice to live or to exist, to survive or to feel *alive* with the joy of living. Fundamentally, to claim our humanitarian right to freedom and choice—or should we say *reclaim* this right—we must first come into right relationship with ourselves, which automatically creates right relationship with others and the world.

The Four Intentions as a Model for Conscious Communication

The four intentions is a model that can really support our quest to establish a new approach in our communications. It is a way of communicating that directly responds to the call of these transformative times.

The First Intention Is to Speak from the Heart

This means speaking not from our heads but from our hearts. It means to communicate as honestly as we can in every moment. Today we may each experience countless thoughts, ideas, or feelings, some that bring us joy and some that may make us feel uncomfortable or emotional.

Let us set an intent to express these truthfully, being mindful to do so from the heart, be it with words, movement, sound, or in conscious, respectful, and connected silence.

Let us trust our capacity to be present as individuals or in a group and seek to find harmonious ways to express our thoughts and feelings, so fostering harmonious outcomes and resolutions.

The Second Intention Is to Listen from the Heart

This means that we try to listen without judgment, to listen with an open mind, even if we disagree with what the person is saying. We simply try to take in what is being said and to hear it completely.

If we feel the need to express a feeling or thought to that person, we must remain mindful to whether we are reacting or responding, for if we are reacting we are not speaking from the heart.

The Third Intention Is to Communicate Respectfully and Wait until the Other Has Finished Speaking

This invites us to wait until the other has finished speaking before we respond. We try not to interject or interrupt. We are mindful not to raise our voice above whoever is speaking in order to be heard ourselves.

Let us be mindful that some voices may be quieter than others and therefore find it difficult to contribute because of that. These voices are to be encouraged as they have equal validity and a right to be heard. Let us not cultivate a communication where the loudest voices rule!

The intent is to wait for the other to make their point to express their thoughts or feelings and then check with them to see if they have finished, at which point we can express our desire to respond and to include our own thoughts and feelings.

The Fourth Intention Is to Speak Leanly

Something that is lean has nothing extra or unnecessary attached to it. Speaking leanly means to keep to the point of what we are trying to say and to let go of any unnecessary details.

When we speak, we need to keep in mind that there is another involved in the communication who may also wish to share and be heard. Speaking leanly fosters the practice of mindfulness in our communications: for example, respecting our own as well as another's time boundaries and doing our best to acknowledge and honor these.

Let us also practice listening from the heart. Through attentive listening, we foster deep sharing and communication that meets the needs of both or all parties. This approach beautifully serves and honors our need to be seen and heard, gracefully serving the cultivation of harmony with others.

The Practice of Authentic Communication—Within a Group

The following suggestions can support us to develop our skills in deep listening, self-expression, conflict resolution, and decision making within a group context.

- Speak from the heart about issues that are important to us, to the group, and to the world.
- Listen from the heart with an open mind and without judgment, even if we are not aligned with what others are saying.
- Speak leanly when expressing ourselves and when communicating with others in the group. Be mindful of time boundaries.
- Develop trust, respect, cooperation, and understanding by communicating authentically.
- Self-monitor—silently check in with ourselves if an emotion is triggered to acknowledge that feeling as our own. Gently and quietly breathe into the emotion, breathe it through, consciously releasing it through the out-breath. Quietly give thanks to whoever it was who triggered the emotion.
- Cultivate deep listening and unconditional positive regard for each person that speaks.
- Be present—the greatest gift we can offer another is our presence. Hold the intent of wishing to be fully present to whoever is speaking and to the group energy, while at the same time remaining present to our felt sense.
- Refine our capacity to be present to another (and ourselves) without judgment.
- In all communication, the need of any individual is to feel seen, heard, and validated. Let us seek to meet this need, even if we do not resonate with what is being expressed.
- Let us remain mindful that the purpose of any communication is not to be right, but to remain present to another, with an unconditional heart.

The ideal setup for a group is to sit in a circle so that all can see each other and everyone is on the same level. This is a nonhierarchical formation and serves to remind us of the importance of each person. We can place something beautiful or meaningful in the center of the circle, as this is the heart of the circle and where we all meet.

If possible, adopt the use of a "talking stick" as a tool to help focus attention on each speaker in the circle, one at a time. When you are holding the stick it is your turn to speak; when you are not, your complete attention is on the person who is speaking.

And remember to breathe in and breathe out peace.

MINDFULNESS

Let us now explore mindfulness, which constitutes another instrumental component of contemporary spirituality for an evolving world. Mindfulness leads to peace and peace leads to a true sense of inner freedom.

Mindfulness clarifies the difference between reaction and response, the former being ego driven and the latter arising from the Self. Ego represents many shadow layers of human expression—the result of a psychologically frozen and wounded inner child and an unintegrated personality—that keep us unconsciously maintaining cycles and patterns of self-sabotaging and self-destructive behaviors.

Eugene Gendlin, the pioneer of *focusing*, developed this system that encourages the individual to cultivate self-awareness and to become mindful. By focusing on self-awareness we become receptive and attuned to what we are really feeling and where in the body we are feeling it. Focusing enables us to empathically connect with our innermost feelings and to cultivate our felt sense and our felt knowing.

The language of focusing comprises simple phraseologies, including, "Yes I know you are there," that encourage a direct dialogue with the thought, feeling, sensation, or image that arises when we focus our awareness on our inner world. We do so to foster an empathic response to that which wants to reveal itself, or make itself known to us, in terms of our inner experience. The psychological shadow most seeks compassion, empathy, and understanding.

And so, I invite you for a moment to practice mindfulness through focusing. I invite you to pause, to breathe, to be still, to hear the subtleties of your inner experience, your deeper and more authentic feelings. I encourage you to become present to yourself, to cultivate honesty with yourself, and to begin to cultivate right relationship with yourself.

◆

Practicing Mindfulness

Take a moment now to practice mindfulness.

Pause . . .
Breathe . . .
Be still . . .
Turn your attention inward . . .
What's there?
What are you noticing?
How are you feeling?
What wants to be known?
What is in need of your attention?
Where do you feel that?
Be in silence . . .
What is there?
Where in your body do you feel it?
Breathe . . .
Be unconditionally present to it . . .
Listen . . .
Sense . . .
Feel . . .
See . . .
Breathe . . .
If the feeling had a voice what would it say?
Listen deeply . . .
Open mind . . .
Open heart . . .
See . . .
Hear . . .
Gently respond, "Yes, I know you are there"
What happens?
What is happening?
What does this feeling need?

It may just be your unconditional attention.

Let that feeling know you care and are wishing to know more . . .

Make an agreement to meet again, very shortly . . .

Complete this visit lovingly and gently . . .

Come back into the room . . .

Sit quietly for a moment . . .

Breathe . . .

◆———————————————————————◆

Becoming mindful within is becoming self-aware. Mindfulness and self-awareness require that we are mindful in every thought, word, action, and deed. It is a threshold moment on the evolutionary journey of the Self when we have mastered the capacity to turn our attention inward.

Mindfulness in the World

When we are not living from mindfulness and awareness we become armchair critics and voyeurs observing the unfolding tragedies, not only in our own lives but in the lives of others. We gaze numbly at the atrocities inflicted upon our fellow humans, as well as the animal and plant kingdoms. We stare past the stories of trauma and war reported by the media, become vaguely preoccupied by such news, but then pacified by a consumer culture that continually vies for our attention.

For many who sit back and watch the unfolding events in the world, over which they feel they have little control, it is as if they are anesthetized with hollow eyes and closed hearts. We remain ineffective, disconnected, and discontented when we are not expressing mindfulness in the world.

If we truly seek world peace, if we really wish to experience inner peace, joy, happiness, and fulfillment as the norm, we must first seek to resolve what has been lost within and, as a result, lost to the world. As we adopt an attitude of mindfulness toward ourselves, we cultivate the capacity for this in the world. And by doing this we begin to wake up to what is going on around us; no longer lost in ourselves, we recognize that the world needs us and is crying out for us to apply mindfulness and awareness in order to cultivate world peace and support global evolution.

When working with a brilliant technique, such as Gendlin's focusing, we become enabled to connect to the unhealed psychological and personal historical trauma that dwells within us. Mindfulness, through such a technique, allows us to deeply explore an emotion and recognize that it is not the emotion itself that unsettles our sense of equilibrium, but what lies behind it. By engaging with ourselves at this level, we begin to heal.

MASTERING THE EMOTIONS

Emotionally we find ourselves in need of ever increasing stimuli, including the use of drugs, alcohol, consumerism, sex, and other psychologically manipulative aspects of our global culture in order to feel. However, we also experience stimuli through the projection of our own unhealed psychological shadow and trauma expressed by reactive emotional outbursts.

When we are caught in the whirlwind of the charge that accompanies reaction, we can choose to pause and ask ourselves, "Does this charge match the situation?" For example, when we find ourselves reacting strongly with anger at the way someone may have spoken to us, does the charge, expressed or felt, match the related experience or does the charge and overreaction far exceed it? A measuring stick such as mindfulness can help us ascertain to what degree we have mastered our emotions as well as support us to analyze the charge that we experienced in relation to the situation.

When the charge is absent, we are located in neutrality—which means we are mindful and aware. When the charge is present, this conveys how disconnected we are from mindfulness and awareness and, because of this, our inner world too. This demonstrates how we are unconsciously projecting our own discord on to others, and out into the external world. We are each co-creators and the world around us mirrors this as a reality.

Unaccustomed to fully experiencing our emotions after a lifetime of their repression, we seem only to be able to withstand the briefest encounter with them before withdrawing rapidly into the twilight zone that is disconnection. We need to consciously move into the emotion—instead of retreating away from it and becoming lost in behaviors that distract us and keep us disconnected from ourselves and from truth.

Becoming mindful requires that we regularly visit our emotions, that we check in with our inner selves to see *what is there* on any given day. Each time we do this, we seek connection with our inner selves a little while longer in order that we may *feel* to *heal*. The longer we can remain present to our emotions, the less likely we are to experience them as overwhelming and out of control and the less probable it is that we will default into ingrained patterns of repression and denial.

For many, to begin to connect with their emotions is a scary thought indeed. They are afraid of what they may find. At first it might feel like peering into Pandora's box. People are afraid that they will be consumed by their emotions, not be able to manage them, and consequently fall apart. Yet conversely, allowing ourselves to fall apart is exactly what is needed as we surrender and let go of the rigid control that keeps us emotionally imprisoned.

It is true that we have lives to live, children to raise, jobs to work at, responsibilities, and so forth. So, how do we find space for a deep encounter with our emotions that facilitates us to surrender to *what is there?*

We need to make an agreement with ourselves to take such a process step by step and consciously turn that focusing tap on slowly when we have created the appropriate time and space to do so. Setting an intent is all important, for when we do this we send a message to the psyche and to the higher Self that we are ready for change, that we are seeking transformation. Sometimes, merely by setting an intent with deep sincerity we set the process in motion in a way that we can manage. So, when setting an intent to heal and grow, we can ask for the process to unfold in a way that supports everything else we have to manage in our day-to-day lives.

Mindfulness is all important in this. Being mindful requires that we ensure we find time for ourselves to allow us to turn our attention inward and ask that beautiful question of self-enquiry, "What is there, today." Then, we can reassure ourselves with what we discover by stating, "Yes, I know you are there."

Little and often is the sacred medicine that supports us to heal. The medicine may taste bitter at times, yet more often it is sweet. No matter what the case, both are sacred medicines that we need if we are to fully heal. Mindfulness invites us to be aware and to be kind to whatever arises when we practice being present to our inner selves. Here is a beautiful mantra on mindfulness by Buddhist meditation teacher Larry Yang.

> *Can I be mindful and loving of whatever arises.*
> *If I cannot be loving in this moment, can I be kind.*
> *If I cannot be kind, can I be nonjudgmental.*
> *If I cannot be nonjudgmental, can I not cause harm.*
> *And, if I cannot not cause harm, can I cause the least*
> *amount of harm possible?*

Now more than ever, it is this we must remember.

EMBRACING THE LIGHT SHADOW

Contemporary spirituality embraces the human shadow, recognizing that when we explore ourselves consciously and with awareness, therefore engaging in our own evolutionary process, the shadow is not dark, but indeed light.

Contemporary spirituality discounts the notion of the existence of a fundamentally dark nature within the human being, to instead acknowledge that there exists within each of us a primal wound of separation from Source/God/Creator/Divinity or our Divine Nature. However, we need not bear this perceived wound just because we are human. We experience it only because we have been steeped in duality, brought about by the misinterpretation or obscuration of what has always lain at the heart of religious and spiritual philosophies throughout human history.

The light shadow is referred to in this way because, by the very process of our becoming aware of the human shadow and healing it, its existence has brought us further enlightenment. When compassion and empathy are offered as balms with which the human shadow can be healed and transformed, it can be integrated and will aid the conscious evolution of the human being.

For thousands of years we have lived under dictatorships, flawed regimes, and a misinterpretation of the fundamental meaning of all religions, which is love. We have lived in duality, personally and collectively. We have been separated from the heart of religion and spirituality, and therefore from our own hearts. The primal wound of humanity, the separation from Source/God/Divine Self, is one that can be healed.

The way to healing all perceived sense of separation (for we have never truly been separate, only perceived ourselves to be so), is to become Love and only Love—to live, breathe, sleep, and live Love in every moment—to be a master of the heart—to reclaim and embody our natural state of being, which is Love. This is what lies at the heart of contemporary spirituality. This the new way forward for the new human and a new world.

PRESENCE

Presence is another fundamental element of contemporary spirituality. It is an important antidote to anger, as more often than not when people are upset or in turmoil, they do not feel that they are being seen or heard or that their feelings are validated and acknowledged. We live in a world where reaction is normal; therefore, we expect this from another when we attempt to share difficult emotions with them. Because this has always been the case, we have learned to express our emotions in a *reactive* way. We accuse, we judge, we blame, we finger point; all are reactions that create more of the same.

Learning to be present to ourselves or another requires that we recognize that where there is reaction, there is always something deeper occurring that has little to do with the trigger and everything to do with unhealed core trauma that often reaches back into childhood or past lives. It is our emotional pain that causes us to react, whether we are on the receiving end of anger or projecting it toward another. When someone is being reactive toward you or you feel that you yourself are reacting, pause for a moment and acknowledge not the behavior or the words, but the emotion behind the reaction.

When you can say to yourself "I feel pain" instead of "I feel anger," you are shifting from reaction to response. When you are able to say to another who is being reactive "I see/hear/feel the pain behind your words," you are supporting them to recognize what they truly feel. This may then allow them to reflect on your response rather than the reaction they expected from you. *Responding* to another can stop them in their tracks and mark a turning point in their self-awareness. This is also true for ourselves.

By being present, patient, and compassionate toward your own pain, or that of another, you are initiating peace. We all have an innate need for our feelings to be acknowledged, validated, and responded to. Presence, patience, and compassion are alchemical practices that will transform reaction into response and anger into peace. Next time you find yourself feeling angry or are on the receiving end of anger, allow yourself to be quietly present, to be patient, to feel compassion, and see what a world of difference it can make.

You will know when you are experiencing a release of pure emotion because the anger or sadness you feel will have no specific hook. You will feel angry or sad, *just because.* When you feel angry or sad and you have no idea of the reason why, this is good news! It means that core and pure emotions are able to rise to the surface to be felt and released. When we truly express pure emotion we do not have mental images of others nor do we feel any compulsion to apportion blame.

Such releases occur spontaneously and are often triggered by something that is totally unrelated. Once you feel calm and centered again, remember to bless whoever or whatever acted as a catalyst for the release. If you do see the image of another person in your mind's eye or harbor feelings of blame or vengeance toward others, stop, breathe, and wait until you can arrive at a place of neutrality within yourself before proceeding to release the emotion. Recognize and remind yourself (and others) that it is okay to feel the way you do, as long as you own it and do not project those emotions onto another.

At the most, all another can do is to act as a trigger for bringing an emotion that was already inside of us to the surface. Others are not causal to our pain, they simply serve as reminders of the unhealed wounds we carry from this and former lives that we now need to heal.

NVC tells us that the more we talk of the past, the less we heal it. NVC encourages us to talk about what is alive in us in the moment, to talk in the present about what is still being felt as a result of the past. NVC explains to us that intellectual understanding does not bring about healing, *empathy* does. Retelling the details of the story deepens the pain.

NVC invites us to refer to the past but not to go into detail about it. It suggests that when we refer to it, that we do so in no more than five words. For example, rather than going into detail and relaying the whole story, which only proves to retraumatize us, we can say, "When she (or he) left me," and then move to what emotion is alive in us in that moment: for example, sadness or anger. Name the emotion you are left with rather than the story, such as "I feel angry," "I feel sad," or "I feel frightened."

By connecting to core emotions we give them space to be seen, heard, and validated, which may be the first time we have ever experienced them as such. Equally, it is not conducive to share our emotions with someone whose own "stuff" gets triggered, who will then offer us advice that is colored by their own unhealed places of wounding.

TRANSPARENCY

Transparency is another key aspect of contemporary spirituality. Transparency is a path that leads to transcendence. By cultivating a transparent heart we can experience transcendence of the ego/personality self.

So just what constitutes a transparent heart? A transparent heart is one that is crystal clear and open. It is an honest heart that is full of goodness and pure intent. A transparent heart is peaceful, caring and kind, empathic, and unconditionally loving and giving. A transparent heart is compassionate and sensitive and is full of humility and humanity. It is a heart of grace, wisdom, and beauty. A transparent heart is understanding and forgiving. It is selfless and peaceful, yet passionate and courageous. A transparent heart is joyful and empathic. It is the heart of a true humanitarian. It is a heart at peace. A transparent heart leads to a transcendent world.

AWAKENING TO OUR TRUE ESSENCE

Our True Essence represents that which is glorious, radiant, and magnificent in each one of us. When we are in touch with our True Essence we radiate pure love and goodness. Our True Essence feels like the most exalted feeling we can ever experience. Recall a time when you felt most happy and filled with joy. This will give you a glimpse into what living your True Essence can feel like.

If we were to imagine the color of True Essence it would be luminous and golden, like the finest champagne bubbles. When in touch with our True Essence we are experienced by others, and experience ourselves, as sparkling, alive, and effervescent. When embodying and radiating our True Essence our presence captivates and enraptures all who encounter us, as we light the spark of curiosity within them to wonder how they too can experience this state of being.

True Essence is like nectar: a fluid energy that sources our very Being, rejuvenating our cells, cleansing and healing our deepest levels, dissolving our physical challenges, balancing our emotions, clarifying and purifying our thoughts, aligning us with the higher purpose of our Soul, and further awakening our Spirit.

When we are in touch with True Essence, it is as if a vast and powerful light shines around us, pours from us through our eyes, our smile, our kind words, our loving presence, permeating everything it touches to reveal the exquisite core beauty of who we truly are. It reveals our very Being.

Is it possible to fully live our True Essence? The answer to this question is yes. Absolutely. What would it feel like to do so? Imagine feeling in love with everything in life, feeling full of compassion, forgiveness, understanding, and empathy. Imagine feeling emotionally stable and possessing a crystal clear mind. Imagine what it would be like to feel a tremendous excitement about life every day, to know your purpose, and to feel fulfilled. Imagine what it would be like to feel no fear, but instead be surrounded only by love. This is how it would feel to be awakened to True Essence. Living our True Essence is as simple as making the choice to cultivate this way of being.

COMING BACK INTO THE HEART

We live in a consciously evolving world that is ready for a contemporary spirituality.

People no longer wish to have sermons read to them, nor measure their souls against the distorted teachings of religion handed down by those who were un-integrated and psychologically split. Fire, brimstone, and damnation belong to a dysfunctional, obsolete religious era, and one that is fast dying. With every death comes rebirth. The twenty-first century is a new epoch for a new spirituality that is based upon the core teachings handed to us by the great masters who have graced this Earth.

The heart of all religion has a unified voice and a unified vision. The time is upon us to ensure the dissolution of the misperception that we have been separated from God, for it is this belief (known as the primal wound) that keeps us locked in separation. Now is the time for us to realize that we have never been separated from God/Creator/Source and that we have only been separated from ourselves.

**Ten Fundamental Values
of Contemporary Spirituality**

- Unconditional Love
- Unconditional Positive Regard
- Compassion
- Empathy
- Understanding
- Transparency
- Mindfulness
- Equality
- Conscious Communication
- Unity Consciousness

When all ten of these fundamental values of contemporary spirituality are lived as an everyday reality, we will finally be living a true expression of spirituality within the world.

◆

The Diamond Heart Prayer Meditation

When you say this prayer speak it from the center of your heart, directing it straight to the center of Source.

With all of my heart, I release all karma, vows, agreements, contracts, promises, and bonds. I request that all such be lifted from my Soul contract and dissolved and transmuted in the divine Light and Love of Source.

With all of my heart, I request that all layers of my energy field are cleared, that all blocks are removed, dissolved, and transmuted in the divine Light and Love of Source.

With all of my heart, I request that all defenses, scars, and such be lifted from my heart and dissolved and transmuted in the divine Light and Love of Source.

With all of my heart, I request that all trauma memories from all incarnations be lifted from my Soul and dissolved and transmuted in the divine Light and Love of Source.

With all of my heart, I request that all blocked or stored negative energy held anywhere in my physical body and all of my energy bodies be removed, dissolved, and transmuted in the divine Light and Love of Source.

With all of my heart, I ask for forgiveness for all transgressions—past, present, and future—that these be lifted from my Soul contract and dissolved and transmuted in the divine Light and Love of Source.

With all of my heart, I request that all cellular and ancestral memory and my genetic DNA be wiped clean of all trauma imprints and negative energies, and that I be flooded with and hold only the purest and highest vibrational Love and Light.

With all of my heart, I request that my life now begins to reflect only the greatest and purest Love and Light, and that I may live immersed in unconditional love, flow, joy, vibrancy, magic, wonder, wellness, positivity, happiness, perfect balance, adventure, purity, and true abundance.

With all of my heart, I ask that my heart become peaceful and that I become joy-full and perfectly centered and anchored in Love—that the Light, Love, and Divine Essence of my Soul radiates and pours forth through my eyes, my smile, my heart, my very Being.

With all of my heart, I request that I become the embodiment of peace and Love—that I experience deep peace within me always and all ways— and that I come to embody the most exalted and purest expression of unconditional love, expressing this to and for humanity, all sentient beings, and all life-forms, in all kingdoms of the Earth.

From this day forth, may my heart, my life, my very being, be filled with love, wonder, joy, happiness, laughter, peace, blessedness, beauty, fulfillment, and true abundance.

With all of my heart, I request that my life unfold to be a joyfully blessed experience.

With all of my heart, I request that I may come to fully know and experience true, deep, sacred, and abiding Love as a lived reality, as a physical being on Earth.

With all of my heart, I request that my time here on Earth bestows upon me unforgettable, magical, and beautiful memories to take with me when it is time for me to return Home.

I am Love.

So shall it be.

———————◆———————

The Diamond Heart Prayer Affirmation

This affirmation can be spoken at any time—it is especially powerful when spoken after speaking the Diamond Heart Prayer Meditation.

I choose only to live from the Love that I Am.

 I choose only to love from the Light that I Am

 I choose only to speak from the Understanding that I Am

 I choose only to hear from the Compassion that I Am

 I choose only to see from the Beauty that I Am

 I choose only to love unconditionally from the Unconditional Love that I Am

 I choose that my every thought, word, action, and deed be in alignment with the Truth that I Am

 The river of Love and Light that I Am never ceases to flow.

 The temple of my heart is a place of refuge and sanctuary for all sentient beings and all kingdoms on Earth.

 I live in the present—this moment, the now—lovingly accepting what is, not what has been or is to come.

 Each day I renew a sacred vow to unconditionally love all—human, winged, furred, insect, plant, mineral, element, ocean, sky.

 Each day I choose to respond, not react.

 In each moment, I hold an attitude of unconditional positive regard toward all.

 I consciously cultivate peace with each step, each breath, and with each thought, word, action, and deed.

 I Am Peace.

 Today is the first day of the rest of my life.

I choose to become the embodiment of unconditional love, compassion, empathy, kindness, and care.

I cultivate humility, grace, and reverence.

Each day, I take a moment to pause and to feel the wonder of the gift of life.

I live in gratitude.

I live from pure truth.

My heart is as a diamond—radiating pristine love, Zen peace, and exquisite beauty to all.

SIX

A Reevaluation of Ego

A New Approach for Our Times

If I were asked what I thought was the single greatest contributing factor to the critical state of the world we live in, as well as what is causal to the deeper malaise that afflicts most of humanity, I would sum it up in one tiny word—ego.

So, what is ego and how can this tiny little word, made up of just three letters, represent the reason why there is so much disharmony within the individual and the world?

Ego is born of trauma. Trauma is born of empathic disconnection. Whenever we have experienced empathic disconnection we register trauma. Nearly every human being on this planet has experienced empathic disconnection at some point in their life. Empathic disconnection equates to any situation where we have not felt seen, heard, held, validated, or acknowledged. It can begin with the way in which we are breast- or bottle-fed: for example, is a mother gazing adoringly at her infant, speaking in loving, soothing tones throughout each feeding, or is she disconnected, preoccupied, and distracted by other things she prioritizes during those crucial developmental moments for the infant?

We can say that empathic disconnection begins with the mother's and father's relationships to the baby in the womb. The symptoms of empathic disconnection are projected out into the world by the traumatized individual, who by adulthood has empathically disconnected to themselves, others, and the world around them. This can prove to be dangerous, destructive, and ultimately catastrophic. Early infancy and childhood trauma are the call to the ego to rise to power, dominance, and control. The ego is driven by survival instincts and fear, and its strategies are defense and attack. Given that nearly seven billion human beings are carrying layers and layers of unhealed trauma and therefore are entirely under the control of the ego, is it any wonder that we face the looming world crisis that we do today?

An exhortation often attributed to Gandhi invited us to "Be the change that you wish to see in the world." Just what exactly is this inviting us to change? The message speaks of inner change in order to bring about world change. So, just what is it that we need to change in ourselves? Could it be a significant and all-encompassing shift from ego (adapted self) based survival, to living from the *I* (Authentic Self)?

As fifteenth-century philosopher Paracelsus wrote, "Inside each one of us is a special piece of heaven whole and unbroken." The ego resides at the borders of this special piece of heaven, which it patrols tirelessly day and night. We could describe this place of inner heaven as the palace of the True Self.

The True Self has the potential to create its kingdom to be not only a piece of, but an entire special heaven: one that is devoid of borders (defenses)—an inner kingdom of peace, love, joy, harmony, and beauty. However, despite the potential we each have to manifest this as our reality, for most, the True Self will remain in hiding in its special piece of heaven. What is reassuring to note is that this special piece of heaven remains so, irrespective of what trauma or tragedies are experienced by an individual.

The Authentic Self is the true expression of who we really are, beyond all conditioning or any physical, emotional, mental, and psychological wounding. We are, by nature, unconditional love. The True Self is all within us that is good and balanced, integrated and wise, peaceful and gentle, creative and gifted, evolved and enlightened. This remains true and never changes, no matter how much suffering and pain we experience, or cause to others. This piece of special heaven remains whole and unbroken, no matter what.

So, how do we begin to live our lives as our True Self? The first step is to acknowledge that our ego has served us and *is* the reason we have managed to arrive this far in our lives as functioning human beings.

Tibetan Buddhist meditation teacher and scholar Lama Surya Das teaches, "Through honest self-inquiry and no-holds-barred meditative introspection, one can take apart and deconstruct the hut that ego built, thus entering the mansion of Authentic Being." Deconstructing the hut that ego built is not without challenges; as the Authentic Self prepares to emerge, the ego devises many clever defense strategies designed to stop it from doing so, for the ego is driven by fear for its own survival.

PRELUDE TO THE EGO/SELF FAIRYTALE

The ego is often spoken of in terms of being the worst enemy of the True Self. Yet, in fact, it is our most loyal friend. In an unintegrated individual the ego is viewed as the enemy. But one who is psychologically awakened recognizes that the role of the ego is to protect the True Self at all costs. However, when we are psychologically unintegrated we become locked into patterns and behaviors that keep us in illusion, powerlessness, lack, and self-sabotaging and destructive patterns of behavior.

Whenever we resolve to heal our body, mind, emotions, and our psychological history, we will encounter the resistance of the ego. The ego is fully preoccupied with survival and will attempt to overthrow anything that threatens its position, even the True Self.

During my training in psychosynthesis psychotherapy, we were taught how the ego can often be seen in this resisting pattern. We were given the example of a new client canceling an appointment at the last minute owing to the car breaking down, the alarm clock having not worked, a bout of unexpected flu, or some other reason. This we learned was a classic sign of the ego resisting the presence of the emerging Self.

However, let us not forget the true purpose of the ego and how it serves us. In early childhood it is the ego that comes to our rescue. As infants, we incarnate as pure Soul energy and it is at this time that the True Self is most present. The Authentic Self is surrendered, trusting, undefended, and open. The ego emerges at a point when the True Self has not been appropriately acknowledged or responded to, feels threatened in any way whatsoever, or is ignored or invalidated.

To a child whose True Self goes unnoticed, the world is perceived as a hostile environment. This perception is then reinforced and reflected through the behavior of the child's parents, caregivers, teachers, and authorities, as well as the dysfunctional systems of the wider community and the world. It is the ego that shields us as infants and children from emotional, mental, psychological, or actual physical death when the harshness and hostility of the environment encroaches upon us.

Jung spoke of the King and the Queen and of love being the center of the Self, when he said, "Somewhere there was once a Flower, a Stone, a Crystal, a Queen, a King, a Palace, a Lover and his Beloved, and this was long ago, on an Island somewhere in the ocean 5,000 years ago. . . . Such is Love, the Mystic Flower of the Soul. This is the Center, the Self."

We could say that the ego is the Warrior who protects and serves the King or Queen and that the *I* is the Authentic Self.

The ego steps into the role that the Self would have taken had it been able to remain present, instead of having to retreat into hiding for its very survival. And so it is that Self withdraws, waiting for a time when the consciousness of the environment is aligned to its own, at which point it begins to emerge. The emergence of the *I* does not require that the consciousness of humanity be aligned to it, only that one or more people of like mind are in alignment with it.

Over the years the True Self remains withdrawn and the ego, which has taken over the role of Self in order to ensure survival, eventually forgets about the existence of the Self, because of the layers of defense it has put in place in order to protect the Self in the first instance. Ego is instinctual, not intuitive, and will react instead of respond. It has a sophisticated set of survival strategies that serve as rigid and set defenses to keep the True Self safely locked into a survival mentality.

The ego will continue to draw to itself challenging life experiences because it is not at peace (like attracts like) and therefore continues to encounter conflict. This, in turn, acts as a feedback system to unconscious programs set up by the ego, which then triggers survival mentality and actions. Ego is driven by fear and it specializes in defense and attack.

Over time, the ego mistakenly comes to believe that it is the King or Queen of the kingdom of the Self. Meanwhile the true regent, the Self, withholds from stepping forward to reclaim its throne until such a time it feels it is appropriate and safe to do so.

Whatever our life circumstances, the Self can be resurrected whenever we feel ready to heal and integrate the ego. In order to do so, however, we must first begin to empathically connect with the ego.

> To learn more about empathy and how to empathically connect, I advise that you study Marshall Rosenberg's nonviolent communication theory and practice or join an NVC training course. It will also serve you well to study Eugene Gendlin's focusing practice or join a focusing group. These two methods will really support you to understand how to empathically connect with your ego, yourself, and others. Their details can be found in the resources directory.

The Self is the phoenix rising from the ashes of a past that can rapidly fall away to make way for a new future of liberation from suffering. We could say that the past represents the ego and the future represents the Self.

When the ego is in the driver's seat of our lives we continue to engage in dysfunctional and destructive patterns of behavior. This does not suggest that we are not spiritual, yet it does point clearly to a psychological split between the ego and the Self. The first step toward self-healing, integration, and self-actualization is to empathically connect with the ego and acknowledge the role it has played in our lives so that the truth of who we are was able to survive.

There comes a point on the journey of the Soul when those who are ardently in search of their True Self begin to experience this preparing to emerge. It is at this stage that the ego becomes aware of the Self. In reaction and panic, the ego devises many defense strategies by which to ensure not only its survival, but its continued rule. An example of this is when someone whose heart is closed, falls in love. Ego views anything that will awaken the heart as a threat to its survival. Self-sabotaging mechanisms instantly come into operation as the ego begins to defend itself against the emerging Self, for if the True Self emerges the ego fears its own death. Ego defense mechanisms are rooted deep within the unconscious mind and, thus, the True Self rising in love (although the ego ensures the experience becomes one of "falling" in love) becomes caught in great confusion, longing to open more to love, yet (unconsciously) sabotaging any possibility of harmonious, true, and lasting love.

This patterning illustrates how we remain caught on the wheel of karma. However, as we raise our consciousness and begin to live from the True Self, old dysfunctional and destructive patterns begin to fall away and we are no longer caught on the karmic wheel, having instead moved into a place of free will and choice.

As the Self begins its journey toward emergence and actualization, it will encounter ego defenses to block its path. Fear, shame, rage, sadness, despair, hopelessness, worthlessness, lack, and pain are just some examples of ego defenses presenting as psychological shadow. With wisdom and openness, insight and awareness, forgiveness and compassion, understanding and unconditional presence, empathy and unconditional love, Self is able to heal and transcend these shadow energies, and thus achieve integrated wholeness.

Most individuals are living as their adapted self, or ego, yet our quest and the natural way for us to live, is from our Authentic Self. Adapted or Authentic—which one do you choose? So, let us now look at how we can reclaim the throne to the kingdom of the Self, which is the true seat of the Authentic Self. If we learn to do this for ourselves and then encourage others to do the same, we can transform a world that currently mirrors the ego into one that reflects the values of the Authentic Self.

For a moment let us go into our imagination and picture the True Self as a King or Queen returning to reclaim its kingdom. Let us imagine the many shadow defenses it will encounter on its journey through the long dark corridors to the throne room, where it will meet the ego.

Ego/Self: A Fairytale

Ego has realized that Self is returning to reclaim its kingdom. Symbolically, Ego, experiencing fear and panic, frantically barricades the throne room door. Eventually, Self arrives and knocks on the door, requesting that Ego let it in and relinquish the throne.

Ego is defensive, refuses to open the door, and prepares to take up arms ready to fight. Ego is prepared to do anything to remain in power and through the closed door tells this to Self. Ego proceeds to try to intimidate Self into submission in the vain hope that Self will scurry away to its place of exile.

However, Self rides the storm whipped up by Ego. Ego feels powerless in the full presence of Self and panics further. What will become of it if Self succeeds in reclaiming the throne? Ego fears it will die. It can see no other outcome. Ego is too afraid to surrender to Self and does not know what to do. Resolutely, Ego digs in its heels and refuses to move. They have reached an impasse.

Days, weeks, and months go by with Self remaining present and Ego, locked in the throne room with no resources to maintain its power, becoming weaker. Ego resolves to die on the throne, for surrendering to Self will surely only result in this outcome, until Self throws Ego a lifeline.

Self begins to speak with Ego ever so gently and with great respect. Ego is struck by the tone of unconditional love and compassion in this voice, believing it to be the kindest and most beautiful voice it has ever heard. Ego begins to feel very, very weary, overwhelmed with exhaustion, and begins to pour out its fears to Self, who listens with great compassion and empathy. Ego feels an inexplicable sense of trust as each of its fears are validated by Self.

Ego begins to consider the possibility of opening the throne room door, yet again is overcome with fear of the consequences. As much as it wants to trust, for it is so, so tired, it is afraid, believing that Self will betray it. Ego pours out these fears to Self.

Self hears Ego's fears and, with the greatest tenderness and compassion, makes a promise. It assures Ego that its life will be safe and offers a written promise with a golden seal, which stands for absolute integrity and authenticity.

Self slides the document under the door for Ego to consider. Ego reads this and notices a separate letter tied with a golden thread. Ego unwraps the letter. It reads:

My dear, dear Ego, I am so glad to finally have the opportunity to thank you for saving my life. I recognize that without you I would not be here; I would not be alive.

You were there when I most needed protecting and, even though I have been in exile for all of these years, you ensured that I was provided for. You have held on to my kingdom and many battles you have endured on my behalf.

I know you are battered and bruised, scarred and weary, yet you never deserted me or left me exposed, unprotected, or vulnerable when I was unable to return to claim my kingdom. This undertaking has been a great burden for you and it took tremendous courage and strength. How can I ever repay you? What price can be placed on a precious life?

You have served me so very well. You have always been and will remain my hero and I know that everything you have done was to protect me. I am humbled in your presence for I know that you have suffered greatly in my name.

I see the pain and hurt you have endured. I see your heart has been broken. I see the anger and rage you have felt and received. I see the loss you have suffered. I see the loneliness you have endured. I see how you stood in the line of fire for me when the first perceived threat to my existence occurred many years ago and how you have repeatedly done so ever since.

All that you have suffered and endured has been to preserve and ensure my existence. You have been the most loyal of friends. You have never abandoned me. You bear the many scars of the trials and ordeals of this life.

My beloved Ego, I have been asleep. For many, many years I was lost in exile. I did not know who I was. During these years I forgot what happened at our first meeting when you shielded me from attack.

However, one day, not so long ago, I heard the most pitiful cries of anguish. I heard a voice scream out in the still of the night, "Help me God. Set me free. I can no longer live like this. I am so lonely and in so much pain. I am so tired. Help me someone, release me from this suffering."

That cry awakened me. It was as if I were resurrected as I felt the life force fully return to me. I heard that cry of anguish, which pierced the very core of my heart. Every cell and fiber of my being heard that call and I recognized that voice as your very own. In that moment I knew that it was now my turn to save you, my dear and loyal Ego.

Ego, I have come once more to be the ruler of my kingdom. I am as new. Even though alone, I have been protected for all of these years and I am unscarred with an unbroken heart.

Dear, dear Ego, would you do me the great honor of being the one to whom I turn for advice when I need it? Let us once more be friends. I have no need of a wounded Ego, yet great need of a healthy one. You no longer need to be lonely, for I am here as your friend.

First, you must rest and heal. Would you trust me to guide you to the people and situations that can help you to heal, to let go of fear, to learn to play, and to experience joy and love? Will you rest? I have prepared new rooms for you to live in and a beautiful garden of peace and serenity. What say you, Ego?

Ego fell to the floor with great sobs and said to Self, "Yes, how very great has been this burden and yet, not a burden, a sacred duty." Ego spoke of the wrong it had done in Self's name, of those it had hurt and how it had hurt itself. Ego hung its head in shame, afraid that by telling the truth of its misdemeanors Self would abandon it.

There was a moment's pause and then Self spoke to Ego in a most compassionate voice saying, "My dear, dear Ego, I love you unconditionally and forgive you; can you forgive yourself? Can you recognize that what you did to others was a result of what had been done to you and, even though this does not justify your actions, it does not make you unworthy?"

Ego replied, "Even if I could forgive myself, how will those who I have harmed forgive me? Without their forgiveness how can I truly heal and be free?"

Self replied, "Dearest Ego, you cannot know the karma of those who have crossed your path. Perhaps you were a catalyst or a teacher. You may have brought an experience into someone's life to help them to redress their karma. There is so much that we do not know in this dimension, why punish yourself forever?

If you stole from someone, now give to someone or to many. You may give your time or your resources. If you abused someone, help those who have also been abused. If you killed someone, now help others to live. Redress the balance of the actions you regret: for example, where there is fear bring unconditional love.

"Know this Ego, all is forgiven—all is forgivable. You only need to forgive yourself and redress your past misdeeds to be free. This is something that you can do every day. Let it be a joy to do so."

Ego stood up and with great courage and a shaky hand unlocked the throne room door and opened it. Their hearts met before their eyes and in unison they said, "I've missed you friend."

From that moment on, a harmonious, positive, and true partnership began. Self took its place upon the throne as ruler of its kingdom, with Ego, now healed, a positive and trusted advisor at its side.

◆

Remember that before we can fully embody the true Self it is the ego that helps us through the tough times in our lives. Once we embrace the true Self we no longer react. Instead we respond from the heart, from our authentic Self, and as a result of this our lives transform.

Ultimately, when healing and integrating the ego we need to first acknowledge its role. The ego deserves our honor and respect no matter what has gone before, as it very likely saved our life when it first emerged in early childhood.

Like any parent, the ego was doing the best it could at the time. Be mindful and recognize that the negative ego needs to heal and retire. The newly emerging positive ego, one that has healed and discovered self-worth and is open to give and receive love, gratitude, and appreciation, is a wonderful companion to assist the Self on the journey of the Soul.

Be gentle with your ego.

Be kind to your ego.

Love your ego unconditionally as the friend and protector it has tried to be and unconditionally love and respect your Self. If you feel that you do not know how to do this, find someone who can remind you, such as an empathic and skilled counselor, therapist, or healer. This in itself is an act of self-love. (There are contacts in the resources directory at the back of the book that can help to support you to heal and integrate the ego.)

PSYCHO-SPIRITUAL INTEGRATION

There are many people across the world who are spiritually awake and communicate with the higher dimensions, spiritual guides, and their loved ones who have passed. Most of these people believe they are integrated human beings. Nearly thirty years of psycho-spiritual research, study, and experience has taught me a fundamental truth—this being that regardless of whether someone is newly spiritually awakened or has been spiritually awake for many years, most are lacking psychological awareness and integration and, therefore, true spiritual balance.

The signs of an unintegrated individual are all too obvious to one who has achieved a psychologically integrated state of being. Many "spiritual" people lack true self-worth, an understanding of conscious communication, or the ability to respond to any given situation, as opposed to reacting. Such people are caught in an egocentric spiral where historical psychological wounding, physical, emotional, and mental trauma, and dysfunctional conditioning and patterns, convey a psychological split between the ego and the Self.

The Self is revived through spiritual awakening, yet not fully awakened. To fully embody the Self, the ego must become integrated. This is only possible when an individual is committed to Self-healing, Self-realization, Self-knowing, and Self-actualization.

I often describe those whose eyes are wide open to the spiritual realities, yet are devoid of any deep psychological Self-knowing, as having *balloon syndrome*. These seekers of spiritual truth float high toward the heavens, yet without any real grounding on the Earth or in the Self. An analogy for psycho-spiritual integration might be that of a great oak tree whose roots run deep into rich, fertile soil, while the tips of its branches aspire high toward the heavens. We must be rooted in the rich, fertile soil of our humanness while, at the same time, aspiring toward our higher ideals.

Understanding the role of the ego in our conscious evolutionary development is essential if we are to accurately describe and experience ourselves as whole and integrated human beings.

Plato is the philosopher most associated with the quote "Know thyself," and never a truer invitation has been offered to humanity. It is our responsibility as consciously evolving human beings to *know thy Self*, both as a Spirit Being experiencing a human life and as a human being awakening more to the spiritual reality of who we really are.

It is not possible to know thyself merely through aligning with the love and light aspects of a spiritual reality. In actual fact, this often further disassociates an individual from their capacity to experience themselves as whole and integrated. This state of being can only be achieved when both the human shadow and the spiritual Self are explored, embraced, healed, and integrated into our day-to-day lives.

Understanding and integrating the ego is a necessary, essential, and critical turning point on the path to full conscious awakening. The Ego/Self fairytale offers the twenty-first-century consciously evolving and spiritually awakening individual the opportunity to do so in the most eloquent, loving, simple, and joyful way. This new and unique approach to the integration of the ego encourages neither blame or shame, guilt or repentance, judgment or defense, pain or suffering, or expensive ongoing therapy. It requires only a sincere desire to become a whole and integrated human being. By so doing, we reap the rewards of true love, peace, joy, and happiness. This ego/Self teaching reminds us that there is only love. That love is the greatest healer. And that love is the answer to everything.

SEVEN

Inner Peace—World Peace

There are many ways in which we can promote peace in the world. There are many campaigns to which we can dedicate ourselves. However, perhaps the most effective way to ensure world peace is to seek and cultivate it within ourselves.

The cultivation of peace, both inner and outer, is dependent upon fundamental human qualities such as compassion, empathy, and understanding. These three qualities promote a feeling of peace in both those who give and those who receive. We could say that when we are compassionate, empathic, and understanding it is a win-win situation.

One of the most profound teachings that our schools and institutes of learning could offer us is peace. Can you imagine if part of our school curriculum included lessons in this? Peace within the Self, between ourselves and others, within the family, the community, and the world—what a wonderful addition this would prove to the educational system. Everyone deserves peace. Peace is what we all strive for and yet so few ever find. The reason for this is because not many look within. Most are preoccupied with searching for peace out there, when it is truly only to be found in here—within the Self.

BEING PEACE

Inner peace equates to being in a state of deep peace at a physical, emotional, mental, psychological, creative, energetic, and psychic level.

When all of these levels are aligned in peace we become as tuning forks, capable of emitting a wonderful and tangible vibration that draws those still searching for peace closer to us. They too may then come to understand this most desirable of all human states and experience it for themselves.

Those at peace also resonate with others who have found the same and all are able to bask in the amplified and unified field created: for example, within a group meditation or at a spiritual retreat center. Peace is catching and it needs to go viral! How? What is it that we must do? Or, to be more accurate, what is it we must *be*? Where must we focus our awareness? To what is it that we must commit ourselves?

What is clear is that we must first find peace within. By cultivating peace—by being peace as Thich Nhat Hanh teaches—by sharing our inner peace with others, by raising and educating our children to cultivate peace as a priority, it can go viral. Peace needs to be a preventative rather than a cure.

Being peace requires that we have developed a strong inner core, rooted in compassion, empathy, understanding, and connection, nevertheless recognizing that we can remain aware of the trauma and suffering of another without losing our own sense of peace. Peace is hard won in these times, and once achieved we need to maintain this state of being in any circumstances and without compromise. And so it is that we can say that the cultivation of peace is a two-fold process: one, the attainment of it and two, the maintaining of it.

When we feel at peace, we feel tranquil, calm, serene, magnanimous, understanding, empathic, compassionate, forgiving, open, expansive, warm, well, vibrant, gentle, and strong.

Zen Buddhist monk and Nobel Peace Prize nominee Thich Nhat Hanh believes that there is no way to peace, peace is the way. Along the way are several places of resource that can support us in the cultivation of inner peace. Self-mastery at a psychological level is perhaps the most important in terms of psychological awareness and development, healing and integration. This I would say is the most profound initiator of true and lasting inner peace. Yet also, there are other practices that can enhance and offer us deep inner-peace experiences, such as meditation, yoga, t'ai chi, being in nature, or a loving relationship with a sentient being—whether this is another human or a beloved pet. (You may wish to watch my Four Minutes and Four Seconds of Peace film on YouTube at www.youtube.com/watch?v=imW1Skieo_4.)

When we have cultivated inner peace, we automatically wish to co-create a world of peace. Having resolved our own inner conflicts, we seek more and more ways to contribute to the establishment of a peaceful world. Conflict resolution seeks to create harmony, equality, peace, and understanding in any situation where there is conflict and confrontation between people, communities, countries, and nations.

One of the six core values for an evolving world that I speak of (see chapter 9) is restorative justice. My dear friend and colleague Wendy Webber has written an in-depth account of restorative justice explaining this core value. However, suffice to say here, restorative justice seeks to ensure the resolution of perceived injustices through either mediation, arbitration, negotiation, community conferencing, restorative circles, community meditation, negotiation of the agreed application of appropriate boundaries, and collaborative conflict-resolution law making.

Peace needs to be a priority in the agendas of all nations during elections for new governments. Political candidates need to be selected and merited on how much importance they give to peace as a priority in their own campaigns, even for initial steps that might include introducing peace as a primary subject to be studied in schools. It could also be offered at B.A., M.A., and Ph.D. levels for universities and adult education.

Mother Teresa was quoted as saying the following: "If we have no peace, it is because we have forgotten that we belong to each other. . . . I was once asked why I don't participate in anti-war demonstrations. I said that I will never do that, but as soon as you have a pro-peace rally, I'll be there." A new paradigm calls for new measures.

A new epoch, such as the one we now are entering into, requires a new global system where antiquated laws that were effective in past centuries are replaced by new laws that address not only the times we are living in, but more importantly the needs of the people. In the corridors of political, governmental, educational, policy- and law-making departments, a new conversation needs to be taking place—one that speaks to the establishing of world-peace committees that consist of peacemakers and humanitarians from across the globe whose job it is to ensure that peace is upheld as a priority. If this is not forthcoming from those who hold power and office then we, the people, must peacefully decline to involve ourselves in election campaigns or support the antiquated laws, reelection policies, or anti-peace and anti-human-rights proposals.

We are a global humanity. With the advent of the Internet we are unified worldwide more now than at any other time in human history. The problems of one are also the problems of all. One nation's plight is the concern of all. When another suffers from a lack of peace, unless we are deeply integrated, this can impact our own capacity to hold that same state within ourselves. It is interesting to note that on Facebook the most responses are not to world affairs, but to people who have the courage to share their personal suffering with others. People are looking beyond nationality, religion, and race. They are recognizing each other as brother and sister, mother and father, elder and innocent child.

We need to work together to co-create a new united global policy where we see the eradication of war, poverty, disease, starvation, and the displacement of peoples; to develop new education and judicial systems; new models for medicine, the economy, and the environment. Right-relationship models for ecology, employment, and for governmental stewardship need to reflect the six core values for an evolving world if we are to progress as an evolving global society.

Ideally, the borders between individuals and countries need to dissolve, with one flag symbolizing a united human race. We are brothers and sisters and citizens of the Earth. The time has come for humanity to stand together in unity, as one voice, one heart, one nation, living in one country—this planet Earth.

We can go through our entire lives with an underlying sense that something is missing. Rarely do we realize that what is missing is a part of ourselves. In the preverbal stages of our development, the environment impacts us in a profound way. Our parents, or primary caregivers, influence our sense of Self and personality enormously and, if the early environment is a dysfunctional one, we very quickly begin to adapt to the incoming messages in order to survive.

We develop an adapted self. As we grow and reach adulthood this adapted self becomes our primary identity and the Authentic Self, who we were born to be, disappears from the conscious mind and everyday experiences of our lives. It is the adapted self that comes to our rescue as infants, when we first perceive a threat to our survival. It is in this moment that the ego is born. Whereas the Authentic Self is undefended, trusting, surrendered, and open, the adapted self is defended, untrusting, suspicious, and closed.

In most cases as we grow into adults, we develop a coping mechanism that keeps us out of sanatoriums or prisons. This coping strategy facilitates our unconscious need to express (via projection and transference) repressed fear, pain, rage, sadness, anger, and hurt.

A DYSFUNCTIONAL MEDIA

Perpetuating or Acting Out the Human Shadow?

We have only to switch on the news or to tune into any one of two-hundred-plus television channels to find that the predominant theme is murder, theft, rape, sexual misconduct, betrayal, rage, and deception. The media culture in particular serves as a representation of and an outlet for the repressed human shadow. Of course, there are aspects of the media that seek to raise consciousness; however, this is the exception rather than the rule and it is not this representation of media to which I refer.

Yet, we have a chicken-and-egg scenario here. For to what degree does the violence depicted in the media, most notably from television and film, exacerbate the human shadow, and how does the unexplored, unhealed, and unintegrated human shadow inflict itself upon the world? Without this capacity to passively express our psychological shadow would the state of the world further degenerate? It seems we are caught between a rock and a hard place. Many people remain totally unaware of what exactly it is that they get caught in, what gets perpetuated and activated, each time they engage with mainstream media.

It is necessary and critical now for us to turn our attention inward to explore, heal, and integrate our own psychological shadow as mirrored by an unconscious media. For example, the more integrated a person is, the less attracted they are to all things representative of the unhealed human shadow. We find that as we refine the Self, we are inclined to turn away from anything that represents conflict, suffering, and pain and empathically disconnects us from others and our True Self, unless in our awakened state we turn toward it to bring healing and restoration.

And so, the more that people become integrated and whole, the less compulsion there will be in the individual and collective human shadow to meet itself out in the media, including films, books, television, radio, and the Internet. People would instead seek stimulation of the heart, the feelings, and the Soul—not the unintegrated human shadow.

All the while people remain comfortably numb, all the time they stay psychologically asleep—without any awareness that they are merely adapted and inauthentic versions of themselves—the more the media will continue to anesthetize the True Self with a lethal cocktail of data to keep them psychologically, consciously, and spiritually asleep.

The time has come to wake up and to ask ourselves: what is this I am reading; what is this I am watching; what is this I am listening to; and what is this I am colluding with and endorsing by my participation in it. The time has come to explore our own psychological shadow through appropriate means so that we may wake up and be liberated, instead of remaining the prisoners of our unintegrated, slumbering, psychological selves.

The main issue with the media is that it is a stimulant for the lower drives and the adapted self. By and large it is a negative force that recognizes the enormous subliminal and overt influence it has over the thoughts and emotions of its viewing public. It prescribes with unnerving accuracy the exact message that will ensure that people will "turn on, tune in, and drop out" from any conscious and authentic participation in their own lives. We need to "turn on, tune in, and wake up" to ourselves, to the reality of the Authentic Self, and to the Truth of who we really are.

Another prime target for the overt playing out of the human shadow is the treatment of the creatures of the land and oceans, all life-forms, and nature herself. Also, we can observe the worldwide addictions to consumerism, drugs, alcohol, sex, and pharmaceuticals to be representative of the further numbing and repressing of the psychological shadow. Repression and suppression lead to depression. In the psychological model, depression is a result of unexpressed emotions. Keeping the masses psychologically asleep, disempowered, dumbed down, and numbed out is a multitrillion-dollar global industry. What happens when truth attempts to break through the global agendas? It gets stamped out.

Look at the pharmaceutical and medical industries that will destroy anything that poses a threat to their all powerful money-making machine, which feeds off the needy, the desperate, and the vulnerable. Industries strike off reputable doctors who try to champion known cancer cures (a list of these can be found in the resource directory at the end of this book), or seek to ban natural remedies. This is because it became apparent just how much money they were losing to the natural remedies industry that promotes the empowerment of the Self with its "healer heal thyself" approach.

Few are actually driven to fully act out their unhealed psychological shadow in the world. There is a fine balance between noncatastrophic projection and the catastrophic acting out of the psychological shadow. The majority of people have a psychological profile that enables a noncatastrophic shadow expression. We need only look around the world, however, to see evidence of those whose psychological profile is so afflicted that its impact is, or has been, catastrophic.

Humanity needs now to experience a shift of evolution. We need to become conscious of and responsible for how we project our shadow selves onto others and out into the world, or conversely how we project it onto a media that is mostly based upon the new seven deadly sins. At the very least this induces further numbing of the emotions and the mind, but at worst those who have been overstimulated by this perpetuation of violence may be influenced to act out their shadow side with innocent victims. This cycle will continue unless we stop it. For the majority, the projection of the shadow is a way of life and mostly unconscious. However, the behavior that results from this is considered normal by an anesthetized culture.

While our focus remains fixated on what is outside of us, while we lament the harrowing stories reported on the news, and then, paradoxically, are entertained by the same subject matter glamorized on television and in films, we will continue to remain numb and blind to the true cause of the lack of peace in the world. Without psychological exploration, with its accompanying healing and integration of the human shadow, humanity will continue to project both the individual and collective shadow onto others and into the environment, thus reinforcing and perpetuating the turmoil and state of crisis the world finds itself in. The global shadow is our shadow. It is representative of anyone who has not looked within themselves for the purpose of psychological healing and integration.

A dysfunctional early environment is not a peaceful environment (this also applies to the experience in the womb), and so it is that the seed of "unpeacefulness" is sown deep into the psyche. We must retrace our steps back to our *felt knowing*, which means to feel something to be true even if we cannot recall it.

Felt knowing is based upon the precept, "It feels like it was." What is important in our inner-healing process is that we listen to the deeper wisdom of "what it feels like," which is beyond our mental recollection. For example, if someone says, "I feel I was abused as a child," they may not have mental recall of this event taking place, yet it may have actually occurred. There is also the possibility that it may not have. However, what is important here is what they feel occurred, as this can give vital clues to what they feel is happening in their lives in the here and now. For example, what they share could indicate that perhaps they are feeling abused by a boss, partner, parent, colleague, or sibling. Abuse can be experienced as overt or subtle. It can also be a physical, emotional, mental, or spiritual trauma memory that arises seemingly spontaneously.

Ask yourself the questions: Have you ever thought, longed for, or campaigned for world peace? Have you ever signed a petition, discussed, debated, or written about it? If your response is a *Yes* to either of these, then ask yourself the following necessary questions: How peaceful do I feel within myself? What active measures am I taking to cultivate inner peace? What is my vision for world peace? True and lasting world peace can only come when we are each at peace within ourselves.

For a positive and sustainable world shift to occur we must first attain a positive and significant inner world shift. This is the only way to establish lasting world peace. Inner peace equates to world peace. This is a fact.

The following was posted by the World Peace Newsletter Facebook Community in October 2011. It was titled "Peace Definition." I think it is a beautiful summary to end this chapter on "Inner Peace—World Peace." And so, I hand the final word over to these Facebook friends.

Peace is a vastly greater concept than the lack of war, violence, poverty, and inner turmoil. Peace is the combination of bodily peace, family peace, local peace, national peace, inner peace, and world peace.

Accordingly, true peace must begin with food, water, vitamin nutrition, and appropriate medical care for both rich and poor alike. Next, peace training starts with the family and in our education systems. Peace needs to surround us in the form of local safety and security, which is best achieved through communication and negotiation with neighbors to attain mutual trust and respect for one another. Governments and state leaders can assist in the peace process by creating and encouraging moral and ethical standards, thus promoting restorative justice, liberty, freedom, ethnic and religious tolerance, and constructive relations with all nations.

Inner peace may be the most important key to peace because through love (both of Self and the world), faith, meditation, self-esteem, compassion, hope, kindness, gratitude, and wisdom (self-cultivation), peace will spread to those around you.

World peace is achieved by combining all the "peaces" together to create "hot peace" (as opposed to cold war). Hot peace is the absolute presence of worldwide justice, freedom, cooperation, negotiation education, mutual respect, sharing, compassion, kindness, happiness, joy, equanimity, human dignity, and harmony with nature, animals, and Mother Earth.

World peace is merely an unsolved puzzle waiting for loving people to put the "peaces" together. Through love, world peace not only becomes possible, peace becomes probable.

The benefits of human beings working together to create peace for all, will reduce poverty, crime, war, hate, injustice, pollution, etc.

The true benefit is living in a world where love, care, and compassion become the standard on this beautiful planet.

EIGHT

A Higher Love
and Sexuality

The musician and songwriter Will Jennings's song "Higher Love," made famous by Stevie Winwood, has the following lament:

Bring me a higher love
Bring me a higher love, oh
Bring me a higher love
I could rise above for this higher love.

This same lament can be found deep within the heart and Soul of each one of us. In our most sublime dreams, we long for such a love. Yet, to experience this we must first embody the extraordinary qualities that a love of this nature requires. For it takes us beyond the realms of what is understood by the old paradigm models of romantic love, beyond the conditions, the expectations, the chocolates and flowers and into the realms of an exalted love that is unconditional, personal, and beyond personal. It is the meeting of heart and Soul with the presence of Spirit in its very fiber.

There are various levels of experience of romantic love, just as there are many levels of learning. Where along the learning curve of love we find ourselves, to what degree our hearts are open, and the capacity we have for love will all determine the type of romantic love we will experience. It is possible to experience a deeply romantic and affectionate love with a partner if we have never explored ourselves psychologically or spiritually. This type of love is one in which the partners have the ability to express their feelings and thoughts to such an extent that the other feels cherished and loved. However, with such a love there will always be a sense of something missing, even if this is not at first apparent. It can be the subtlest of feelings, which can easily be brushed aside or ignored. Nevertheless, that feeling will come and go throughout the relationship.

The reason for this is that our capacity for the deepest, highest, and most exalted love only becomes possible when we have that experience within ourselves. If our identity is wrapped up with the way in which we are loved by another and we find ourselves fearing the loss of the partner, then this indicates that there is a psychological split within ourselves and we are projecting our need for love onto them. However, if we have not developed our love of Self enough, we find that there is no *I,* in our romantic relating, only *we.*

In every healthy relationship there needs to be an *I* and a separate *we.* As individuals, we need to know where we begin and the other ends. We need to have a clear experience of our *I* and *we,* and recognize that the two are not the same. Only when we can fully experience the Self and the other (*I* and *we*) in heart-to-heart love, can we transcend identification with either, to elevate the relationship to a realm that is beyond personal.

In the wonderful book *The Prophet,* Khalil Gibran shares:

Let there be spaces in your togetherness, And let the winds of the heavens dance between you. Love one another but make not a bond of love: Let it rather be a moving sea between the shores of your souls. Fill each other's cup but drink not from one cup. Give one another of your bread but eat not from the same loaf. Sing and dance together and be joyous, but let each one of you be alone, Even as the strings of a lute are alone though they quiver with the same music. Give your hearts, but not into each other's keeping. For only the hand of Life can contain your hearts. And stand together, yet not too near together: For the pillars of the temple stand apart, And the oak tree and the cypress grow not in each other's shadow.*

So, what is it that differentiates a higher love from what may be termed normal romantic love? Let us begin with the qualities that each express. Normal romantic love is often dependent and codependent. Normal love seeks security and the known. In normal love, we find the first attraction is often a physical one: in particular a physical attribute such as nice eyes, smile, teeth, hair, physique, or figure. For men, it is often the woman's overall appearance that is desirable and for women it can be a man's standing in the world or her perception of how he relates to and expresses his "power." And then there is the greatest influencer of all—unconscious projection.

The pitfalls of a lack of psychological awareness or integration have a detrimental impact on the relationship, often leaving both partners confused and in pain. Because they do not understand what is really happening, they get caught in a cycle of separating and reuniting. This is because the unconscious hope for both is that out of the suffering that comes through separation, the consequent reuniting will bring back what brought them into the partnership in the first place, which was an unconscious desire for their unmet needs to be healed. And so ensues a spiral of experience where each traumatic event in the relationship creates further separation. If only there was an understanding of the psychological dynamics at play, so much healing and the subsequent breakthroughs to a higher experience of love could be possible.

So what constitutes a higher love? A higher love is independent and interdependent. A higher love seeks deep fulfillment and is continually ready to step into the unknown. With higher love the attraction is first to the *feeling* of the person, to the quality of the Soul, the mind, the emotional intelligence, the energy, and Spirit. It is the quality of conversation that lights a fire within the Self, the moral and ethical values that become apparent, the inner and worldly perspective, a sense of the

---

*Khalil Gibran, *The Prophet* (New York: Alfred A. Knopf, 1923).

other having a good degree of self-knowing and the greatest influence of all—what is *known* and seen when looking into the eyes.

This experience is nothing to do with the size, shape, or color of the eyes. It is beyond those physical factors. However, it has everything to do with the quality of Soul awareness, of the inner knowing, of a connection to something beyond the Self that extends not only to one's fellow human beings, but to the whole of nature and to the heavens. It is a tangible felt sense of the openness and enormity of the heart of the other and a light that radiates from and around them.

It is the electric charge that is not sparked by sexual attraction but by something more, a charge that is ignited when two awakened Souls reencounter each other in this lifetime. It is an unequivocal familiarity, a profound sense of déjà vu, a gnosis that a great love is about to unfold. Sexual attraction in this type of encounter is secondary, the physical appearance almost an afterthought. It is two Souls colliding at the exact predestined moment in time.

At this level of attraction both individuals seek the same, for they are psychologically integrated and spiritually awake. What they seek is the complement to themselves, one who possesses similar qualities, not one who can bring inner qualities they lack, as is often the case in a normal romantic love. These are relationships in which the heart, mind, Soul, and Spirit of each partner are developed to the same level and in which their work and vision for the world is a humanitarian one. It is for people who feel complete in themselves, whether in a romantic relationship or not. If and when that comes along, it proves to be the icing on the cake, as it were.

In such a relationship all aspects of life can be shared. He shops, she shops. He cooks, she cooks. She works, he works. She cleans, he cleans. He takes care of the children, she takes care of the children or, at the very least, he supports her if it is her preference to primarily do this.

When it comes to the sexual expression of a higher love, whereas a normal romantic relationship places great emphasis on the body, in terms of physical "assets" or sexual sensations, clothing to enhance attraction, sexual performance, and so forth, higher love focuses on the energy between partners. It is the feeling, the heart, the importance of the windows of the Soul, when an entire sexual experience can be solely gazing into the eyes of the beloved.

The experience takes both beyond the physical and into higher and higher realms of ecstatic love. Orgasm involves the whole body, with or without the emission of semen, which is often retained, as this type of lovemaking is not about the destination, but the journey.

Whereas in normal romantic sexual encounters the primal drives tend to be the main focus, in the lovemaking of those engaged at a higher level of love, the superconscious is activated, which can lead to altered states of consciousness, out-of-body, and extradimensional experiences. Normal sexual contact can be stimulated by alcohol and drugs, whereas the sacred sexual union of higher love is catalyzed by the intoxication of love and love alone.

It is also important to distinguish between those sexual couplings that some might term sacred union, and temporary intense sexual encounters, which may be experienced at festivals, parties, or gatherings. Again, any type of union that is experienced outside of the realm of what constitutes true and higher love is not the type of love of which I speak. More often than not, even those who can claim some degree of awakening or psychological awareness, are still genitally driven in their sexual encounters.

The higher love to which I refer here is the type that has often been described as *twin flame* love. There is only ever one, and although it is rare to meet them in any lifetime, it is possible. Only twin flame union, or the closest love to this, which I now refer to as *twin soul* love, can catapult us into the highest human expression of true love and sacred sexuality. Both of these categories will be explained in depth later in the chapter; first let us begin to explore and understand the profound reality of sacred sexuality.

SACRED SEXUALITY AND CONTEMPORARY SPIRITUALITY

Sexual union should be like a rite, a ritual performed in mindfulness with great respect, care, and love. If you are

motivated by some desire, that is not love. Desire is not love.
Love is something much more responsible. It has care in it. We
must look upon ourselves and the other as a human being, with
the capacity of becoming a Buddha.

THICH NHAT HANH

To see an image of a tantric yogi sitting in the lotus position, penis erect while in deep meditation, in deep inner union with his Self and the Absolute, is an experience few people can lay claim to and which can create a powerful reaction in one who gazes upon such an image.

When I was researching images for the "Seven Dark, Seven Light, and Seven Rainbow Arrows," I came across just such a tantric yogi. It was startling and had a profound impact upon me, for I had never before seen such an image of sacred sexuality, particularly one of a male sitting in the silence and sacredness of meditation.

I posted the image, along with the text for the "Light Arrow of Self-Pleasure," on my Facebook wall. The usual *likes* or *comments* disappeared and I could sense the confusion, shock, judgments, curiosity, excitement, embarrassment, upset, and denial of those who looked upon the erect penis of this tantric yogi, in sublime and deep meditation.

Such an image is representative of the unknown. People feel safe with the known, but it is the unknown that either draws or repels them. As we throw off the shackles of the old paradigm and prepare ourselves for the new, the time has come to lift the dark veil that has shrouded the truth of sexuality. For in truth, sexuality is sacred and a pathway to enlightenment. This reality has been lost to humankind and now it must be rediscovered, reclaimed, and reestablished.

Sexual energy is the most powerful and potent on the planet. It is the creative force of all of life. Distorted misrepresentations of true religion have castrated the sexual nature of both male and female to reduce the act of sexual union to a basic animal level. For most, this induces feelings of shame, guilt, rage, disgust, self-loathing, and depression.

The two most powerful forces in the world are the sexual drive and Spirit. Sex is the creative energy and Spirit is Creator energy. Throughout millennia, these have been manipulated and distorted by those in power in order to control the minds of the masses and maintain their wealth. As such, the nature of sexuality has become an unrecognizable impulse, an animalistic urge, and used to manipulate all systems that make up the components of a dysfunctional mechanism by which global society is run. From consumerism to politics, religion to media, corporate level to international trade, and including the fashion and beauty industry, the entire global business and social systems are saturated by sex.

What is known without a doubt by the dysfunctional global establishment, is that "sex sells." Sex is commerce and currency. Sexuality has been manipulated to the point of having acquired a murky shadow called glamour. In Latin, *glamour* means "illusion." Over millennia, the human being has acquired a sexual shadow and this is played out and projected into the world.

At a personal level, the sexual shadow not only exists in the few, but is a reality for the majority. The sexual shadow equates to any attitude that constitutes a reactive behavior of personal sexual expression, be that in the form of self-pleasure (masturbation), or soulless sexual experience with another. Any other thoughtform or feeling about sexuality that is not part of a sacred, deeply loving union with Self or between two people, has shadow energy surrounding it.

We have been conditioned by the system and by our parents and caregivers, who were themselves conditioned by generations before them. Religion has held the heart and sacred sexuality hostage. When combined with the way the establishment uses sex for commercial gain by surrounding us with distorted images and representations of sexuality, is it any wonder most people are in dysfunctional sexual relationships with themselves and others?

Sexual dysfunction begins from conception with the emotional and physical conditions in which we were conceived. It is colored by the quality of the experience in the womb in terms of the consciousness of the mother and the father during sexual intimacy, the mother's emotions and the father's supporting presence. The way we are birthed, and the associated trauma of what may be an entirely unnatural birth process (for example sterile hospital conditions), further alienates us from the felt sense. This felt sense is initially stimulated by intimacy and the quality of innocent naked bodily contact. This is vital immediately following birth, throughout infancy, and in the formative years of a child.

Breastfeeding; toilet training; early handling; the physical, emotional, and psychological environment; and the relationship between parents and grandparents and the immediate household and local community all further impact the messages we absorb about intimacy and help influence and shape us. Added to this are the imprints of sexual attitudes within our genetic or ancestral historical memory.

Furthermore, there is the impact of the environment, the television, the newspapers, magazines, radio, advertisements, billboards, Internet, fashion and beauty, and—the final nail in the coffin—pornography, which is now blatantly widespread and easily accessible. Is it any wonder that we arrive in our teenage years with an attitude toward sexuality that has lost all trace of the sacred? In fact, the term *sacred* may only serve to further distort a person's attitude toward sexuality, as it may well be associated with religious conditioning. Sacred has become *scared*—a simple shift of letters that pinpoints the hidden agendas of religion.

It is time now to understand the true nature and use of the sexual force, our own sexual energy, and the sexual being that we each are. This energy is potent, powerful, and profound and can heal the most wounded of hearts and the deepest trauma imprints and memories held within the psyche. It can support the cultivation of the Self and self-mastery, the evolution of the Soul, and facilitate us to evolve ever closer to God/Source/Creator. The sexual force is the driving force and a way to enlightenment: from ego to I—I to I Am—I Am to I AM—I AM to God/Source/Creator.

Let us now return to the image of the tantric yogi I mentioned earlier. This spiritually aware being sat in the lotus position, eyes closed in deep meditation, in sacred sexual union with himself, with his hands held in a position to represent some sublime mudra and in communion with God/Source/Creator.

When gazing upon such an image, some may have to look twice to believe their eyes, or to even notice the erect penis. However, by allowing a moment to pause and breathe, we can rest our eyes on such an image and allow ourselves to gaze upon it with interested curiosity. It is a new experience for both a man and a woman to be confronted with a nonpornographic image of a peaceful young man in meditation fully aroused. Who has seen such an image before?

Yet, if we adjust our vision and look at this image through the eyes of the heart, we experience something extraordinary beginning to occur. We notice a feeling sensation in our bodies, our hearts, and our minds. This is not a sexual arousal, but a remembrance—a knowing, a gnosis—that what we are looking at is sacred sexual Truth. By doing so, we come to experience a felt sense of this extraordinary truth and so activate a longing to know exactly what that pure state of being would feel like. We sense somewhere deep inside, in that place of truth that exists within us all, that this is an exalted expression of sexuality. We are left with a knowing that anything we have experienced is not comparable to what is being conveyed in the image of the tantric yogi. He reminds us of what is possible in terms of our own spiritual practice for sacred sexual reunion with ourselves and other, and of a noble and true path to enlightenment and to the Divine.

And through the practice of sacred sexuality, let us heal and transcend a history of sexual dysfunction, one that we have been caught up in throughout history. Now is the time to write not "his-story" or "her-story," but this story—our story. Love is transcendent. It is Love that will blaze a trail straight to the heart of God/Creator/Source—which is the true heart of religion.

SACRED SEXUAL UNION WITH SELF

Before we begin our exploration into romantic partnering, I would like to spend a moment here exploring sacred sexual union with Self. There are two categories to this level of experiencing; self with a small *s* and Self with a capital *S*.

Sexual Union with Self

What am I referring to when I differentiate *self* from *Self*? Self with a small *s* denotes the unhealed ego, the unintegrated aspects of ourselves and the psychologically wounded inner child who sits in the driver's seat of our life.

Sacred sexual union, when located in the place of self, is not sacred and is not union. It is not a sacred union.

Unnatural Sexual Experiencing versus Natural Sexual Expression

Unnatural Stimuli

When we are located in self, sexual stimulation and arousal are triggered by the dysfunctional processes that form that level of self-expression. It is desire, fantasy, and a pornographic culture that tend to be dominant, if the sexuality is not repressed or split off as in those who are single or celibate. And so we can say that this expression and experience of sexual energy is unnatural because it is stimulated by unhealed psychological history, an unintegrated ego/personality, and sexually dysfunctional cultural conditioning.

Continual exposure to sexual stimuli, be that through a dysfunctional media, the Internet, or within the home environment or wider community and culture, unnaturally impacts our natural sexual cycles and rhythms. They are forced to adapt to the signals and messages coming from the external environment. These can have a devastating impact on the natural expression of sexual energy, to the point where it may become deeply suppressed, or replaced by an unnatural response to the quagmire of sexual dysfunction in which the majority of the world is immersed.

An unnatural and disharmonious relationship to, and expression of, our sexual energy is detrimental to the body, feelings, and mind. It leads to imbalance and illness, whether physical, emotional, or mental. The natural sexual nature of an individual has been manipulated and over-stimulated by exposure to the dysfunctional representation of sexuality that is all pervading in a sexually fixated global culture.

Sexuality in its natural and purest essence cannot be aroused by any of the triggers or stimuli of a dysfunctional sexual paradigm. This unevolved level of sexual expression is only experienced through the self. At this level, we are talking about sex. When expressed and experienced through the Self however, we are talking about sexuality and sacred union. The self *has sex* with self or other. The Self *makes love,* in the truest sense, with Self or other.

Just as in many other arenas of life, sexuality has become distorted beyond all recognition. It has become so far removed from its original expression that 99 percent of sexually active people are experiencing a hybrid of sexuality that bears little resemblance to natural sexuality. When unnatural sexual stimulation and arousal occurs, it inappropriately activates a sexual reaction and floods the system with chemicals, fluids, messages, and triggers that result in the body, feelings, and mind falling out of balance. Whether the catalyst for sexual arousal is a mental thought, an image, film or reading material, or an actual physical sexual experience, the base and sacral chakras become inappropriately stimulated and send a message that releases a physio-sexual chemical reaction into the system. This negatively impacts the physical, emotional, and mental levels of the individual.

Unnatural sexual stimulation can be compared to salivating. We are meant to ingest natural food substances only when the body feels in need of fuel for survival. We feel hungry and so we eat. (Let us also note that in affluent societies our relationship to food and beverages has become entirely unnatural and therefore the rhythms and cycles of natural hunger is a phenomenon that most are unaware of.) In order to help break down the food, the body releases various particles, chemicals, and acids within the saliva to serve that purpose. However, if we were to obsess about thoughts of all our favorite types of foods and beverages (mostly unnatural), we would be salivating excessively and unnaturally and this would impact the overall balance and experience of our health and well-being.

I raise this point because the sexual energy is meant to lie dormant (kundalini at the base of the spine) and become active in entirely natural ways that totally preclude unnatural stimulation. Instead kundalini is meant to be stimulated *only* by the heart and a pure mind. When kundalini is naturally active, it releases internally as ever-increasing waves and natural rhythms and cycles. Kundalini informs us when an actual physical release is needed, via orgasm, to enable further integration and amplification of internal energies. Such a rhythm brings a sense of overall well-being, radiance, and clarity.

Natural Stimuli

Kundalini energy, to a greater or lesser degree depending upon the conscious evolution of the individual, surges throughout the entire system, including the cells, molecules, organs, and blood. It literally permeates the bones, both the physical and energetic bodies, the genetic blueprint, the DNA, the mind, consciousness, the luminous energy field, the light body, the Soul, and beyond, into the atmosphere flowing to the stars and out to the universe.

Kundalini is the most potent force on the planet; and the power of its far-reaching multidimensional impact on Self, the collective, the Earth, and the universe is still little known, because nearly seven billion people experience sexuality only as self. We can but imagine what would happen if nearly seven billion people were in sacred sexual union with Self and significant other.

To express sexuality in its purest and most natural form requires a very high level of self-development and self-mastery. When we are at this level of personal evolution, dysfunctional external stimuli cease to impact as triggers for stimulation of the sexual energy. The kundalini (also known as the serpent at the base of the spine) rests and slumbers and then awakens and activates in entirely natural rhythms and cycles: just as the sun rises in the morning and sets in the evening, and the moon rises at night and sets in the morning. The entire system— physical, emotional, feeling, mental, mind, energetic, psychic, and Soul—comes into alignment when naturally stimulated by the expression of kundalini energy. When that energy naturally rises and is responded to it brings all the systems into perfect balance.

So what constitutes natural stimuli? First and foremost the prerequisite is to live from the heart. Without this, we cannot align our kundalini energy to an entirely natural rhythm and cycle. So, living from the heart; purity of the body, the feelings, and the mind; alignment of the personality with the Soul (not the other way around); living love and living light in every moment; being connected from the root to the crown chakra; and feeling the deep connection with the Earth and matter, while at the same time being profoundly connected to the heavens and spirit, all constitute natural stimuli.

When we are fully in our hearts; when love and light radiate from our eyes and pour from us; when we live located in the center of peace and love within ourselves; when we are empathically connected on all levels with ourselves and all sentient beings and all kingdoms on Earth, including human, animal, nature, mineral, then we fully experience natural sexual energy. Then we are stimulated and aroused by the feelings of intense love that wash through us in that state of being. The very essence and multi-nuances of nature and the stars themselves become stimuli for sacred sexual arousal. Our whole Being is aligned with the All that Is and this triggers an entirely natural kundalini response.

How Do We Begin to Evolve from self to Self in Our Sexual Expression?

First, we consciously choose an entirely natural relationship to our sexuality and reclaim it. Then we consciously choose to enter a period of celibacy which may be one month, three months, six months, or longer. It must certainly be at least one month of no sexual activity at all with ourselves or anyone else. But ideally, three months of abstinence is preferable if we are to begin to rebalance the sexual rhythm and cycles.

We begin to become mindful of what is out there in the environment and culture that is subtly or overtly manipulating our sexual energy. In each moment therefore we consciously choose to unhook ourselves. In the early days of evolving our sexuality, the neural pathways within our brains are deeply wired to react to this manipulation, which results in our becoming hooked into a sexually dysfunctional culture. Choosing to unhook from these stimuli may entail switching off a television program or advertisements, closing a magazine or a book, staying away from the Internet, removing ourselves from sexually dysfunctional conversations, or from anything at all that involves unnatural sexuality.

In regard to our sexual relationship with ourselves, by abstaining from all sexual activity and stimuli for a predetermined period we will find that, like fasting, the physical, emotional, and mental levels of our being will react. The sexual force may intensify, the battle for our minds in terms of the flooding of past visual/thought stimuli will increase, and the body will feel extra sensitive as each day and week passes. The first three-month period will be experienced as the most intense.

Bramacharyaism— A Support for Evolving Sexuality

During the period of abstinence, a sexual release will occur in sleep or the dream state. Gandhi walked the path of the Bramacharya of which celibacy is an intricate part. It involves the practice of seeing all males as brothers and all females as sisters. To do so from a place of integration is self-mastery and it will take much dedication and commitment and the deepest desire (in its true meaning) to achieve this. Otherwise, seeing through such eyes could ultimately prove to be a splitting off or repression from a psychological perspective.

So, the path of the Bramacharya is not for all. However, certain principles and moral codes of conduct could be supportive for those in the early stages of reclaiming their natural sexuality. For Gandhi, one of the most challenging aspects of his own path as a Bramacharya were the occasional moments (rare at the highest levels of this path) of night releases during his sleep. This informed him that he had not yet attained the absoluteness of Bramacharyaism. And yet even so, he would have been at the higher levels of this. Bramacharyaism is the attainment of total neutrality and transcendence of sexuality and is an entirely nonsexual expression and utilization of the kundalini.

Ultimately, in sacred sexual union with Self, we are literally outside of our minds. There is only neutrality at this level. We are entirely located in the heart, ensouled in an act of lovemaking as Self with Self. Stimuli comes via our total connection with the sensations we are experiencing in the body and from feelings that are a pure and untainted expression of sexual self-loving. We experience being intimately connected with the Divine. Sacred sexual union with Self is true intimacy between Self and Divine.

Only when we have mastered and embodied sacred sexual union with Self are we able to truly enter into that space with another. We do not need to have attained the higher levels of a Bramacharya state to do so. Two people merely need to have unhooked from the cultural conditioning and historical patterning of sex in regard to self. Two simply need to be located in Self, free from the paradigm of glamour.

When one has attained a state of Self and experiences sexual energy from this place, one has become like a crystal clear pool of water. Even one droplet of anything other than sacred sexuality will be seen and felt to be magnified a thousandfold. Because of the dysfunctional culture we live in, we must each choose to be sexually "response-able." It is our human right to experience sexuality in its most natural form. We must unravel and unknot the serpent coil of kundalini in which self has tied up its sexuality. We do this by refusing to be hooked in, collude with, or participate in any sexual activity that is anything other than sacred.

Tantra became renowned for its ability to potentially prolong life, increase the life force, and amplify well-being. However, endless practicing of tantra will not achieve this if the mental level is imprisoned by or at the mercy of unnatural sexuality and an entirely sexually dysfunctional global society. What is life-enhancing and brings us into true balance and natural sexual rhythm and cycles within ourselves is when we live and love from a pure heart, a pure mind, aligned with Soul, connected with Spirit, and rooted into the Earth.

Enlightenment

Sacred, natural, and conscious sexuality with Self and/or our beloved can transport us to inexplicable heights we never dreamed possible. If we really wish to know what it feels like to fully merge with the Absolute, first we must fully merge with the Absolute within ourselves, and then with the Absolute within our beloved.

Sacred sexuality has long been overlooked as a spiritual gateway to enlightenment. It is. We are meant to experience this as spiritual beings in a human body. We do not have to be with our beloved to do so. By merging Self with Absolute we can experience enlightenment as deeply and profoundly as the spiritual aesthetic who sits in meditation for years on a mountaintop, or the spiritual aspirant who has chosen a path of celibacy. There are many rivers leading to the ocean of enlightenment—sacred sexual union with Self and/or other is one of them.

THE FOUR CATEGORIES OF ROMANTIC PARTNERSHIP

Much has been written on the subject of romantic love. I have categorized what I perceive to be the four levels of romantic partnerships.

Companions
Soul Mates
Twin Souls
Twin Flames

Let us begin by taking an in-depth look at companions.

Companions

The relationships that fall into the category of unawakened, unconscious, and barely awakened are those partnerships we can term companions. Sexuality expressed within a companion relationship tends to be sporadic, loaded, or dormant.

This level of relating tends to represent those partnerships that begin romantically: usually involving drama, affairs, convenience, neediness, fear, or with an aversion to remaining single. There can be a psychological history that results in the individual unconsciously seeking "mother" or "father" in a mate. Often, such relationships are born out of fear, or a need for security, safety, or acceptance within a specific culture or social environment.

For those who are for the main part consciously asleep, companion pairings serve as a safe way of relating, requiring no depth or quest for truth on any level: physically, sexually, emotionally, mentally, psychologically, or spiritually. Those comfortable in such a relationship are able to experience a feeling of belonging or an escape from loneliness, without having to look at their own or the other's psycho-spiritual Self.

Soul Mates

There are two general understandings of the term soul mates. The first is in the context of romantic connections, and the second extends to family members, including children, friends, associates, working colleagues, pets, and even our so-called adversaries. In essence, a soul mate is anyone who we feel an intense connection with, for better or worse. So, the term soul mate does not always designate someone we have a romantic attraction to or connection with.

A soul mate is anyone who plays an important role in your life, one way or another. They can be someone who you have met just fleetingly and yet their presence brings irrevocable changes.

It is to soul mates more than any other partnership that the term *contract* most applies, because soul contracts are playing out. Pre-agreed (preincarnation) agreements or contracts to support the evolutionary growth and healing of an individual are the mark of a soul mate connection. Soul mates are inextricably drawn to each other because of this fact. Somewhere deep within, they know it is not by chance the other is in their lives and they term the relationship fate or destiny.

Soul mate relationships can be a brief encounter or they can last for a lifetime. The full spectrum of emotions can be present—including loathing or lust, love and hate, can't live with yet can't live without—and can apparently be beyond or out of a person's control. These types of connections are marked by intensity. With soul mates there often is no middle way, no middle ground and they find themselves in an all-or-nothing type of relationship. Soul mate relationships are often indicated by extreme emotional struggle, suffering, and challenges, which are needed to crack open the shell around the heart and pierce the veil of truth.

Soul mates are those we have encountered in many lifetimes and those with whom we journey closely in the higher realms in between earthly lives. This is the reason why the feeling of familiarity is predominant on first meeting—that undeniable sense of déjà vu.

Soul mate relationships do not fulfill the longing in either party for the love of the twin flame. Soul mates tend to feel attracted to others, to celebrities and such, because there is no concept at this level that when one has found true love all attraction toward others dissolves—unlike the twin soul and twin flame that provide all that is sought and longed for.

Soul mates who are on a more difficult journey, whose hearts are being wrenched open, who run kicking and screaming from the relationship only to be compelled to return to it, are in touch with the part of themselves that seeks absoluteness with the One. Thus, they attempt over and over to be what the other wants and needs, prepared to change themselves and curb their sexual interest outside of the relationship, as a deeper longing begins to ripple through their consciousness. Yet, soul mates cannot ever be considered twin flames or even twin souls, for the healing edges (those edges within ourselves that need healing) of both partners are deep and the consciousness is not yet at a level that places either in the center of the Self, as a psycho-spiritually integrated and consciously evolved individual.

We could describe the love experienced between companions as the platform at a train station, soul mates as the train journey, twin souls as the penultimate stop, and twin flames as the ultimate destination. And, just like a train journey, we know it is not possible to arrive at the penultimate stop or the ultimate destination when we are only at the beginning or midway into the journey. Thus it is with soul mates.

There are several levels to soul mate relationships, from the earliest awakening of the heart, then rising through the higher levels as each partner becomes more conscious of the psychological and spiritual Self. Soul mates are the greatest warriors of the heart, for they will die for Love; and the death most required from the evolutionary teaching of soul mate love is the death of the ego—the death of the adapted self. In soul mate relating we *fall* in love, as the relationship calls upon us to die to old selves. By doing this, at the very highest level of soul mate relationship, we *rise* in love to the level of twin souls.

Twin Souls

The Rainbow Bridge

For many years, I have meditated on the phenomenon of true love. Recently I came to a deep understanding and realization of what I perceive to constitute a higher love.

My meditations have led me to understand that there is a level of higher love positioned just beneath the most exalted of all levels of romantic relationship, this being twin flames, and this I have termed *twin soul love*. I have yet to come across any writings on twin soul love that do not confuse this term and interchange it with twin flame love. Twin flames are mistakenly referred to as twin souls, yet there is a difference.

In the existing hierarchy of romantic couplings the least evolved level of these is companions, moving on to the varying degrees (from lowest to the highest levels) of soul mate unions, and to what is considered the highest level of beloved union, the twin flame.

For so long, I felt that there was a missing piece in this existing hierarchical model of romantic partnerships and my attention was always drawn to what I perceived was a space between the level of soul mates and twin flames. I have now understood (because awakening consciousness allows for awakening understanding that takes our awareness and evolution to ever-ascending levels) that this space is filled by the phenomenon that is twin soul love.

Manifesting or cultivating a higher love (with Self, other, Source/ Creator/God) is an essential aspect of the profound process of transformation in which awakened ones are now deeply immersed in these unprecedented times of personal and global awakening. This transformational process of conscious evolution and awakening compels us toward a higher love—the beloved (Self), in search of the beloved (Self in other/other in Self), and seeking absolute union with the beloved (beloved with Source/Creator/God).

Through many years of contemplation, meditation, and observation, I have come to understand that the highest level of soul mate love precedes the exalted relationship of twin soul love. Twin soul love can be defined as the penultimate level of union between the heart, body, mind, Soul, and Spirit of two people in love.

The Secondary Summit on the Highest Mountain of Love

So, just exactly what is the difference between the exalted levels of twin soul and twin flame love? I would like to approach this question by focusing on what constitutes a twin soul relationship, as I will speak of twin flame love later.

Twin souls have arrived at a threshold point in the journey of the heart and the journey of the Soul. These beings are termed *awakened*. They have reached a greater degree of psychological integration, conscious evolution, and spiritual awareness and thus enter into the realm of twin soul love.

Those who have achieved the level of twin soul relationship will have experienced trial and initiation by the fire of love. What they have known from childhood is that they were always drawn to finding that one special friend and a special love. So, they may have had a rich and diverse history of relationships, suffered many trials and tribulations of the heart, journeyed to the depths of their being, and bared their Soul in the quest for that one true love.

Soul mate relationships are the gauge by which we can measure the extent of our evolutionary development, psychologically, consciously, and spiritually. Soul mates are the mirror into which we can gaze, that reflect back to us the truth of where exactly the deepest healing edges are to be found within ourselves. All that occurs in soul mate relationships conveys messages about the self, and the Self. Were we to imagine the four levels of romantic relationship to be likened to a mountain, companions would be at the bottom, which would be a small and easy climb with few views and no vantage points. Soul mate relationships prove to be the greatest trek up the mountain. To travel this path can be a grueling, arduous, exhausting, at times punishing, distressing, painful, excruciatingly heartbreaking (the rigid defenses of the heart need to be broken down), and bittersweet journey of awakening.

And so, all those who are to experience twin soul love in this lifetime have had to endure the unendurable, the highest of highs and the lowest of lows, the breakdown to the breakthrough, to the breaking of the defenses of the heart and of dearly cherished love relationships. The greatest distance to cover in terms of the assent of our metaphorical mountain is a crucial part of the heart and Soul's evolutionary journey.

All those we feel we have done battle with, who we believe have harmed us or deliberately hurt us, are actually soul mates, albeit unconscious in their understanding of the Soul contract. Nevertheless, they are really the allies of the heart and Soul. It is only when we transition from our earthly life, returning home to the heavenly realms, that conversations had with those who caused us suffering and pain will reveal the true nature of our relationships.

All experiences of conflict are a means by which we can heal, grow, and evolve. No matter how dire or distressing an experience appears to be, it holds a profound and liberating teaching and an opportunity for us, if only we open our evolutionary eyes to see it clearly for what it really is, which is a pathway forward for our own evolution and liberation.

And so, those who we label as our perpetrators, abusers, betrayers, and adversaries are in fact soul mates in disguise fulfilling a Soul contract for us, as we do for them. For all the experiences we may have of neglect, abandonment, any form of abuse, victimization, bullying, prejudice, annihilation, emotional absence, mental cruelty, physical violence, religious conditioning or spiritual indoctrination, deprivation or conditioning from atheist mentality, or other conditioning, the sacred truth is that such perpetrators are soul mates with whom we have a Soul contract.

When people become stuck in their history and frozen in time, when evolutionary development becomes arrested, when we are rooted to the spot and become as an immovable object on the time line of our lives, this is when we fail to see the meaning and purpose or ask ourselves from the very depth of our Soul, Why?

If we are of the mind that *everything* happens for a reason, that we attract *everything* that happens in our lives, that *nothing* happens by chance, that *everything* is an opportunity for self-healing, growth, evolution, and ultimate liberation, then we make it possible for twin soul love to enter into our lives. Only an open heart, an open mind, an inquiring Soul, and an awakened Spirit can reach this point just beneath the very summit of the mountain of exalted love. However, for those who choose not to look at their own or another's suffering, then the journey of the heart and the attainment of the Soul's longing ends just above the foot of the mountain where the companions are camped out.

So, for those whose quest it is to experience the heart-to-heart, soul-to-soul union that is twin soul love, the highest levels of soul mate relationship will have been transcended and they will arrive into this sublime and unique experience.

Attributes of Twin Soul Love

Here we will focus specifically on what constitutes a twin soul. We recognize that a twin flame is the ultimate union between two self-actualized human beings. We are aware that to merit such a rare union, we must have traversed the hierarchal evolutionary ladder from companions, through soul mate relationships, to the penultimate union of twin souls, culminating in the ultimate reunion of twin flames.

In many respects, twin soul love reflects the multiple diamond facets of twin flame love. Twin soul love is a love that is founded upon consciousness, awareness, and integration. Souls vibrating at this level of union are usually world-servers; humanitarians; global-, human-, or Earth-rights activists; consciously evolved and spiritually awakened new paradigm voices of conscience; highly evolved and deeply conscious healers; visionaries; teachers for conscious evolution and spiritual awakening; and conscious writers, poets, artists, and musicians.

To have arrived at the level of twin soul love indicates that we are in the final stages of personal evolution and integration. Imagine it as a long distance marathon, where we have passed the flag that signals we are on the home run. Passing that flag informs us that there is a still a distance to cover before we reach the finishing line, which is twin flame love, but we are almost there.

On this final run, one is flooded with a newfound energy. We can breathe a sigh of relief. We have learned much and every grueling mile has been covered and we have almost completed the quest. So, as we pass the flag that heralds the home run, it is there we find the twin soul who will accompany us to our destination, and who may even prove ultimately to be our twin flame.

And so, twin soul love is a meeting of hearts, of minds, and of Souls. It is a love that enables both to experience harmony, peace, and togetherness unlike any previous relationship. Twin soul love is free of conflict, is highly conscious, and at its very foundation is an integrated love that is unconditional and accepting. Twin soul unions differ from those of soul mates in the degree of loving harmony experienced by the couple. Twin soul unions are like swans and usually pair for life, unless the purpose of the union is to lead the individual to the twin flame, but this is rare.

Twin soul relationships are not only for life once the encounter takes place, but are unions that retain the magic, the feeling of being in love, and the wonder of each other throughout the partnership. Such is the depth of connection and elevation of consciousness, that for twin souls they are each other's ultimate partner. The reason for this is that those who are at the evolutionary level of twin soul relationship no longer seek or need powerful mirrors to reflect their psychological shadow and wounds for healing and integration. These have already been dissolved and therefore no longer exist. Those at this level of relating are no longer clearing trauma. What they are continuing to release is cellular memory, not the trauma itself. Waves of emotion and physical symptoms may arise; however, there is no associated reactionary charge felt by either partner.

Twin souls attract each other. One who is at a twin soul level cannot be in relationship with one who is at a soul mate or twin flame level. Twin souls are drawn to each other because their consciousness is in resonance. Twin souls seek only a harmonious and consciously awakened evolutionary relationship.

Consciousness is all pervading and twin souls move from minute to minute, day to day, week to week, month to month, year to year, and decade to decade with consciousness at the foreground of every aspect of their relationship. Twin souls never argue, nor does one bring conflict into the life of the other. They calmly, respectfully, lovingly, and gracefully talk things through for as long as is required in order to release the cellular memory, or the physical symptom that twin soul love catalyzes. Twin souls prioritize their beloved's well-being above all else. They are mindful to maintain harmony, balance, peace, and tranquillity within the heart of the relationship.

Most who encounter twin souls would describe them as twin flames, for this is a relationship that stands head and shoulders above any other, save for twin flame love. Those who are close to twin souls live in wonder at what is possible between two people and bathe in the glow of the shining love that they emit.

The qualities that underpin twin soul love are consciousness, awareness, mindfulness, transparency, honesty, integrity, honor, responsibility, empathy, compassion, reliability, loyalty, dependability, unity, inner beauty, balance, tranquillity, grace, gentleness, respect, autonomy, refinement, support, commitment, conscious communication, dedication, devotion, and unconditional love and acceptance.

Twin Soul Sexuality

Sexuality between twin souls is the closest experience to that of the absolute union of twin flames. In the beginning phase of a companion relationship, sexuality is experienced at a purely physical level. However, in those types of relationships sexual intimacy is short-lived, as they are mostly celibate unions. Soul mates experience the uniting of the physical bodies and, depending upon the frequency they vibrate at, the heart and Self become more present through the eyes, the touch, and the energy between them. However, the sexual experience of twin souls is entirely different.

Sexual intimacy between twin souls is entirely conscious and awakened. It is a conscious sexuality that is an "all-consuming yet not consumed by" experience. Such unions involve *all* the bodies: the physical and energetic. Sexuality at this level draws the emphasis away from the physical sensations (although these are still present) and from the need for physical orgasm. Orgasm is no longer desired and is not the prime focus. It occurs at times but is not always invited by either as part of the experience. When orgasm is not present, it is not because the couple is engaging in upholding a tantric practice, for in twin soul sexuality the mind is mostly absent. This level of sexuality is solely about the heart and the Soul. Physical orgasm is sporadic and spontaneous as the energetic orgasm takes precedence.

Energetic orgasm is only possible when two Beings are merged at the heart, energetically and at a Soul level. When in this state, the Light Bodies merge to create a feeling of sublime ecstasy and bliss. An intense sensation of love and of Light rushes through the energy bodies and the entire energy system of each individual. This occurs in unison, as wave after wave transports the twin soul lovers to higher dimensions and holds them in the highest possible frequencies. Intense waves of Light flow through all of their bodies, their hearts, their minds, and their whole being. Two words that aptly describe this level of sexuality are *ecstatic* and *enraptured*. When one considers the ecstatic merging with the Divine, which is the experience of the whirling dervishes, this is the intoxicating sexual union between twin souls.

Companion and soul mate sexuality involves a strong procreative element in order to bring through those souls who will further support the healing of their family ancestry. Twin soul unions are far less likely to conceive, and if they do, the result is mostly only one soul who is raised in unconditional love, consciousness, and truth. They themselves usually experience a twin soul relationship when they reach adulthood, with the purpose of serving global evolution, humanity, and world peace.

Twin soul sexuality is an expression of pure love. It is experiencing each other as an energetic being of Light. It is a merging of Light Bodies, hearts, and Souls. This invokes the first real felt sense of two becoming one, which is fully experienced during sexual intimacy, to begin the process of Soul alignment and preparation for the final union with the twin flame. This experience is a state of Being that twin flames are in—all of the time.

Twin Flames

Omraam Mikhael Aivanhov has written an oft-quoted description of the twin flame relationship. Although the translation refers to "twin soul," the description, which is set out below, is that of the twin flame.

Every human being has a twin soul. When man leapt like a spark from the bosom of his Creator he was two-in-one, and these two parts complemented each other perfectly, each was the others twin.

These two halves became separated, they took different directions, and they have evolved separately. If they come to recognize each other at any point in their evolution, it is because each carries the image of the other in the depth of his being, each has put his seal upon the other. Thus, each carries the image of his twin-soul within. The image may be blurred but it is there. For this reason, everyone who comes to Earth has a vague hope that he will find a soul who will be everything he needs, and that with this soul he will find indescribable harmony and perfect fusion.

Twin souls complete each other; no other person in the world can so complete them.

Thus, all beings you have met since the beginning of your multiple incarnations, all the husbands and wives you've had, all the lovers or mistresses, have all left you, because they were not for you.

Perhaps you were together for a while, like a pot with a lid that doesn't match. Whereas two Souls whom God has created together are absolutely made one for the other, and nothing can separate them, truly, they have no fear of being separated.

In married couple, when one or the other is AFRAID that someone may "rob" him of his partner (and nothing can keep this from happening), it is because that partner is not truly the beloved, not the TRUE beloved, the twin-soul. . . . Twin souls recognize each other with absolute certainty and can never truly leave one another.*

The Origins of Twin Flames

It is said that twin flames first incarnated on Earth in Lemuria in an area of the Pacific Ocean. It was during the time of Atlantis that they were physically separated. It was there that they began consciously disconnecting from Source to allow themselves to descend further into matter.

A highly advanced community of Lemurians relocated to Atlantis. The division into separate bodies proved a profoundly tragic and deeply traumatizing experience, which embedded deep into the Soul memory and the psyche as *the* core human wound.

For eons of time a veil of forgetfulness fell across the memory of the Soul. Yet, millions are now awakening, and as they awaken, they are remembering. The memory of the trauma of separation remains alive within all lightworkers† to this day. Millions now find themselves, consciously or unconsciously, in the continual search for their other half.

Even in the most conscious of relationships, the wounds of separation may remain. It is not something that can be rationalized, but is a felt sense at a core level of something that is not fused in the absolute totality of oneness. Twin flames tend to continue to be divided. Often

---

*Omraam Mikhael Aivanhov, *Love and Sexuality, Part I* (North Hatley, Quebec: Prosveta, 1976).

†A lightworker is a psycho-spiritually and consciously awakened individual. Please see my book *2012: A Clarion Call* for more information on lightworkers.

one twin remains in the higher realms as the other incarnates.

For those awakened ones who are not ready to close the cycle of earthly lives, they will unite with the closest love to the twin flame, which is the twin soul. True twin flames will not choose to reincarnate again, for they will complete their life cycles on the Earth as they began—as one.

Twin flame reunion requires the highest level of evolution of the incarnated Soul. We now know that what is needed more than anything in the world is love. The Love and Light frequency emitted by twin flames and twin souls will raise human and planetary consciousness.

For Souls who have attained an advanced level of conscious evolution and even for those who have not, there are spiritual realities that are imprinted into molecular and cellular memory—the biospiritual blueprint and the Divine genetic coding of our very Being. Many people believe in past lives, most in a supreme divine force, whether God/Source/Creator, and yet will not have had a direct conscious experience of either.

My gnosis or intuition and the guidance that comes through me from my own spiritual guides inform me of the following. As we evolve toward human perfection, the energy bodies are released of all old imprints and memories, are cleared, cleansed, and purified. This increases the rate at which they vibrate and raises the energetic frequency of the individual. At this point, the Truth of twin flame love downloads into the energetic fields, which in turn informs an aligned consciousness that this is possible. At this stage, we come to know, "gnosis," and intuit the truth of twin flame love.

It is revealed to me that the physical is the final body to be permeated by this experience, and when this occurs, *all* levels of our Being come to fully know this truth. Until this point, it remains exclusively in the superconscious mind and the felt sense. My perception informs me that awakened and awakening incarnate Souls inherently know the truth of twin flame love at varying levels, depending on their consciousness. Even souls who remain consciously asleep feel compelled toward romance. This may be a fleeting experience, as the high of falling in love quickly fades. Their attention can quickly become drawn to another in order to recapture the initial high.

Even at these earlier levels of conscious awakening, the psyche senses something of the heart and is compelled toward a romantic connection. In the case of those who remain consciously asleep or who are just beginning to stir, the light of revelation has too many psychological and karmic layers to penetrate to reveal the "more than" that their compulsion drives them toward.

So, to conclude, my perception is that awakening and awakened Souls "gnosis" twin flame love through information the Self receives from the energetic levels of the nonphysical bodies. The physical experience is but the icing on the cake as the anchoring of such a love is an evolutionary contribution to humanity and the Earth. Twin flame love is about two as one, in service of bringing more Light and Love to the world and to the collective consciousness.

The physical embodiment of twin flame love is the completion point of a journey of gnosis that began eons ago, following their initial separation. The memory and reality of twin flames has increasingly emerged as the Soul has become more and more awakened.

The greatest spiritual teachers and Lights to have walked this world were, or are, most likely two as one incarnate. If not, their twin flame walks with them in the higher realms, working with them to bridge heaven and Earth. Avatars, as Beings with no history of earthly lives who have spoken of twin flame love, know of this, for such is their evolutionary advancement.

The pure truth of twin flame love is a reality that comes to all Souls who have achieved a certain level of evolutionary development. Yet, the experience of physical reunion is the reality of incarnate Souls who have attained the greatest degree of evolutionary advancement. It is a rare phenomenon to be reunited with our twin flame, yet, the times in which we are living offer an unprecedented exception to this universal law. Spiritual teacher, Omraam Mikhael Aivanhov taught how twin flames reunite just twelve times during the innumerable incarnations of a Soul's experience here on Earth.

The New Human

Awakened humans are becoming crystalline. Pineal crystals are forming and activating in awakened humans. This is an evolutionary process, and activation of the new human prototype template is now occurring as a result. Medical science terms this process *biomineralization*, and is able to capture, in visual data, crystals forming in the pineal gland. It views such phenomena with both interest and, at the same time, caution, because such a process also highlights resultant challenges being noted in the human physiological structure.

These crystals are activating to enable awakened humans to receive powerful electromagnetic frequencies and anchor "galactic downloads" in the human physical and energy bodies. This process is what is responsible for ascension symptoms.

The physical body of humans, especially lightworkers, is in an evolutionary state of profound change. The human body is literally rewiring, especially the heart and brain, enabling the activation of the new human prototype template. This template has remained dormant in the human body awaiting the auspicious times we are now living in.

The awakened human is becoming the "New Human." Carbon and silicon based structures within the human body are transforming into crystalline structures. Crystal seeds that have been lying dormant since the first wave of lightworkers incarnated in the late 1930s, are now activating. Those whose new human template is now activating will feel an overwhelming need to align with light, in every aspect of their lives. The experience of inner Light will become all pervading. A powerful urge to be surrounded by light colors, and to eat light foods will become a necessity.

The next evolutionary stage for lightworkers is to become light-beings. So, surround yourself with Light—radiate Light—be Light—become a beacon of Light for the world. And, remember your spiritual heritage, and how you are an ambassador for the Light.

The Ultimate Union

For a twin flame reunion an incarnate Soul must have attained Self-mastery. For this to be so, an individual must have achieved full Self-actualization. Clearly, this is a very rare and exceptional state of being while in the human form, and this is why the twin flame reunion is so very rare.

Such a human being will have attained the most advanced levels of psychological, conscious, and spiritual evolution to merit the reunion with their twin flame, for such a meeting heralds the last earthly incarnation before returning home—together. If twin flames choose to return to the physical, they do so in service of humanity and the Earth, often as one being. Throughout history, many of humanity's greatest teachers and lights appear in the guise of one individual. Yet, many of these great beings are in fact two—as one.

Twin flames can also be relationships between the same sex, for at this level of loving, all associations with human identity are transcended and the integration of the inner male and female is in perfect balance. The act of intimacy is experienced at the highest possible level for human sexual union. The body and body sensations dissolve as the focal point of sexual union is to seek absolute transcendence.

Neptune Love

Twin flames can experience nothing other than divine union. Sexual union becomes a merging process with Self, beloved, and Beloved (God/Source/Creator). Twin souls can also experience the same, for this relationship is the lower octave of twin flame love. Therefore, the purity and completeness experienced by twin flames is also experienced by twin souls, but to a lesser degree.

When the sexual union is solely about heart and Soul, when the focus of the gaze is deeply locked into the windows of the Soul of the beloved (the eyes), it is here we experience the truth of who we are, who we are in union with, and where we are from. The age or age gap, the physical appearance or gender, are irrelevant. Such a union, at a sexual level, is beyond the physical and is instead akin to the merging of two Light Bodies.

So, even though sexual expression takes place through the physical, it is beyond this. It moves from what I call a "Venus and Mars" love, with its flamboyant and dramatic displays of sentimental romance, to that of a "Neptune" love, which is beyond the personal, beyond physical gratification, and not an unconscious mating in which the two partners remain disconnected.

In astrology, Neptune is the higher octave of Venus and represents unconditional love and ethereal, spiritual, awakened union. Neptune stands as the bridge between beloved and Beloved, between I and other. Love is exalted by Neptune and Neptune is an exalted expression of love.

Whereas Venus and Mars offer chocolates, flowers, wine, and sensory indulgence with the ultimate aim being localized physical orgasm, Neptune invites a total merging, a sublime union, an energetic sacred orgasm by which the lovers are transported to other realms and other dimensions. They share inner and out-of-body experiences and visions; have access to vivid memories of their lives, past, present, and future; and exchange gifts that symbolize the perfection of such a sacred union. Neptune love is a transcendent love. It is a love that brings together heaven and Earth. It is a love that draws heavenly beings forth, in celebration of such a union. It is a love that fully serves the divine plan—the creation of heaven on Earth.

Sacred sexual union with the beloved (twin flame or twin soul) is an experience beyond mind, beyond emotions, beyond words. It triggers an altered state of consciousness, an out-of-body experience, a merging of both the inner and outer with the divine. It is an experience of the purest love, the purest light, and the purest joy.

The evolutionary process of self-actualization propels us toward a higher love, the highest love of all—that of the twin flame. This is the ultimate love that carries us home together and marks the closing and completion of the learning process of our lives on Earth. The search for the beloved and the Beloved, as the beloved (Self), seeking the beloved (Self in other/other in Self), and seeking the Beloved (Self with Source/Creator/God) is complete.

And so, I conclude our sojourn into the subject of a higher love with this quote:

> *For Aeons of Time*
> *The veil of forgetfulness has befallen the Soul*
> *Yet now . . . this veil is lifting as millions of Souls*
>   *awaken*
> *And, as they do so,*
> *So comes . . . Remembrance.*
> *What is now needed more than anything in this world*
>   *is LOVE,*
> *The frequency of love emitted by twin flames—or a*
>   *love closest to twin flame love, twin souls—is so*
>   *elevated that it can raise human and planetary*
>   *consciousness into a higher-dimensional reality.*
> *And, the amplification of the light of twin flame/*
>   *twin soul love will light up the world and the way*
>   *forward for humanity.*
>
> NICOLYA CHRISTI

NINE

Six Core Values for an Evolving World

It has been said that our generation is the first in history that can decide whether it is the last in history. We need to add that our generation is also the first in history that can decide whether it will be the first generation of a new phase in history. We have reached a watershed in our social and cultural evolution.

ERVIN LASZLO

In September 2009 I became deeply involved with WorldShift. I went on to found WorldShift Movement in 2010 and, one year later, co-found WorldShift International with my dear friend and colleague Kingsley Dennis. WorldShift Movement is an online global initiative for the people of the world to come together to co-create the foundations of a new world.

Upon founding WorldShift Movement (WSM), I felt a need to reevaluate the five original core values of WorldShift (peace, justice, sustainability, social innovation, and conscious evolution) and revise these in the context of promoting core values for WorldShift Movement that would accurately reflect its core message as a "Movement for the

People." And so, a reworked set of core values became the six core values for WorldShift Movement, now also held by WorldShift International (WSI), to represent the vision and purpose that both hold for a new epoch with a new paradigm consciousness.

The six core values held by WSM and WSI address that which the personal and collective are most in need of establishing in these unprecedented times. The six core values that underpin WSM and WSI are peace, restorative justice, sustainability, compassionate action, conscious communication, and conscious evolution.

These six core values for an evolving world along with the twelve foundation stones for a new world paradigm (see chapter 10) need to form part of the bedrock of a new paradigm and conscious global society. These core values and foundation stones can positively impact both the individual and collective psyche and can beautifully serve the establishment of new sociopolitical policy that simply must be revised if we are ever to manifest and experience such core values and foundation stones as a living global reality.

PEACE

Pema Chodron, author of *Practicing Peace in Times of War,* asks the question, "Why is it that we all want a peaceful existence, yet our actions or reactions produce just the opposite?"

Pema speaks of a moment of choice when we can either react with anger, or respond with patience and compassion. When asking her teacher Dzigar Kongtrul Rinpoche, a Tibetan Buddhist master, why is this moment so uncomfortable when we choose not to give in to anger, he referred to this moment as *the burn.* He stated that when we can be fully present to this moment, we are able to burn up seeds of aggressive behavior. He then continued to explain that we can consciously choose to view this as an opportunity for "burning the seeds of negative karma and planting the seeds of peacefulness."

Most of us live in anxiety, afraid to let down our guard for fear of exposing a vulnerable and soft heart. Yet, in order to experience deep and lasting peace we must find the inner strength and courage to allow the dissolution of the walls of defense that we have placed around our heart in order to protect it.

By imagining our hearts to be like a beautiful white dove locked away in a small cage, we can gain some idea of why they are unable to fly high and free to touch heaven. No matter how gilded the cage may be, the dove is unable to fulfill its full potential or experience its very essence and nature. It will never experience love, joy, wonder, healing, and beauty or know that it can bring these to others. A dove locked inside a cage will experience only deep sorrow. It may know security, but never fulfillment.

For this, it must leave the security of the cage: leave the known for the unknown. If it remains in the cage, it will stop singing and its furtive attempts to fly in such a confined space will eventually result in broken wings. An imprisoned heart becomes a broken heart.

If we wish to experience peace at the deepest levels then it is time to fling the doors wide open and set our hearts free. It is our heart that leads us to true fulfillment and to an experience of peace that surpasses anything we could have imagined. What would it feel like to be in deep peace every day, especially when a challenging situation arises?

How can we cultivate inner peace? How can we encourage ourselves to allow our hearts to become visible? Whenever we feel the stirrings of a reactionary charge, we need to catch it before it erupts. How we can do so is to acknowledge this charge, pause for that moment to take a few deep breaths, and then ask ourselves the simple yet profound question: If my heart had a voice what would it say? Whenever we find ourselves on the edge of reason—this is what we ask ourselves. Peace is to be found through a gentle, open, undefended, and unconditional heart.

Buddhism is a wonderful example that teaches us how to respond instead of react. At the core of Buddhist philosophy we will find the teachings and practices of right action, mindfulness, nonattachment, forgiveness, and compassion. If we seek to embody these fundamental Buddhist qualities, we will come to experience lasting inner peace and joy.

Whenever you find yourself asking, what is my Soul's higher purpose? or, what can I offer to the world? know that by being peace your life is making a difference. If you live in peace, the world is one step closer to peace. As Thich Nhat Hanh teaches, peace is every step.

When you next find yourself in that moment that Pema Chodron speaks of, pause . . . breathe . . . and make a choice to respond from your heart. Do so with compassion, sensitivity, empathy, and understanding. You will then come to experience a peace that permeates every atom of your Being.

It is time to remove the defenses from the heart. It is time to listen to the wisdom of the heart. By doing this we become the embodiment of peace. We can choose to cultivate inner peace as a priority. We can transform our life into one of grace and gracefulness. There are two choices—reaction or response.

We can choose to prioritize inner peace while at the same time remaining mindful that we are no longer willing to compromise our sense of this. We can choose to walk in peace, to talk peace, to be peace. It is a step we can take right now.

Remember . . .

Peace in Every Step.

◆

Peace, Harmony, and Love as a Lived Reality

From today, this very moment, you can create a reality that is one of permanent peace, harmony, and love. This requires the practicing of mindfulness and absolute alignment with the ever-present Now. For when we do this we are empowered—we empower ourselves to create a reality of peace, harmony, and love.

Every choice we make in each moment is creating our reality. Let us not view this phenomenon as merely a concept, but let us really understand the fundamental truth of it.

In each moment we are either creating peace and happiness, or conflict, drama, and upset for ourselves as our immediate and future reality.

If we truly long or wish for a life of peace, joy, happiness, and love, then we must become acutely and mindfully aware of each and every choice we make.

Is each choice, decision, agreement, commitment, or intention that we make ultimately going to prove peace-serving or peace-denying?

We must trust our intuitive felt sense, the quiet voice inside, and our gnosis when it comes to making decisions and choices in our lives. The outcome of these is already felt in our bodies when we are in the process of choice and decision making. As we do this, the body is already informing us. However, most people ignore what their bodies are feeling and revealing, and go against their instincts, only to find the outcome of the choice or decision made is one that has brought disharmony or upset.

Yes, we can say that ultimately all experience serves us. However, when we have reached a certain level of psycho-spiritual evolution we need to be mindful that there comes a point when we no longer need experiences that bring us pain or upset. We only continue to attract these when caught in the groove of an old pattern that has acted as a facilitator for healing, but has now been dissolved.

Every single choice we make today will shape tomorrow. If we truly seek a harmonious, peaceful, and love-filled life, then we must listen to the all-knowing wisdom of the inner voice and tune in to what our bodies are telling us. The body is the most sophisticated, wise counsel we will ever have. It will tell us, every time, if a choice or decision is one that will bring us peace and happiness.

If we feel apprehension or a deeper felt sense that an inner warning is being brought to our attention about a direction we are moving in, and yet we are still drawn and proceed in that direction, then we know that we still have a healing edge in that area of our lives. However, if we find ourselves hesitating over and over again, it is because we are aligning with the wisdom of the inner voice and the body and, instead, allowing it to direct our choices and decisions. In this way, we will maintain a feeling of peace, harmony, and love in our lives and continue to evolve, refine, and liberate ourselves from the experience of pain and upset being our teacher.

We reach a level in our evolution where these are no longer required to teach us the lessons we are here to learn, or to heal karma or historical inner wounding. There is a plateau we arrive at where all choices and decisions made bring us further experiences of peace, harmony, and love.

We arrive at a place in ourselves where we are no longer willing to negotiate or compromise inner peace, holding this as a priority in all our words, thoughts, actions, decisions, and choices. Know that every decision or choice that you make will either take you further away from, or bring you ever closer to, fully embodying and living peace as a reality.

From today, commit to noticing every nuance in your body, listening to the wise inner voice and consciously and mindfully make decisions and choices that are sourced only from these.

You can choose. You are choosing in every moment. What do you choose? Inner peace or inner conflict?

Listen to your body—it knows. Listen to your inner-voice—it knows.

If you really do feel ready to take that next evolutionary leap into living a life of peace, harmony, and love—then today is a good day to listen to the wisdom that you are. When your body and inner voice are in harmonious union, and a feeling of peace washes through you as you make a decision or a choice—then know you are making the right one.

Remember, there is no way to peace—peace is the way.

◆————————————————————————◆

RESTORATIVE JUSTICE
By Wendy Webber

Howard Zehr is widely recognized as a major restorative justice pioneer (*Changing Lenses: A New Focus for Crime and Justice* and *The Little Book of Restorative Justice*); he utilizes the metaphor of restorative justice as a river, with its source as a spring that is then fed by countless streams. Zehr writes of a variety of indigenous traditions and current adaptations that draw upon those traditions: family group conferences adapted from Maori traditions in New Zealand, for example; sentencing circles from aboriginal communities in the Canadian north; Navajo peacemaking courts; African customary law; or the Afghani practice of *jirga*. The field of mediation and conflict resolution feeds into that river, as do the victims' rights movements, and alternatives-to-prison movements of the past decades. A variety of religious traditions flow into this river.

An overview (taken from www.restorativejustice.org) explains that: "Restorative justice is a theory of justice that emphasizes repairing the harm caused by criminal behaviour. It is best accomplished when the parties themselves meet cooperatively to decide how to do this. [Although other approaches may be used when that is not possible. Sometimes these meetings] lead to transformation of people, relationships, and communities."

Notice three big ideas:

- Repair—crime causes harm and justice requires repairing that harm
- Encounter—the best way to determine how to do that is to have the parties decide together
- Transformation—this can cause fundamental changes in people, relationships, and communities

The Differences between Retributive Justice and Restorative Justice

Rather than seeing them as opposing we can simply say that each system asks different questions, and therefore there are different consequences and outcomes. Retributive justice (the current criminal justice system) asks the questions: What laws have been broken? Who did it? What do they deserve?

Restorative justice asks the questions: Who has been harmed or hurt? What do they need? Whose obligations and responsibilities are these? Who has a stake in this situation? What is the process that can involve the stakeholders in finding a solution?

Howard Zehr notes how restorative justice argues that what truly vindicates is acknowledgment of victims' harms and needs, combined with an active effort to encourage offenders to take responsibility, make right the wrongs, and address the causes of their behavior. Currently, restorative justice practices are often offered as choices within or alongside the existing legal system. Of note is that since 1989, New Zealand has made restorative justice the hub of its entire juvenile justice system.

A Personal Account of Restorative Justice

My early exposure to this concept and application of restorative justice a decade or so ago came through my study and practice of nonviolent communication, developed by Dr. Marshall Rosenberg, and then in the last few years by being a volunteer at my local community restorative justice center, and also by undertaking training and practice in a process called *restorative circles,* pioneered by Dominic Barter in Brazil.

The process model of nonviolent communication spoke directly to me of the way human beings have been educated to think and speak over thousands of years. It showed me that our habitual lens and mode of relating is characterized by a language and system of dominance; power is unevenly distributed so some have more external power than others. In this system there are winners and losers, there is good and bad, right and wrong, and there are those who place themselves or are placed in authority positions to decide on that. Our education, political, economic, health, legal, and corrections systems are all based on that.

In the life-serving system that nonviolent communication is pointing to in its approach, we are not focusing through the lens of what is right or wrong or who will win and who will lose, but through the lens of what serves life—and life is flowing through every life-form on this planet.

It reflects the natural intelligence of life to know how to course correct and bring itself back into dynamic balance and harmony (one that is evolving, not static), if we learn how to listen and follow the guidance! When we look through the lens of what is life serving, we immediately enter a world of interdependence, of relationship, and understand our connectedness in the web of life—that we cannot just meet our own needs at the expense of others.

Responsibility and accountability are key concepts and practices here. When an imbalance has occurred it is usually because someone has tried to meet their own needs at the expense of others. This does not only happen at the individual level, but it is modeled by many corporations and institutions at the macrolevel. Sadly we do not see much responsibility or accountability here in relation to the common good, or the good of the whole.

I like to think of restorative justice as not only serving as an alternative to the criminal justice system, but one that applies to all our human systems and endeavors, internally and externally. This is why I have been very drawn to one of the tributaries that feed the restorative justice river: that of restorative circles, pioneered by Dominic Barter in the shantytowns of Rio de Janeiro and that now continues to spread, both in Brazil and internationally.

Restorative circles (RC) is a process for individuals and communities to address conflict in ways that restore connections on profound levels. Within an intentional dialogue of people with equal power—even if outside the circle their power is not equal—participants invite each other and attend voluntarily. A very precise process is used to restore connection out of which agreed actions can arise. The circles bring the profoundly openhearted clarity and tangible power-sharing dynamics of nonviolent communication to restorative practices.

The dialogue process is shared openly and is guided by a community member. Key concepts and practices here are shared power, mutual understanding, self-responsibility, and effective action. Ideally they happen within and are supported by a restorative system, one in which there are agreed-upon structures that allow a group to care for and take ownership of its conflict. Any group of people (families, schools, workplaces, communities, and such) can decide to become a restorative system, and learn to use restorative circles as their only response to conflict or as another option alongside already existing approaches to conflict.

Lastly, I'll speak from the very personal experience of being a member of a COSA for two and a half years. COSA stands for circle of support and accountability, and it can be offered through a restorative

justice center (such as the one in my hometown in Vermont) to returning offenders when they are attempting to reenter the community,
sometimes after many years in jail.

I, along with three colleagues, have been the COSA for a core member: for a year while he was still in jail, and then for one and a half years
since his release on parole. I would say that *relationship* is the key word
here. For the first year it was very hard for him to understand why we
would be willing to volunteer our time for him, such was his self-image
and his habitual mode of thinking that was steeped in "deserve" thinking from our prevailing culture.

Gradually over the months, as we have fulfilled our role both of
support and holding him accountable, meeting weekly with additional
ad hoc visits and support, he has come to see us as a deeply valued and
essential bridge, without which he is sure he would have been back in
jail by now. (Recidivism, meaning offenders returning to jail again and
again, is a profoundly worrying statistic in the United States, not to
mention the astronomical cost to the nation.) Through the AA meet-
ings and community that makes up a large part of his current social life,
he has found a way to contribute, and to begin the journey of feeling
that he has worth and value.

I'll end this article with a quote from The Freedom Project, which
I had the privilege to train with a number of years ago. It is a nonprofit organization that does wonderful restorative work with returning offenders in Seattle, Washington. For me their work epitomizes
an understanding of how the web of life can only be rewoven through
restoring relationship and recognizing our interconnectedness and
interdependence.

"The Freedom Project strengthens community through supporting
the transformation of prisoners into peacemakers. We offer training in
concrete skills of nonviolence leading to reconciliation with ourselves,
our loved ones, and the community. Our work addresses the healing
of relationships ruptured by violence and the forging of community
founded on genuine safety through connection."

SUSTAINABILITY

By Kingsley Dennis

The term *sustainability* refers to how various systems—ecological, cultural, biological, and the like—remain diverse and productive over time. For many of us, sustainability suggests the potential for long-term maintenance of our well-being, which has environmental, economic, and social dimensions. However, many of these systems that once kept sustainability within natural limits are breaking down.

Many of the world's nations have been living the high life as a result of the prosperity afforded by rapid industrial, technological, and material growth. The long tail of this—the technological revolution—has been fundamental in stretching tentacles of dependency far and wide. Complex structures of supply, demand, and energy are now near to their breaking points. According to social commentator James Howard Kunstler, those of us who presently live in the comfortable Western countries are facing "the comprehensive downscaling, rescaling, downsizing, and relocalizing of all our activities, a radical reorganization of the way we live in the most fundamental particulars." However, just as humans are a social species, individuals are the building blocks of society. Social philosopher Duane Elgin states that for a sustainable future to be viable it needs six requirements: to dismantle consumerism; to return to ecological living; to engage with sustainable futures; to create a conscious democracy; to embrace a reflective paradigm; and to work with reconciliation.

All these features support a communal immersion: the very opposite of what has been occurring within the Western urban landscape. To a large degree, modern urban living has contributed to isolating individuals from their wider social community and from the influence of their peers. What is needed is for us to revitalize our social communities.

Revitalizing social communities is necessary because urban life is increasingly out of balance with the needs of the people. This is especially so if the individual is dependent upon supermarket food supplies, gas station fuel, and other necessary external amenities. In short, the average urbanite is partly (and sometimes wholly) dependent upon the plentiful supply of always available goods, such as food and energy.

It is important that creative individuals view the upcoming years (or even decades) as opportunities to transform these dense urban zones into more compact, sustainable living centers. For example, instead of segregated areas the city could be functionally integrated between living, working, and leisure areas; mixed-income communities integrated as different skill sets are likely to be important, rather than traditional income status. Also, public spaces can be transformed into well-integrated and interconnected walkable networks and easy-access corridors.

A sense of community needs to be revitalized through open spaces, parks, and community landscaping projects, such as communal gardens and food gardens. Superstores and large shopping complexes should be replaced with local shopping areas and farmers' markets. While this may sound the death knell for many corporate giants, their presence will be replaced by something more beneficial to the community. The large supermarkets have exploited and manipulated consumer demand for too long, and many smaller retailers and farmers have suffered greatly over their monopoly. There are already positive signs that groups of individuals are recognizing the urgent need to transform urban living centers.

A recent movement called *new urbanism* was established online in 1998 and has grown to promote good urbanism, smart transportation, transit-oriented development, and sustainability.

The organization promotes policies for national and local governments to revitalize many existing cities and towns into walkable, car-free, mixed-use communities. Out of this new urbanism movement has also emerged a trend in urban development called transit-oriented development, or TOD. For example, in the town of Orenco Station (15 miles west of Portland, Oregon) transit-oriented development has been successfully implemented. It was designed as a neighborhood community and organized around a pedestrian spine that extends out toward a grid of walkable, tree-lined streets and parks.

The town promotes a walkable, pedestrian-friendly community and discourages the use of the car and other fossil fuel transit. Similarly, the *transition towns* movement was established as a means to design a strategy for helping small towns move away from fossil fuel dependency. It also promotes public participation and citizen action within the context of a sustainable and self-sufficient community. The first United Kingdom transition town was Totnes, in Devon, where local town forums were created for citizens to come together and decide on ways to develop low-carbon energy resources. In other words, how better to survive in a "post-peak oil" world.

A prescient report from 1997 forecasted a possible future social scenario that was termed the *great transition,* which involved a social shift toward new paradigms of sustainability in the form of eco-communalism. In this, the report envisioned a network of self-reliant communities.

Eco-communalism could emerge from a new sustainability paradigm world if a powerful consensus arose for localism, diversity, and autonomy. Eco-communalism might emerge in the recovery from breakdown. Under conditions of reduced population and a rupture in modern institutions, a network of societies, guided by a small-is-beautiful philosophy conceivably could arise. (Gilberto Gallopin, Al Hammond, Paul Raskin, and Rob Swart. "Branch Points: Global Scenarios and Human Choice." Resource Paper, Global Scenario Group. [Stockholm Environment Institute, 1997])

Physical social networks modeled on self-reliant communities could be established that are based around ecological practices. Another example of creative architectural thinking is that of the compact city proposal from celebrity architect Richard Rogers. Rogers proposes that the creation of the modern compact city rejects the dominance of the car and instead favors a design whereby communities thrive and the streets are rebalanced in favor of the pedestrian and the community.

Further, Rogers's compact city design proposes that home, work, and leisure districts/regions/zones become more densely interrelated and overlapped rather than as separated areas. The compact city idea is to increase the density of shared spaces so that there are increased opportunities for social connection and interaction. There is a rise worldwide in urban innovation that seeks to move toward constructing more compact, sustainable communities. This will become more of an imperative, rather than luxury thinking, in the ensuing years. Such changes will need to be implemented if our social systems are to be resilient enough to adapt to the coming global changes. The emphasis needs to be upon recycling of goods and waste, efficient alternative energy production, localized distribution, and change in such social drivers as consumerism, economics, and general well-being. Over recent years there has been a vigorous interest in permaculture as a way of combining living centers with agricultural systems.

Permaculture is a way of integrating the ecology of natural agricultural practices with the needs of the community. The word *permaculture*, as a combination of permanent agriculture and permanent culture, reflects the social aspects of the system. Permaculture encourages the construction of self-sufficient communities that work with nature's cycles within the surrounding ecosystem. Permaculture is often seen as a more holistic system as it looks at both the natural (agricultural) and human systems as a whole, rather than as separate systems. In this way localized communities could benefit tremendously from incorporating permaculture practices into their way of life. Not only would it provide a means for self-sufficiency, but also help to sustain the local ecosystems at a time of increased strain. However, one of the immediate concerns will be energy requirements.

A variety of energy sources will likely be explored by local economies. Given that a true free-energy revolution is still an uncertainty, alternative energy will need to be harnessed from solar, wind, water, and other natural sources. The corporate red herring of agro-fuels (mass-produced biofuels) is likely to be rejected by local communities that are seeking to shift to low-carbon alternatives using real biofuels. True biofuels are produced from waste such as biogas from manure or landfill or waste vegetable oil. Their development, however, is so far limited. This situation is likely to change once necessity becomes a key factor. Already some local communities are developing their own low-key diesel manufacturing through recycling waste vegetable oil. These DIY projects can be developed further by well-organized communities using agricultural processes.

There are a range of oilseed crops, such as sunflower, rapeseeds, soy, palm, and jatropha, that can be converted into biodiesel used on its own or blended with conventional diesel. A range of cellulosic materials, such as various waste products from crops (including grasses, trees, and wood), can be broken down with enzymes and turned into bioethanol. Bioethanol can also be produced from a number of crops including sugarcane, sugar beet, barley, corn/maize, grain, and cotton. Using cellulosic biomass to produce ethanol would lessen the strain placed upon standard agricultural land needed for growing crops.

Butanol is currently a potential second-generation biofuel produced by fermentation from a range of organic material, such as molasses left behind by sugar production or whey from cheese production. Butanol has several advantages over ethanol in terms of higher energy output and being easily blended with diesel. In the future we may see regional areas, and localized communities, adopting a bottom-up biofuels market that would serve to create energy-sufficient lifestyles.

This can be achieved not only through a supply of recyclable waste but also through citizen-managed low-scale farming. Genuine biofuel schemes could be located within sustainable programs based within active communities and separate from corporate top-down energy suppliers. This would involve a move from mass production to distributed and localized schemes, which would aid many communities. It is foreseeable that these, and more, energy innovations will begin to manifest through grassroots pioneering and newly emerging citizen information networks. The corporate control and monopoly upon such natural resources, and primary human needs, will be rejected for local empowerment projects.

Alternative technologies are arising that seek to bypass traditional dependencies as the civil movement grows in power and determination. There are now markets for rocket stoves, vegetable oil generators, solar fridges, cheap wind generators, and reusable water bottles used as solar lamps. Innovations are also turning shipping containers into virtually cost-free homes.

Social information networks are advising people how to make their own soap, toothpaste, clothes, and much more. Instead of recycling there is now a movement toward "pre-cycling": that is, training people how to exist not only on what they have but to transform their conception of necessity so that non-primary needs are taken out of the equation. Individuals and communities are learning how to live more on less. Part of this reeducation is a perceptual paradigm (a new mind for a new world). For many of us, if we don't choose to think and behave differently in the upcoming years, then we may be forced into change.

Also on the increase are localized microfinances whereby communities are issuing their own specific local currencies as a means of promoting local business growth. This is a Depression-era idea and helps to tie-in local consumers with their neighborhood suppliers. It works by local businesses printing money and then consumers exchanging national currencies for the locally issued one and redeeming them in participating stores. Communities throughout Europe, North America, and Asia are buying food and fuel with such currencies as the Detroit Cheers and the Bia Kut Chum.

Exchange and credit/barter systems have also been running successfully as in the "Local Exchange Trading Systems" (LETS) that are local exchange networks that trade goods and services without using a currency. Instead, a credit system is in operation whereby individuals can earn credits by performing services, which can then be swapped for gaining the services of others. At present it is estimated that over four hundred such schemes operate in the UK alone, with others in France, Australia, and Switzerland.

Cultivating sustainable food tastes is also gaining in popularity. Projects and schemes already underway around the world include gardening workshops for growing-your-own. Information made available for self-farmers will encourage food production to be once again a prime aspect of family and civic life. There is currently a growth in the number of urban gardens and communal composting. Neighborhoods are sourcing water supplies and introducing local permaculture schemes. Social networks are already established that seek to bring home gardeners together to share tips, advice, and friendship. One such social network—Freedom Gardens—describes itself as a food security movement, person to person.

A modern gardening era/movement for the twenty-first century is underway, resulting in efforts to become free of foreign oil, corporate controls, contamination, and food miles while creating a sustainable future by promoting local food production. Inspired innovators are currently developing new sustainable alternatives to industrial agriculture that push toward forming a post-industrial food system that is less resource intensive and more locally based and managed. An array of such start-ups include BrightFarm Systems, SPIN-Farming, Virtually Green, Aquacopia, and NewSeed Advisors. Similarly, new networks are emerging of investors, donors, entrepreneurs, farmers, and activists who are committed to building local food systems and local economies.

There has also been a huge interest in the Slow Food Movement. This international organization, originating in Italy, advocates that the education of taste is imperative and people need to develop and deepen their knowledge about food by eating produce that is produced, sourced, sold, and prepared in sustainable and equitable ways. In three years membership in the Slow Food Movement grew from five hundred to eight thousand. The emphasis is upon the enjoyment of food as well as, importantly, the cultivation of awareness of food culture as an effort to conserve distinctive local food products. The Slow Food Movement operates through local groups or chapters known as convivia. Twenty years after the formation of Slow Food, there are 1,000 convivia with more than 100,000 members in 132 countries from all over the world.

Not only are our tastes changing, but so is the very manner of how we make use of our resources in all areas of our lives. Being a global citizen also requires that we are locally responsible. Sustainability is a core value for a harmonious, well-balanced future.

COMPASSIONATE ACTION

In these days of increasing global unrest, with mass protests taking place across the world calling for change, we experience our hearts going out to all those who are caught up in demonstrations that demand basic human rights and autonomy be addressed in the policies of global authorities.

Protestors take action on behalf of all living beings and nature herself. These brave few are calling for change for themselves, their families, communities, countries, and for the world. Their unified voice acts as a sounding call for all of humanity caught in dysfunctional and repressive systems of authority. Voices that state, "Enough!" The wave of uprisings has increased exponentially.

For the most part, the intention and motive behind the actions of these "new paradigm crusaders" is humanitarian, except for the few who descend into rioting and looting. However, these must not be polarized or judged, but instead recognized as representative of the dark underbelly of a humanity that has been suppressed for millennia.

This shadow aspect of the collective has been split off, for fear of the potential consequences of challenging or resisting a repressive system. Resistance has resulted in the death of millions who dared to stand up for human rights and equality. This includes the untimely death of some of the greatest humanitarian leaders who stood for peace, restorative justice, equality, and human rights.

The rioters and looters need exemplary, nonviolent role models who they can trust and believe, who speak their language and are able to permeate all hearts and minds in order to achieve change: role models who, through nonviolent means, can elicit a response that brings real hope and potential for change.

At the core of the wound of humanity lies a cauldron of deeply repressed, unexpressed emotions that go back for thousands of years and are contained within our genetic blueprint. These include anger, rage, grief, sadness, hurt, and pain. Where do these emotions go if there is no appropriate system in place to ensure that they are seen, heard, and validated? What happens is that these repressed emotions hide behind the insidious veils of consumerism and addiction and, unexpectedly and spontaneously, erupt like a volcano. This release at both a personal and collective level is dangerous and has a destructive impact rather than a constructive outcome.

The times we now live in call for compassionate action and acting with compassion. It is time for us to feel compassion for those who need to see, hear, and validate us. Throughout history, humanity has attempted to live in peace and harmony, in equality and freedom. To date, all attempts to achieve this have mostly resulted in violence, blame, and attack. As Gandhi stated, "Nonviolence which is the quality of the heart, cannot come by an appeal to the brain."

Humanity has been stuck in a pattern of reaction (instead of response) and, because of this, has been caught in an ever-decreasing spiral that continues to maintain a model of duality. Now is the time to appeal to the hearts of those in authority by aligning with and co-creating a model for unity, through the means of nonviolence, nonparticipation, and peaceful protest.

Sometimes we have to lose a battle to win a war. In our modern global society, the battle that needs to be lost is the desire for revenge through violence, and the war to be won is equality and unity gained by engaging the heart and mind and the ethics of nonviolence.

As Gandhi so eloquently shared, "Remember that all through history the way of truth and love has always won."

The Compassionate Heart

At the very core of the human heart lies an innate capacity for deep reflection, contemplation, perception, and unconditional acceptance, which can inform, expand, and transform our experience and outlook on life. A perception of the world that is cultivated and expressed through the heart, as well as the mind, leads us through liberation and understanding into a new landscape of insight and experience.

Compassion constitutes a deep awareness of the suffering of another without the need to relieve or fix it, while remaining totally present to another: feeling deep appreciation for the value that can be taken from the suffering and remaining in a nonjudgmental state. Compassionate action is unconditional. Compassionate action is devoid of blame, shame, or finger pointing. Instead, it calls for us to maintain an open heart and to unconditionally extend our hand in support of the need that lies behind the perceived dysfunctional behavior of another.

There are many resources available to us that speak of, promote, and teach how to reconnect to compassion and engage in compassionate action. Some examples are the legacy of Mahatma Gandhi, the ongoing influence and impact of Martin Luther King Jr., the teachings of H.H. The Dalai Lama and Thich Nhat Hanh, the role model of Nelson Mandela, the establishment of the Truth and Reconciliation Commission with the support of Nelson Mandela and Bishop Desmond Tutu, the introduction into the mainstream of nonviolent communication via Marshall Rosenberg, and the teachings of Buddhism, which in its many forms extols the virtues of compassion.

Mahayana Buddhism teaches:

- Boundless loving kindness
- Boundless compassion for all beings
- Boundless joy (in the happiness of others)
- Boundless equanimity—the desire to help all beings regardless of size or status

Compassionate action requires the presence of an unconditional heart and a total commitment to nonviolence in word, action, and deed. Our capacity for compassionate action lies in our ability to identify with others, including those who are in pain, anger, or are deeply hurt.

Compassionate action requires us to be empathic—to *feel*. Empathy allows us to feel the difficult emotions of another as if they were our own. Empathy allows us to literally put ourselves in the shoes of another. We imagine what it might feel like to experience what the other is sharing. When one shares sadness, we can relate to a time when we felt sad.

When another expresses anger, we can recall how it feels to be angry.

If we can respond to others with empathy and compassion, the potential for a deeper and richer connection—for unity between people, nations, and the world becomes possible.

Commitment to Nonviolence

Compassionate action, in a group context, must bear in mind one defining fact, one that Gandhi, the father of nonviolence, espoused in his teachings. It can be described as follows (see www.michaellewin.org/articles/gandhi/gandhi):

- Compassionate action is not about defeating an "opponent"; it is more about winning them over, exposing them to the real truth inherent within any given situation. It reveals to them the injustice that they are involved in so that they can move forward to some degree of compromise, which creates liberation for both the "opposition" and the "compassionate actionist."
- Both parties can pull away from their dispute with dignity because the perpetuation of force and wrongdoing by the oppressor have been effectively neutralized through the peaceful and ethically based responses of the compassionate actionist.
- No amount of contemplation and deliberation, discussion and consultation, investigation and study, is of any real value unless it is supported by compassionate action.

Conflict and tension are unwanted forces that are to be found in the lives of the majority of us, as well as in most parts of the world. This is an issue that stretches us to our very limits and robs us of the harmonious world we know could be our reality, if only the conflict and disharmony that currently has us in its grip could be resolved.

To establish a harmonious world we must prioritize the cultivation and embodiment of compassion and seek to ensure that it is from this our responses and actions emerge. With perseverance and dedication to the establishment of global harmony, we can co-create a more compassionate world and experience lasting peace within ourselves, and with each other.

The great and good throughout history, including those currently alive and active in the world who are dedicated to the manifestation of global peace, remind us that where there is compassion, there is healing and where there is healing, there is peace. We must come to realize that it is only through deep listening, true understanding, empathy, and compassion that we will dissolve tension and resolve conflict both within ourselves, in our relationships with others, and in the world.

One who is dedicated to acting from compassion offers the greatest gift to humanity, that of peace. One who embodies compassion and whose responses to life's challenges and trials serve as a role model for compassion in action is one who is walking the walk and not just talking the talk. These compassionate actionists are the co-creators of world peace and the visionaries for unity consciousness to become a lived reality at a global level.

Compassion, empathy, understanding, acceptance, humility, gratitude, hope, trust, and compassionate action in service to Self, other, and the world are the qualities to refine if we are ever to establish world peace. Embrace all in compassion and understanding. Serve all through compassionate action.

CONSCIOUS USE OF LANGUAGE

Words can heal or harm. Words can lead to peace or war. In the briefest of moments, words can resolve or create conflict. Most people use words without giving any thought or contemplation to the negative impact or influence their words may have on others or the world. People have learned to relate to each other through violent and inappropriate expression of words.

Is it any wonder that the world in which we live is in the state it is when we think about how it is dominated by the left brain and an ego and personality that are unintegrated. When we live in a world devoid of balance among a majority whose actions are a result of an uninte-grated Self, we bear witness to a humanity that has become discon-nected from its very heart and soul.

Without a deep connection to Self and other, without sharing a unified reverence for nature and a deeper understanding of the nature of the heart and soul, humanity will remain disconnected and lost in a never-ending stream of inappropriate words expressed in an uncon-scious way. The heart is the compass. The language of the heart is the language of the soul. We must become mindful ("heartful") in thought, word, action, and deed.

Inner peace and world peace are to be found through a gentle, lov-ing heart that speaks only the language of unconditional love, under-standing, empathy, compassion, and loving kindness. Mindfulness in every word spoken is but one small step. However, seven billion small steps would prove to be one giant leap for humankind. Let us be poets, masters, and artists in our expression of words.

CONSCIOUS EVOLUTION
By Kingsley Dennis

We can say that life is an evolutionary journey and humankind is on an evolutionary path. This journey toward more evolved forms of intel-lect, understanding, compassion, and creativity requires capacities that lie latent within each person. To accept conscious evolution then is to accept that individually and collectively we have a responsibility toward our future. This involves purposeful thinking and action: to use our creative capacities to guide our lives and the communities in which we live. To envision a creative, dynamic, and positive future is a prelimi-nary step upon the path of conscious evolution.

First, we make the choice for ourselves; then we give intention and commitment in order to give life to those choices. At its core, conscious evolution is a spiritual endeavor in that it affirms the potential capacity of each human to participate within a creative cosmos. It affirms our use and commitment of powerful physical and spiritual energies. It also gives rise to a new worldview—a new perceptual paradigm that views our evolutional process as a lesser step within grander processes. The opposite of this (which has been prevalent for far too long) is for unconscious human energies to be used without our knowledge or knowing participation.

Conscious evolution is also a very real social movement providing for a higher level of cooperative communication and action. It is a collaborative understanding that offers personal development and learning, community building and assistance, and ways toward practical, positive social change. Conscious evolution also implies that each human is an integral and interrelated part of the whole. The beginning of humankind's exploration into consciousness, however, goes back through millennia and is not only a relatively recent phenomenon.

The experimentation with transcendent states of consciousness goes back even as far as the rock paintings of therianthropes (representations of human-like entities with animal features) that date back 35,000 years, and which have been speculated to be the early origins of human religious traditions. Early experiments in consciousness have also been a core element in the ageless perennial wisdom traditions, the shamanic rituals, the earliest recorded otherworldly creatures on ancient cave walls, as well as the ongoing presence in human societies of the inherent search for meaning and the yearning for self-revelation.

As some validation of this it has recently been discovered that the Chauvet-Pont-d'Arc Cave in southern France is full of painted monsters 400 meters below the surface, where a mixture of carbon dioxide and radon gas leads to hallucinations. In these cave chambers the wall paintings become so strange and otherworldly that scientists now think that heading down to the chamber may have formed part of a ritual for prehistoric man. These rituals may in fact be one of the earliest known examples of using substances (in this case the natural mixture of carbon dioxide and radon gas) to induce altered states of consciousness: in other words, a shamanistic experience.

The symbolic paintings/drawings on cave walls and traces of ancient rituals that appear throughout the Paleolithic era display a "primitive" people in touch with the unseen realm, with a creative world beyond that of the human, and a transcendental space, which modern humans, in effect, have never stopped attempting to access. In recognition of this, noted anthropologist David Lewis-Williams has built a theory, after extensive investigations, which explains how the people of the Upper Paleolithic era harnessed altered states of consciousness to fashion their society and also used such imagery as a means of establishing and defining social relationships.

In spite of the tens of thousands of years that separate modern humanity from its ancestral cave dwellers, the notion of entering into a more dynamic and creative union with the larger cosmos has been, it appears, a hard-wired aspect of our deeper selves. Throughout the millennia those persons more able to access this capacity, such as shamans, mystics, and prophets, have often done so to the benefit of their communities, and to bring knowledge and aid to the human family (whether local or on a wider global scale).

To many who negotiate these realms, and maintain or sustain these capacities, the notion that the wider cosmos is a living, intelligent realm is second nature. It is perhaps also fair to say that virtually all human beings have the capacity to access these latent abilities; further, that many people are already doing so without actually realizing it, or casting it off as coincidences, flukes, good luck, or weird anomalies. However, in our current times there has been a great increase in the number of people reaching the understanding that the universe can be connected with, and aligned with, human intentions.

Consciousness researcher Graham Hancock notes in his book *Supernatural* that "Once we have entered a state of consciousness that has been altered deeply enough—itself a universal neurological capacity of the human race—it seems that everyone, everywhere, experiences visions containing very much the same combinations of patterns and shapes." What this seems to suggest is that the human brain (our neurological capacity) may function as an antenna into the finer realms that form a part of the larger creative cosmos.

This could be one of the primary reasons for the great emphasis in wisdom traditions on fostering an altered state of consciousness through such practices as fasting, deprivation, and meditation (as practiced by the early ascetics); to sweat lodges; exhaustive ritual dancing/spinning in circles; and prolonged chanting and prostration.

Humanity has been experimenting with countless methods to induce an alternate state of consciousness for millennia, as if inherent within the deeper self there is a remnant, a trace, of an ability to transcend to a finer state of being that has now become lost to us. Yet modern rational science has remained blind to this, or considers it a fringe, esoteric irrational belief system.

The experimentation of the 1960s with altered states of consciousness has helped to prepare the way for a generation more in tune with transpersonal concepts and values. It may well be that the actual experience that extrasensory states exist may be the foundation for a future that contains extrasensory experience as a widespread attribute. It is important that we embrace ideas now so that they may become acceptable mental currency in advance of their actualization.

Conscious evolution is about acquiring evolutionary consciousness—to engage with both the internal and external worlds. It is our evolutionary imperative to engage actively in conscious and intentional evolutionary transformation if we are to remain as a viable living species upon planet Earth. A new consciousness needs to emerge in order to embrace a new world.

TEN

Twelve Foundation Stones for a New World Paradigm

When the power of love overcomes the love of power—
the world will know peace.

JIMI HENDRIX

Alongside the six core values for an evolving world, I have set out a vision of what I see as twelve foundation stones for a new world paradigm. If we can establish such foundation stones within a new system of values and ethics with which to rebuild a community, a country, a nation, and the world, we will be well on our way to establishing the "One thousand years of peace" and "A New Golden Age" that ancient wisdomkeepers have prophesied to occur at this time.

The question of "how to" must now take precedence at the forefront of our awareness. It is we, as individuals and as a collective, and not the establishment who can, must, and will co-create a progressive global society built upon such values and foundation stones as set out in this book.

The twelve foundation stones are: unconditional giving, receiving, and doing; deep understanding; forgiveness; equality; inclusivity;

empathy; conscious co-creation; cooperation; co-support; collaboration; nonmonetary transactions; and nonviolent/compassionate communication.

Let us now take a brief overview of what constitutes each foundation stone.

UNCONDITIONAL GIVING, RECEIVING, AND DOING

Gandhi taught us, if a thief tries to rob the coat off your back, give it to him, for he needs it more than you.

Unconditional giving and doing is when we give without expectation of ever receiving back. The First Nations Peoples referred to this form of giving as "the giveaway," where one was asked to give away what was most precious to them as a true act of giving, and as a practice of nonattachment and unconditional giving and doing. Giving away something we no longer need is a throwaway, not a giveaway. When we give with conditions, we rob. Why is this? It is because we rob another of their dignity.

We live in a world that measures value by paper, metals, or plastic (notes, coins, and credit cards). The value of presence, love, compassion, empathy, understanding, and our time often remains unacknowledged. The pure qualities of the human heart are seldom recognized as a valued exchange in the same way as the material. Our role in the co-creation of a new global society and a new world invites us to embrace what it is to be a new human. The evolutionary progress of a human being in the twenty-first century is not measured by the development of the intellect, but by the intelligence of the heart.

If you have given or are giving to another materially, check within yourself to what degree you are attached to the repayment. How conditional is your giving? What are your expectations of your action? If you are giving of your heart, your presence, your free time, know that this has as much value as one who gives materially. All giving is of equal value whether it is giving money to one who needs to put food on the table, or empathy and support to one who is materially wealthy, yet whose heart may be hurting.

Give unconditionally. Do unconditionally. Love unconditionally. Be unconditional—for true receiving is found in true giving. Give without conditions, attachment, or expectation: only with unconditional love, thus encouraging joy, dignity, and freedom for all parties involved. When we give from our hearts we find that Source, Creator, God, Universe, Higher Self, spirit guides, Soul, the heavens, and Mother Earth always give back to us a hundredfold or more.

DEEP UNDERSTANDING: THE NEW FORGIVENESS

The true and sacred act of forgiveness has been lost to us. We have been conditioned to a limited understanding of what constitutes true forgiveness by the misrepresentative and distorted "teachings" of religion. Conscious evolution, with its emphasis on conscious communication for a new paradigm, is calling to those of us who are awakened, to reclaim and embody the true act of forgiveness, which offers a sacred and spiritual opportunity to practice unconditional love and for co-creating unity consciousness within the Self, with others, and the world.

The act of forgiveness is fundamentally an altruistic one, yet has been grossly distorted throughout history by a misrepresentative and manipulative religious culture whose version of forgiveness invokes the energy of power dynamics. When forgiveness is sought or given from one who is unaware and unawakened, it can be expressed and experienced as a disempowered or "power over" dynamic. However, when forgiveness is offered by one who is consciously aware and awakened, it is experienced as empowering for both parties.

The true act of forgiveness is a unifying one. However, for the main part, it has become a polarizing act where often the one who is forgiven is viewed through a lens of blame and shame, giving rise to feelings of guilt, self-loathing, and so forth. And so, this never truly allows for deep peace to be the felt experience between the respective parties, or within the Self.

Forgiveness tends to polarize people into a mentality of right or wrong. New paradigm consciousness invites us not to forgive, as in the old paradigm and conditioned sense of the act, yet instead, to deeply understand. The experience and energy of feeling deeply understood, facilitates peace and harmony between the one who does the understanding and the one who is understood.

◆

Feeling the Difference between Forgiving and Deep Understanding

When you can, set aside some sacred time to feel into the difference between forgiving (in the respect of right-or-wrong old paradigm conditioning) versus deep understanding (in alignment with new paradigm consciousness).

Think of someone whose actions you feel the need to forgive. How does the thought of forgiving them feel for you? Now, gain a sense of how this may feel for the other.

Try now to gain a sense of how you and they might feel if you offered only your deep understanding.

Now think of someone that you feel you need forgiveness from. How does it feel if you imagine being forgiven? How do you imagine the other might feel for having forgiven you?

Finally, experience how it would feel if you were deeply understood by the one you needed forgiveness from. And, how they might feel having offered you deep understanding.

◆

Unless we are forgiving from a place of deep understanding, heart connection, and conscious awareness, then this truly sacred act (in its purest expression) continues to run the risk of resulting in a separating experience (in a subtle or overt sense), rather than transpiring to be the unifying act that it is truly meant to be.

Understanding requires us to delve deeper into the psychology, history, and feelings of ourselves and another. It invites us to become curious and conscious as to what was triggered and was really behind the action that hurt us; in that way, we can care about and be mindful of the other's feelings too. True forgiveness invites us to become ever more conscious, to heal, grow, and consciously evolve.

Understanding also invites us to apply the same care and mindfulness toward ourselves to discover how our own dysfunctional actions, from a psychological, historical, and feeling perspective, may have caused hurt to another. So, we do not sit in blame and shame, rather we sit in interested curiosity. What is most important is to gain a sense of what the need is behind our own or another's negative action and to be curious about just what need in ourselves or the other was or is not being met.

True forgiveness requires an elevated level of consciousness, compassion, empathy, and unconditional love in order to deeply understand ourselves and others. The act of forgiveness originated as a pure and altruistic vision for the fostering of peace and love within the Self, with others, and ultimately within the world. However, the pure and original intent of forgiveness has, like religion, become distorted beyond recognition.

True and pure forgiveness is not meant to be experienced as disempowering or "power over." It is meant to be empowering, empowered, graceful, and humble. If either party involved in an act of forgiveness is left with any other feeling than one of grace, humility, and empowerment by the experience, then true forgiveness has not taken place. The act of forgiveness calls upon us to deeply understand both ourselves and others, and by doing so we rediscover this sacred and true act.

EQUALITY

When we define equality, we find its basic meaning refers to the equal rights of all, regardless of age, race, creed, gender, religion, social position, political affiliation, physical ability or disability, or sexual orientation. Equality stands for human rights and the very fact that we are human implies that we are all equal.

As a foundation stone for a new paradigm consciousness, equality does not simply refer to human rights, but also the rights of all sentient beings and Mother Nature herself.

Many feel that equality means to be treated as equals in every way. It is the "every way" I wish to question here, as taking this literally could result in the co-creation of a generic society where there was no individuality and uniqueness of expression.

New consciousness equality is one in which all have equal opportunities and regardless of age, gender, race, or religious leaning are all treated in an equal fashion. However, individual and unique characteristics and the nature and needs of each person must also be validated, honored, acknowledged, valued, and respected.

If all were to be treated as equals, how would we honor and respect our differences? We are different. We have different needs and requirements, different visions for our lives and goals and dreams. We are also very different by nature. Some of us are quiet types, others are the life and soul of the party. Some of us are deep and contemplative, others are light and fun loving. Some of us like to travel and be in company, others like to be alone. So, if one who prefers to be alone were expected to be an entertainer at an event, or one who likes to entertain were required to sit in studious contemplation alone because we had to remain equal, then the diverse nature of human beings would be lost to us, along with the rich tapestry that it weaves.

For just a moment, let us imagine a generic equality. Imagine if when going out for a meal, we all have the same car, we are all dressed the same, and we arrive at the restaurant to eat the same dish, which is the only meal on offer. Some may like the meal and others may not. So some are happy with the evening and others are not. The same could be said for our clothes and our cars. So, with a generic equality we are fostering duality, not unity, as individuals become polarized feeling either happy or unhappy. And so, we have a perfect mix for creating reaction, rebellion, and revolution! Equality, if established in the literal sense, would prove counterproductive, as generic equality is unequal.

So, what constitutes a fair and unifying equality? The equality to which the twelve foundation stones for a new world paradigm speaks is one that is unifying and supports individuals to feel seen, heard, acknowledged, validated, valued, and celebrated in their differences.

True equality considers the needs of everyone. It seeks to meet the needs of the individual, while at the same time establishing a system that also meets the overall needs of the collective. True equality invites each of us to view each other only through the lens of the heart, to recognize that we are all human beings with all that constitutes.

Physically, emotionally, mentally, psychologically, energetically, and spiritually we are all made of the same basic human matter. And in that, we are no different. We all have emotions and feelings. We all have a brain and a mind. We all have a history, karma, and a current life. We all are made up of energy and have the same energetic systems, bodies, and fields. We are all Souls incarnate as spiritual Beings having a human experience. The gender, nationality, and color of our skin in this life is the choice we have each made at Soul level in order to heal, grow, and evolve.

True equality seeks to meet the needs of all, including sentient beings and Mother Earth. True equality values difference and therefore celebrates the rich diversity that is the human being.

INCLUSIVITY

Inclusivity, as a foundation stone for a new paradigm consciousness, has as its basic meaning "all have a place at the table." Like all twelve of the foundation stones, it has a unity consciousness value that is nondivisive, nondualistic, nonseparatist, nonpunishing, nonblaming or shaming, and nonexclusive.

Inclusivity does not exclude others: especially in regard to age, race, creed, gender, religion, social position, political affiliation, physical ability or disability, or sexual orientation.

In terms of conflict resolution within the family, community, workplace, social arena, religious community, and sociopolitical establishment, inclusivity plays a key role. It is a nonjudgmental, noncomparative, nonaccusatory, and nonpunishing value by which to build a new world paradigm based upon the six core values and the twelve foundation stones. With inclusivity, we seek to find ways in which to ensure all have a place at the table. We compassionately and empathically hold all in unconditional positive regard. As such, if a reason arises to suggest that the placement of an individual needs to be reconsidered, we seek to ensure that their individual place continues to be held and honored at the proverbial table.

If a critical decision arises to physically exclude an individual because it is deemed they are a destructive and disruptive influence, then we can still adopt a value of inclusivity. Such an individual's conduct will be arising from unresolved and unhealed trauma and emotional/mental/psychological pain within themselves. Inclusivity always includes a "wholistic" and holistic understanding of the potential cause of an individual's dysfunctional behavior. It holds sacred the individual's place at the table while, at the same time, encouraging and supporting the individual to seek the appropriate psychological counsel.

Having agreed to do so, an individual finds that upon their return to the table they are held in high esteem and deep understanding. The individual will then share with the group what they have come to understand from their healing journey. The group members will then express their own feelings that resulted from the earlier misconduct of the individual, together with their positive feedback of what is now being shared.

In those rarer cases where an individual's conduct is deemed to be dangerous and threatening, they will be asked to physically leave their seat, although this will be held until such time that they have become integrated enough to be able to return. If not, their place will continue to be honored and only empathic and compassionate communication will be expressed about them if their absence becomes permanent. Inclusivity, in the context of the above example, further facilitates compassion and empathy within the individuals in the group: facilitating learning, healing, and growth to result from the teaching that such an individual's presence has afforded to all.

Nothing happens by chance, including the particular group of Souls who gather around any table, from the political, to the corporate, the general workplace, or within communities and families. Everyone at the table is a teacher, a healer, a guide, a mirror, a brother, a sister, and a friend, regardless of their conduct. Even one who has posed a threat or danger is all of the above, and though they may no longer be physically present, the presence of their Soul remains. So, too, does the gift of the teaching and the opportunity given to the rest of the group for processing and healing what has been invoked.

Remember a comment attributed to Gandhi: You will find my friend, that there is room for us all.

EMPATHY

Empathy is the humblest expression of feeling and demonstrates our capacity to recognize the emotions and feelings that are being experienced by another.

Compassion is the emotional quality that is refined through empathy. Empathy precedes compassion, for when we make an empathic connection with a human being, an animal, a bird, an insect, a flower, or a plant, compassion flows. Empathy bestows upon an individual a marked ability for mutually experiencing the thoughts, emotions, and feelings of others.

The Difference between Empathy and Sympathy

Whereas empathy is our capacity to experience the thoughts, emotions, and feelings of others, sympathy represents a feeling of understanding and care for their suffering. It invokes within us a memory of our own experience. And so, sympathy triggers an emotional reaction or response within us and we often find ourselves in tears or anger at what is shared with us.

With empathy we remain fully present, but with sympathy we can find ourselves emotionally identifying with the other's story and be unable to remain fully present and neutral to it. Sympathy identifies; empathy relates. Sympathy offers comfort; empathy offers validation.

Empathy is a deeper emotional quality. It is an unspoken, deeply felt understanding of another's experience. Sympathy provides support and a profound capacity to identify with the pain and suffering of another. However, it also has a shadow side, as it can invoke the "rescuer" within us to respond to others as if they were birds with broken wings.

The Qualities of Empathy

Empathy, as a foundation stone for a new paradigm consciousness, fulfills the need of all human beings to feel seen, heard, validated, valued, and acknowledged. Meeting the need for empathy has far-reaching consequences of unimaginable proportions. The act of empathy tremendously accelerates personal and global healing. All individuals long to feel an empathic connection. All human beings carry the wound of empathic disconnection.

I would like to include here a beautiful wisdom statement: *All wounds are formed in relationship, and therefore all wounds are healed in relationship.* I include this because it is empathic disconnection that creates the wounds that arise out of dysfunctional relationship, and therefore it is empathic connection that heals those wounds.

---◆---

Empathic Connection Decree

From this day forth I choose to empathically connect with myself to heal my psychological wounding, which has occurred as a result of the times I have been on the receiving end of empathic disconnection from others.

I have reached an understanding that it is empathic disconnection that is to be found at the root of all trauma. Therefore, today I choose to empathically connect with myself, to heal the wound of disconnection within me.

I choose to empathically connect with all sentient beings and recognize how empathic disconnection is at the root of all trauma and suffering of human, animal, or nature.

By empathically connecting with all sentient beings, I contribute to the co-creation of a peaceful world.

I Am an empathic, compassionate, understanding, and unconditionally loving human being.

From this day forth, my intention is to empathically connect with all sentient beings: mineral, plant, insect, bird, marine life, animal, and human.

Today, I will empathically connect with at least one sentient, living energy, especially one that is considered to be deserving of the least empathy and love.

I commit to empathically reconnect with myself from this day forth, for doing so is the key to my own depth healing and inner peace, which will contribute to healing and peace in the world.

◆————————————————————————◆

CONSCIOUS CO-CREATION

A new paradigm, which speaks to a new consciousness and is founded in unity, urges us to begin to co-create *consciously*. We are all co-creators and we have been co-creating for millennia. This is fact.

However, we have been co-creating from fear and negative conditioning. Throughout human history, every individual who has ever walked the Earth has been a co-creator. Throughout history, aside from those few enlightened ones who have graced this planet as great teachers, human beings have been unconsciously co-creating a world that cannot sustain peace.

If we ask ourselves why is it that after thousands of years of longing for peace and liberation, which continues to elude us to this day, we are left with the fact that it is the collective who have co-created the world as it has unfolded throughout history. When we look back and even by studying the global situation in our current times, we can see that it is fear and conditioning that kept humanity from the peace and liberation it so desires. By aligning our thoughts with unity consciousness and love, we can co-create a new global reality from this inner state of being.

For decades now we have been hearing and reading about positive thinking. Many of us have engaged with this solely as a mental concept, as our evolutionary process did not make it possible for it to be a felt experience. However, we have reached a watershed in our conscious evolution and find ourselves on the threshold of a new epoch for humanity and a new consciousness for a new paradigm. For the many of us who have devotedly committed to inner healing and integration, we are ready now to embrace a new consciousness founded upon conscious evolution, conscious communication, and conscious co-creation.

Conscious co-creation is a collaborative, co-supportive, co-collective experience catalyzed through deep understanding and conscious awareness. Any co-creation that seeks to reestablish a new twist on the old is born out of fear and conditioning.

Our own conscious evolution is key to our capacity to consciously co-create, for as we psychologically heal and consciously awaken, our attention and focus begins to shift from our personal evolution to global evolution. We come to realize how our thoughts, intentions, and actions co-create the global situation. We begin to feel an undeniable urge to participate in the co-creation of a better world, recognizing that we are not merely powerless onlookers, but an active part of the global dysfunction we can see all around us. We come to understand how our thoughts and actions have co-created a dysfunctional world. To acknowledge that we collude and play our role in the dysfunctional and broken expression that is our world today may feel like one small step, but is in fact one giant leap for humankind.

Creating Reality Consciousness

When we are integrated and living from our authentic selves, we are fully present in each moment and consciously creating our reality. Many who have attained this level of awareness and reached this stage of their personal evolution report that if they ask for, think of, or need something it manifests immediately, or within twenty-four hours. Often those who have given to others report that very soon afterward, they are given to by someone else!

Remembrance

When we live from the True Self and are consciously awakened, a natural phenomenon of remembrance occurs. We begin to remember who we really are. We begin to realize that we are the creators of our own reality. We recall that we are the choosers and our choices not only shape our own lives, but the lives of others too.

Self-Realization

The psycho-spiritual journey consists of many layers as we unfold and reclaim who we really are. It also serves as a process to decondition us from the family myths and cultural identities we have had projected onto us. As we begin to decondition from the illusion and myth under which we have been operating, we begin to align with our own truth and to see what is actually happening in our personal world and in our larger environment. We cease to act as if we are on automatic pilot and begin to disconnect from all that is disempowering and does not serve a peaceful and free world. Instead we turn our attention to how we can support the world around us. We empower ourselves, we find our voices, and we reconnect to a sense of meaning and purpose in our lives that proved elusive until our conscious awakening.

Our Thoughts Manifest as Reality

When we are living from a place of integration, balance, and awareness, we understand that our thoughts do indeed manifest our reality. Because of this it is our responsibility to ensure that every thought, word, action, and deed is a conscious one.

To be co-creative is to be active, even if not in the physical sense. Our feelings and the mind are the all-important active force of creation. Various experiments have been conducted around the world in the past decades that reveal that it only takes a small number of the population to significantly affect global consciousness. (Refer to my book *2012: A Clarion Call* to read about this in detail.) However, what has been proven is that if just seven thousand people meditate together, crime rates and accident admissions to hospital emergency rooms reduce by 75 percent.

Remember this whenever you find yourself falling into a way of thinking that nothing can be influenced by the power of your own thoughts. Your thoughts, intentions, and actions influence the global reality, every second of every day. Change your thoughts and you can change the world.

COOPERATION

Cooperation is fundamentally about people "co-operating" with each other. It can often be seen in action when danger poses a very real threat to human life. However, it is also evident in our willingness to unite in order to co-create communities and nations and to ensure that these run as smoothly as possible.

This type of cooperation meets the needs of our basic levels of survival. Cooperation needs to be upgraded to fit a new paradigm that has consciousness at its heart and, therefore, could be redefined as conscious cooperation. For any act of support, which is driven by the heart and soul with a specific aim of helping to ease the suffering of a fellow human, is cooperation that is conscious.

For millennia, heart-centered human beings have naturally and instinctively sought to protect each other. This is an inborn quality of the heart. However, until now, most people have never paused to really understand the *why* or *how* in terms of their capacity for altruism in the face of suffering or co-creation. For the main part cooperation has been an *instinctive* urge, most noticeable during wars, natural disasters, and in any kind of tragic or traumatizing experience that calls for people to unify and pull together. Yet now, as we become more and more conscious, we can contemplate the *why* and the *how* to become conscious cooperators.

There is another level of cooperation that we could term responsive. This is a conscious cooperation and an *intuitive* response that invites us to offer ourselves in loving support to assist our friends, family, neighbors, and community with the tasks, projects, duties, and responsibilities they are charged with.

Conscious cooperation does not invite us to *turn the other cheek*. Instead, it asks us to remain ever open to those arenas in life where the joining of two or more people can ease the suffering of human, animal, or nature itself by helping to co-create a positive outcome for all.

Conscious cooperation calls to the foreground another level of our capacity to respond: our capacity to respond not from a survival mentality, but from an expression of soulful conscience, so we may ease the suffering that is to be found on our very doorsteps. Cooperation that is driven by a soulful conscience develops our capacity to become more intimately connected with those we encounter in our everyday lives.

Conscious cooperation could be described as a harmonious cooperative unification involving two or more people. It is an expression of cooperating that invokes our basic need to ease the suffering of others and to co-create. Cooperation becomes conscious when it involves conscious awareness, which notices and feels connected to those around us. Cooperation differs from co-support in the respect that it is an innate basic drive to ease suffering and co-create, whereas co-support is a natural need present within us, to meet and support the needs of others.

Conscious cooperation is a unifying joining of energies and action for a greater cause. Conscious cooperation invites us to look among our family and friends, toward our neighbors, within the community, the nation, and the world, to wonder what we may do to ease suffering and co-create.

CO-SUPPORT

Co-support invites us to be mindful of others and to do our best to meet their needs if we so choose. Co-support is a more localized action in contrast to one that is national and international. Co-supporting is all about caring and sharing, loving and supporting, helping and assisting, and random acts of kindness, all of which we know will make someone's day that little bit more special or easier.

Co-support especially extends to those we interact and share our lives with on a daily basis. It can involve anything from offering to walk someone's dog, to watering their plants, feeding their cat, or keeping an eye on their home when they are away. It may involve giving an elderly or a physically challenged neighbor a lift to and from the shops, or doing their shopping for them. It could be helping someone carry a heavy load to their car, or offering the few extra pennies or dollars someone is short of in the supermarket queue.

Co-support is any act that supports another at a personal level and makes their lives easier or more harmonious. It invites us to give of ourselves from the heart, minus any "shoulds," "oughts," or personal agendas. There is no superiority or power dynamics whatsoever in co-support, only a sincere desire to bring joy, peace, and love to another.

Co-support, like cooperation, is a unifying act. It fosters a heart connection and a deepening capacity for intimacy within ourselves and toward others. It is entirely without judgment or comparison and carries no trace of the seven dark arrows. It does, however, carry all the qualities of the seven light and seven rainbow arrows.

COLLABORATION

Collaboration is an openness to join with another or others to co-create, to co-support, and to collaborate for the purpose of honoring a vision, a dream, a hope, or taking part in an altruistic act that has a benevolent purpose.

Collaboration is a selfless offering of our presence, our skills, our talents, our gifts, and our resources. By contributing to an individual or a family, a community, a country, or the world, there is a sense of fulfillment in the co-creation and establishment of an inspiration that touches all involved. For example, collaboration in action can be seen in any voluntary movement or organization where those working together do so for the higher good. It can be seen in action in any group endeavor where the motivational force is not financial, but has as its focus the mutual co-creating of a vision.

Collaboration is a combination of cooperation and co-support. It can be experienced both at a personal and localized level, for example, by helping our neighbor build a garden shed, or by gathering together to refurbish the local town hall, or organizing and/or participating in a sponsored walk to raise money for a charity that is important to family or to the community itself. Collaboration is about joining together to support, be that for a worthy cause, the design of a structure, a launch of a global movement, or taking turns to support our elderly neighbors to feel loved and not so alone or isolated.

Just like cooperation and co-support, collaboration is a unifying experience. It comes from our hearts and connects us to the true values in life. It leaves the collaborator with a real feel-good factor and connects us to the beauty and love within ourselves, which we can express to others. Collaboration must never belong exclusively to the working environment, nor must its focus be on money or agendas. It is an unconditional act of grace founded in integrity and a sincere desire to join with others to co-create something that makes everyone's heart sing.

NONMONETARY TRANSACTIONS

Whenever we engage in an exchange that does not involve money, it is a nonmonetary transaction. Nonmonetary transactions are any exchanges that involve the sharing of items, resources, time, expertise, co-support, or love. Nonmonetary transactions ask us to examine the true value of something in terms of how much love and peace it brings to our own, or another's, world. For example, mowing someone's lawn could be an exchange for someone helping to fix the gutters on your house. We could help a person solve a problem in return for them baking us a cake or cooking us a meal. Minding each other's children, or walking someone's dog, could be an exchange for a lift to the supermarket for the weekly shopping or to the dentist or doctor. These are all nonmonetary transactions that serve both parties and foster the deepening of connections, the birth of new friendships, more meaningful relationships, and interactions with our neighbors as well as those in our local communities or at work.

It is heartbreaking to see parents or their children using money to bribe one another so beds can be made, the dog walked, or some "peace and quiet" can be bought. When we offer our time and our good intention to another, without a need or expectation for payment, the value placed on this far exceeds any monetary exchange. When we give of ourselves from our hearts without a care for financial reward or payment, we experience an energetic wave of love that makes our hearts swell: a conscious clarity and a pure experience of our own or another's innate goodness.

Nonmonetary exchanges are an essential social medicine if we are to heal the separation that money has created between people. Monetary exchanges can serve to unify and yet, more often than not, they cause separation. Our current approach toward money needs to change. If we continue to maintain old paradigm attitudes toward it, we will continue to remain in duality consciousness. Unity consciousness asks us to share, to unite, to give of ourselves from the heart and Soul, not from the wallet.

Nonmonetary transactions are the way to bond people, families, communities and nations together at a heart level. Instead of giving your child twenty dollars to make their bed, give them a warm hug and tell them how much they are loved. Instead of passing by an elderly neighbor's house each day, ask if they need any shopping or any help.

On a larger scale, for example, in Greece where the economy has virtually collapsed and people no longer have the financial resources, I came across a story of a woman who is by profession a teacher of art and piano. However, people were no longer able to afford her lessons. The students dearly wished to continue studying with her, so their parents were willing to offer food and gardening services in exchange for their lessons. This was mutually beneficial and met the needs of both.

The core experience of nonmonetary transactions however is the *feel-good factor* that it bestows. Nothing feels more wonderful than giving to another from the heart, without the exchange of money having to take place.

NONVIOLENT/COMPASSIONATE COMMUNICATION

Most cultures in the world remain locked in a survival-mode mentality. In general, communications between people involve a fight-or-flight mentality with its usual outcome of reaction leading to separation. When we express our true feelings without fear and speak from the heart, communicating openly and honestly, we are able to do so because we are emotionally stable, psychologically integrated, and mindful. These qualities of the Self allow for a responsive mode of communication that fosters unity.

Let us celebrate the beauty of words, the healing influence of words, the wonder of words. When we cease using words as weapons, then we will initiate peace in the world. No longer will we desire to use words to harm people.

ELEVEN

An Evolutionary Leap

A New Vision for a New Epoch

Since December 2011 I have been meditating deeply on exactly what it would take to support the full unfolding and expression of ourselves as human *beings*—as opposed to our current reality (which has been the case for millennia) in which we are humans *doing*.

I have come to the conclusion that in the old paradigm global system, in order to meet our basic survival needs, most people are doing what they do not want to do, rather than being what they most long to be. The old paradigm is set up to reward those who collude with it. Humanity has become enmeshed in a dysfunctional global system. It has become anesthetized by a cultural conditioning that begins at birth, by those who themselves have been conditioned by the generations before them.

THE HUMAN BALL OF DOING

During a conversation with a friend in late summer 2012, he spoke of something he calls "the human ball of doing." In this ball he views humanity "running around doing." He spoke of his wish to no longer be a part of this ball.

I was struck by this analogy when he shared it and had a flash of seeing myself free-floating outside of the ball: looking at it and noting that it was indeed very busy—doing! However, since sitting in deep contemplation of the ball, I have come to view it as a representation of the old world—the old paradigm.

At a practical level the most challenging aspect of releasing ourselves from the "ball of doing" brings us to this fundamental question, how do we meet our basic survival needs? Speaking for myself, my rent is due, my car payment is due, and my bills are due. I need to sustain my body with the nutrition, nourishment, protection, and care that it requires. How can I meet my basic survival needs in the current culture if I choose to follow the wisdom that calls from the depths of my heart and soul, urging me to manifest a more creative, harmonious, and fulfilling life?

THE PHYSICAL BODY AS SEER

For the past twenty years I have consciously sought to cultivate the capacity to deeply trust the wise counsel of my physical body. I came to realize, over a period of several consciously experiential years, that the greatest psychic and seer in the world is the human body. If we learn to listen intently to it, not only will it guide us further and further toward self-liberation, but it will also lead us to a level of physical, emotional, and mental well-being unlike anything we have known before.

Conversely, if we do not listen to its wise counsel, then it will force upon us unquestionable and unequivocal signs and symptoms alerting us to the fact that we have either erred directly onto a path of imbalance or disharmony, or that we are about to consider or, indeed, do something that will take us out of alignment with our deeper Truth. In my own life I have been engaged in a deep existential process that has led me to an increasing realization that there is indeed an aspect of my work that I no longer experience myself in full alignment with. What has imprinted this realization as a felt knowing is the powerful impact that accompanies any attempt on my part to make any plans in relation to this aspect of my work. What immediately follows is an intense reaction at a physical level. I become physically ill, suffer intense nausea and headaches, and become overwhelmed with crippling exhaustion. Not surprisingly, when I state a firm "No" to continuing with those plans, all symptoms immediately begin to disappear and, once again, my body is relaxed and in harmony.

Abraham Maslow once said, "all are well who have a vocation"; never truer words could be said. Over the years, I have witnessed my own health go from strength to strength each time I was deeply immersed in the totality of the moment of what I was working on—even if that "moment" lasted for months at a time. And yet, as soon as I considered doing something that I did not really want to do, because I needed the income, my health would deteriorate within minutes.

What we do has a direct and profound impact, for better or worse, on our overall health and sense of well-being. Ninety-nine percent of us are doing what we do not want to do in order to earn an income. It's as if we sell our souls in order to survive. Yet, is that what God wants for us? Is that what Creator desires for us? Is that what Source wishes for us?

We have become lost to ourselves, and so have lost sight of who we really are. We have been brainwashed and conditioned to conform, as robots, like cogs locked into the global dysfunctional machine. We have become the compliant manifestation of the agenda of the global system. And so, I return to the existential question of *doing* versus *being*.

ADAPTED SELF VERSUS AUTHENTIC SELF

"Doing" what we do not want to do creates catastrophic disharmony within the Self. Whenever we do something we do not truly wish to do, even if we believe that we really do want to, our health and well-being are catastrophically impacted. The level of disharmony and disconnection with Self penetrates us at a cellular level, and it is here that the cells begin to absorb a *life-denying* message, in contrast to the *life-affirming* one of living and speaking our truth.

We live a lie when we get caught in doing what we do not want to do, or when we end up saying "yes" to what we long to say "no" to. This takes us out of integrity with ourselves and with others. If we think about this in terms of the cells within our bodies, then we are out of integrity with these too. Enter "dis-ease."

Human intelligence, at any level of society, is extremely sophisticated and cleverly manipulates any compromising situation by setting up strategies in order to manage and cope. Such strategies include addictions to food, alcohol, sex, television, Facebook, the Internet, consumerism, the media, and so forth. These only serve to further repress a deeper felt sense of our truth—sabotaging our physical, emotional, mental, and spiritual health.

The general cause of illness and disease ("dis-ease") originates from the fact that most people are living repressed lives. To put it bluntly, most individuals are living a lie in order to survive, or to suppress an underlying sense of existential fear. And so, we perpetuate a never-ending cycle that keeps us out of alignment with the truth of who we are. Instead, we acquiesce to the demands and expectations of a dysfunctional culture and thus remain locked inside the human ball of doing. The old paradigm system is not set up to support those who wish to step outside of this.

We need to feel free to forge ahead with inspiration. We need to feel encouraged to manifest our personal dreams and visions, supported by a healthy global system with a fundamental policy that invites the individual to create an enriching and fulfilling personal life. This, in turn, supports the attainment of sustainable world peace. Such a system is not yet in place, but it can become so. It is only by locating our consciousness and awareness outside of the ball of doing that a new global society can be established—founded upon new consciousness values and ethics.

SEISMIC SHIFT

For the current system to change, it would amount to nothing less than the wholesale transformation of global sociopolitical, environmental, and economic policy. Also to fall under the spotlight of radical questioning would be religion and its dysfunctional impact on the individual and the world.

The current global system would need to terminate or adapt existing policies and initiate new ones that prioritize the physical, emotional, mental, psychological, and spiritual well-being of both the individual and the collective. A seismic shift from consumerism to humanitarianism would be required at every level of policy, in every country in the world.

How do we begin to manifest this evolutionary imperative? This is an in-depth question that I address in the Monthly Messages section of my website, www.nicolyachristi.com. To do so here would make this chapter inordinately long!

FROM DOING TO BEING

For now, I shall continue with the theme of this chapter, which has as its focus how to shift from doing to being.

For those of us who resonate with the existential crisis that is this evolutionary leap, we find ourselves immersed in deep contemplation, asking such questions as, how do we sustain ourselves during such a transition? not only in relation to the accelerated evolution of personal consciousness that occurs when one decides to make the evolutionary leap between an old and new paradigm, but also in the context of navigating the physical reality between the two.

We ponder on how to refrain from continuing to give in to old paradigm ways to ensure that our basic survival needs are met. We begin to realize that by maintaining these, we are colluding with the old system and its suppression of the human spirit—for this is the agenda of the old paradigm.

We wonder how to move forward responsibly, with integrity, authenticity, care, and respect in ways that are nonconfrontational and yet enable us to stand firm in our choice of nonparticipation in a dysfunctional system that simply does not align with our highest personal ideals and values and altruistic vision for a better world. We question how we can remain true to our authentic values when caught in the old system and, at the same time, survive.

Where is the place for those of us who no longer wish to collude with a globally dysfunctional system, with its agenda to manipulate, dominate, and control the human spirit through covert and overt wholesale anesthetizing and conditioning of an uninformed humanity?

GLIMPSES OF A NEW GLOBAL SOCIETY

Let us imagine for a moment the kind of new global society that could begin to unfold if a system was in place that served the true needs and values of all people, animals, nature, and the Earth. What would happen if the money spent on perpetuating consumerism and defense was instead allocated to health, wellness, and harmony programs for all citizens?

What could be if government policy and public resources were focused on care for the entire community? What if fully funded "family health and harmony" programs were widely available to all? What if psychological counseling, therapeutic healing, and peace and rejuvenation retreats were available to all as a gift, at specific age thresholds throughout life: for example, at the ages of eighteen, twenty-one, thirty, forty, fifty, sixty, and so on?

What would happen if a fraction of the money spent on maintaining a dysfunctional global system was reallocated to support gifted philosophers, artists, writers, poets, visionaries, and brilliant pioneers in those fields aligned with new paradigm consciousness and humanitarian values? The time is upon us to support those gifted individuals whose sole focus and intent is to bring love, wellness, beauty, wisdom, evolution, harmony, balance, grace, and prosperity to all, and to guide humanity toward the manifestation of sustainable and lasting world peace.

What might happen if the values and practice of deep care for all sentient beings and nonsentient life-forms were instilled as core-teaching elements within the global educational curriculum, and as fundamental values within the working environment? What could be possible if funding were there for all who wish to follow their greatest altruistic or artistic dream and vision? What kind of world could we live in if everyone had the opportunity to explore and cultivate higher ideals and to come to know true abundance and prosperity?

Many years ago, my mother revealed to me that she had once longed to be an opera singer or a designer. Yet, owing to an absence of funding or support to realize her dream, she instead took a job as a waitress. One day, several years later, she found herself managing a branch of a warehouse. As she shared her dream with me, the light of it once again danced across her face and lit up her eyes, yet rapidly disappeared as she returned back to the here and now and to what had transpired to be the reality of her life. I could see how that light had been extinguished by the time she had entered her early twenties when faced with the realization of having to let go of her dream in order to survive. How many have held a vision of how life could be, only to have lost it to the harsh reality that is the archaic system in which we currently live?

We need to co-create a new system—one that will honor, support, and validate the highest ideal of each individual, one that is devoid of gain at the expense of another. We need to cultivate a system of nonduality that seeks to unify Self, other, community, and the world. We need to co-envision and to manifest a new system, where none are sentenced to fall through the gap when their heart's desire leads them to the perfect moment to take a small step or a giant evolutionary leap. *One small step for man or woman leads to one giant leap for humanity.*

A visionary new system is needed that supports conscious evolution and recognizes that each time an individual takes an evolutionary leap, so too does the community, the country, and the world.

SO, WHERE TO FROM HERE?

How do we remain fully present and rooted in the truth of who we are, when caught in a system that cares not for the soul of the individual, or the collective, yet instead is fixated on money? An archaic system that conditions us to believe that happiness is derived from security, and that our level of happiness is determined by our material wealth.

A question to ponder upon is this: Do we need to feel secure, or do we wish to be fulfilled? Security is driven by fear, keeping us caught in the known, whereas fulfillment is of heart and soul, calling for something far beyond what the current system can offer. Our quest for true and deep fulfillment leads us into the unknown and it is only in this sacred place that we become intimately acquainted with it. Fulfillment nourishes the very essence of who we are. True freedom is to be found in fulfillment, not security.

How many of our hopes and dreams become lost to us? How many of our own dreams and values do we fail to honor? And, what of the essential needs of the heart and soul? To what extent do we dismiss or adapt these in order to survive—and at what cost?

To what extent are we caught in fear? To what degree do we live our lives from fear? How many of our choices are made from fear? How much do we collude with a consumer culture that strives to keep us distracted from the truth of who we really are? What type of system do we support that numbs us from the wisdom and truth to be found within our heart, and denies the magnificence of our soul?

How much do we consciously or unconsciously live a lie, caught in a global culture that promotes survival of the adapted? To what degree is our inborn natural, organic, and creative expression suppressed by a dysfunctional culture that we ourselves support?

What happens to those who desire, above all else, to live the truth of who they are? How do we extricate ourselves from the ball of doing and still keep a roof over our heads and food on the table? It will take no less than the highest vision, the deepest faith, and the greatest courage to step outside of the old system to live our truth more fully.

How do we begin to establish the altruistic, humanitarian values and ethos of a new consciousness in a new epoch? What happens to those of us who no longer choose to exist in the old paradigm? Just how much longer are we willing to adapt in order to survive?

At what point do we say "Enough!" and step out of the ball of doing? What will it take for us to do so? How can we take that evolutionary leap and land on both feet, able to sustain ourselves and our families, and manifest our highest vision for our own lives and for the world? These are the questions that we need to ask ourselves if we truly wish to embody and live the Authentic Self and further our own conscious evolution.

LOVE AS ACTION IN THE WORLD

There is a world (a paradigm) of difference between that which we have been conditioned to call *work* versus our vocational calling. The foundations of the type of work we might describe as a *job* or a *career* are mostly set in fear, whereas what we may describe as a *vocation* or a *calling* arises out of an intense, undeniable passion, absolute devotion, and unequivocal, unquestionable, unwavering, and uncompromising dedication to something that feels inspired, something we aspire to, and to which we are willing to give our all.

Our vocational calling is driven by love, and at this level we come to recognize, with crystal clarity, that our work is no longer *work* in the old sense of the term, but instead our calling is an act of love—it is *our love in action in the world*. I have ceased to refer to my own calling as work, for I recognize that my way of being in my own life, and in the wider global community, is an expression of *my love in action in the world*.

The new epoch with a new consciousness urges the individual and the collective to more fully express love as action in the world. It implores each of us to pour our heart and soul, our creativity, our vision, our light, our gift, our unique individuality, our love, our brilliance, and our humanity into its very foundations.

And so, I conclude here.

What price Truth?
What price freedom?
What price adapted to Authentic Self?
What price from human doing to human being?

What price an evolutionary leap from the ball of doing to Authentic
Being?

What price living unbridled, unequivocal, uncompromising, non-
negotiable, and unconditional love and truth?

LOVE IS THE COMPASS

How do we transcend that which remains adapted within ourselves
and embody the Authentic Truth of who we are?

How do we decondition from a lifetime of conditioning that has
required us to live an adapted expression of who we really are in
order to fit in, survive, and conform?

How do we transcend fear in order to live from the center of Love—to
be rooted in Love—to be Love?

What is it that will support us to take that evolutionary leap from an
old to a new paradigm?

How do we rise like the phoenix from the ashes of the old paradigm
and begin to fully live the truth of who we are?

How do we release ourselves from the human ball of doing?

The answer to all of the above questions requires no less than the greatest faith in love, truth, courage, transparency, integrity, inner strength,
trust, surrender, vision, unity, co-support, and collaboration. These are
just some of the qualities we must now call upon, embody, and embrace
wholeheartedly.

We need to align the personality with the Soul—and not the other
way around as is the usual case. It is this that will support and ensure
such an evolutionary leap. We must support each other wholeheartedly
in whatever ways we can—be that through nonmonetary transactions;
unconditional giving, receiving, and doing; co-support; and co-creation.
A key is togetherness—unity—being there for each other. We can
attempt to take such a leap alone; however, with the support of one or
more like-hearts and like-minds, we will successfully make that evolutionary leap out of the ball of doing into Authentic Living.

We are not meant to become like robots as a human *doing*. This is a gross misrepresentation and distortion of who we really are. We are here to evolve into our highest expression of a spiritual being. We must recall that we are a Spirit in human form. We need to remember that our Soul incarnated here on Earth to experience the phenomena of human *being*.

A new epoch founded upon a new consciousness that holds at its core a visionary new global system is dependent entirely upon those fearless individuals, groups, and communities who are willing to blaze a trail and light the way for the establishment of a new global culture—one that fulfills its primary role to nurture the well-being of the individual and the collective and, by so doing, manifest sustainable world peace.

These are early days and everything is possible.

TWELVE

The Other Side of the Shift

DECEMBER 21, 2012: THE GREAT SHIFT

For millions of people around the world, 2012 marked the pinnacle of an unprecedented human and global evolutionary shift.

Ancient prophecy foretold that the year 2012 would be a time when the old world would end and a new world would be born. Many past civilizations, especially, considered the date December 21, 2012, to be of great importance, including the ancient peoples of the Americas, Sumer, China, and Egypt.

The Qu'ero, direct descendents of the Incas, spoke of "An age of conquest and domination coming to an end and a new human being born." They called this process the "Turning of the Earth" and they identified 2012 as the time when this would unfold. The Hopi spoke of 12/21/12 as being the moment humanity enters "One thousand years of peace," and the Maya and other ancient indigenous peoples spoke of 12/21/12 as the threshold into "A New Golden Age."

The year 2012 also witnessed an extraordinary unfolding of rare cosmic events. Ancient prophecy appeared to be engaged in a sophisticated and synchronistic union of astronomical, astrological, and Great

This is a piece I wrote especially for a new book by Ervin Laszlo and Kingsley Dennis titled *Dawn of the Akashic Age.*

Calendar Completion Cycles. One example is the completion of the 5,126-year Mayan Long Count Calendar on 12/21/12—the same date as the completion of the 26,000-year Galactic Cycle.

A total solar eclipse occurred on August 11, 1999, at 11:11 a.m. Greenwich Mean Time (the same time as the 2012 winter solstice—11:11 a.m. Universal Time), which, according to Mayan prophecy, took humanity into a thirteen-year completion cycle that the Maya referred to as the Quickening.

The Maya foretold that these final thirteen years of the 5,126-year Long Count Calendar would be the last opportunity for our civilization to embrace the changes due to unfold at the moment of our collective spiritual regeneration in December 2012.

Millions across the globe could sense that something of an unprecedented nature was occurring during the time of the Quickening, and indeed throughout all of 2012. Millions of people around the world shared their extraordinary experiences of immense challenges and extraordinary potential via social media networks and related websites.

The date 12/21/12 marked the precise moment when important ancient prophecy and rare astronomical alignments converged, signaling a phenomenon unlike anything humanity had witnessed—the Great Shift.

Mayan messenger Carlos Barrios perfectly summed up the meaning of 2012:

The world will not end. It will be transformed. . . . Everything will change. . . . Change is accelerating now and it will continue to accelerate. If the people of the Earth can get to this 2012 date without having destroyed too much of the Earth, we will rise to a new, higher level. But to get there we must transform enormously powerful forces that seek to block the way.

Humanity will continue, but in a different way. Material structures will change. From this we will have the opportunity to be more human. Our planet can be renewed or ravaged. Now is the time to awaken and take action. The prophesied changes are going to happen, but our attitude and actions determine how harsh or mild they are.

This is a crucially important moment for humanity and for Earth. Each person is important. If you have incarnated into this era, you have spiritual work to do balancing the planet.

The greatest wisdom is in simplicity. Love, respect, tolerance, sharing, gratitude, forgiveness. It's not complex or elaborate. The real knowledge is free. It's encoded in your DNA. All you need is within you. Great teachers have said that from the beginning. Find your heart, and you will find your way.*

2013–2020: THE OTHER SIDE OF THE SHIFT

So where do we find ourselves placed post–2012 Shift, in terms of our personal and collective evolutionary development? Let us now journey in our imaginations to visit the year 2020, as observers, and consider the following questions:

1. What do we notice about the inner-development process of the individual?
2. What tangible signs are there of individual and collective integration and evolution?
3. What has transpired in the eight years between 2013 and 2020 to reveal that world peace is a progressive and sustainable reality unfolding between people, communities, countries, and nations?
4. What new values and foundation stones are being set in place to ensure the establishment of sustainable world peace?

My own responses are as follows:

1. The evolution of consciousness has taken a progressive evolutionary leap forward. The awakened human in 2020 has embodied

---

*Oziris M. Stoltz, *Spiritual Awakening* (Bloomington, Ind.: Balboa Press, 2012).

the authentic self, transcended the ego, is psychologically integrated and spiritually balanced. Such an individual understands not only the concept, but the living reality, that an inner shift is a prerequisite for a positive and lasting world shift, and how true inner peace creates lasting world peace.

2. Psychologically and spiritually balanced individuals have undergone a rapid phase of personal evolution. Thus, they qualify as co-creators and evolutionary guides for a new world paradigm. It is widely recognized that only those who have achieved an integrated balance, at a psychological and spiritual level, can successfully establish a positive, new, global, sociopolitical system.

3. The year 2020 holds a greater potential for world peace than at any other time. The millions of integrated individuals are the new evolutionary guides for humanity. They qualify to guide humanity into a new paradigm not merely because of their intellectual capacity, but, equally important, because they possess a highly refined emotional intelligence, and thus are able to develop and implement new holistic systems for all, including those between political authority and people.

What is clear from a 2020 vantage point is that not only are people tired of the old paradigm models that keep government and people in duality, but governments, too, are tired of trying to stem the flow of a dysfunctional economic, ecological, sociological, and political system that runs deep in the fabric of society and that can never be resolved through old paradigm governing patterns. Through new and global 2020 Advisory Councils, 2020 governing authorities are beginning to recognize that cooperation, collaboration, and co-creation with the people is the only way to ensure a win-win situation.

For millennia, humanity has endured extreme trauma, fundamentalism, war, conflict, dictatorship, uprisings, rebellion, cruelty, and revolution. We have been polarized in either fight or flight mentality and actions. Where is peace in the annals of our history?

There has never been a system of rule that has created a healthy economy that sustains us all. There has never been a unified political system that supports the needs and respects the rights of all. Despite the wealth of previous fallen empires, despite all the revolutions, protests, and campaigns, never has there been peace on Earth, in the entire history of humankind.

The fact remains that, pre-2020, global authoritarians were not fully qualified to organize human society in ways that are crucial to human and global evolution.

We are mistaken or naive if we believe that most Western nations are living in peacetime. A war rages under our very noses and plays out in the political landscape and the media every day. It is an endless war that polarizes us in either fight mode or flight mode. We continue to remain unseen and unheard in any attempt to integrate an intelligent and sophisticated vision of collaboration with global authority systems.

Our human right to peace continues to elude us, even after millions and millions of deaths and casualties in the name of peace. It is blatantly obvious that many of the wars that cause untold human suffering and death are fought solely over resources and money. Even after wholesale tragedies—the people's removal of dictators who have decimated or ravaged entire countries, the unimaginable cruelty and torture that has been inflicted on our global brothers and sisters—we find that thousands of years later we are still experiencing the same entrenched patterns of duality governance* and heartbreaking realities of the abuse of people and planet for individual profit and national self-interest.

The stories of our ancestors and the consequences of their own fight for freedom has left a deep, traumatic imprint encoded in our DNA. If we are to transcend this traumatic pattern, we must establish conscious, intelligent, compassionate, and peaceful means in order to co-create together with existing global authority.

The need to integrate and heal the psychological split within ourselves and embrace a unified and harmonious political partnership

---

*A governance that has a dualistic approach, that is, an "us-versus-them" mentality that polarizes and splits rather than unifies people.

is essential if we are ever to shift the balance and co-create with the system-wide sociopolitical systems in existence today. It will require psychologically integrated and spiritually balanced humanitarians to guide twenty-first-century humanity in a new direction. It is such people who can offer the greatest potential for the evolutionary transformation of humanity and a peaceful and sustainable global community.

4. The year 2020 holds promise of contemporary spirituality for an evolving world. The premises and suggestions that I have discussed in this book support that promise and provide the necessary steps to cross the bridge into a new epoch with a new consciousness.

STEPPING OFF THE EDGE

The year 2012 took those of us who are psychologically and spiritually awake to the very edge of our evolutionary process in order to reveal the vast potential of all that lies beyond that point. The period leading to 2020 invites us to step off the edge of the old and into a new world paradigm—one that urgently requires wise stewardship.

I conclude with a simple yet appropriate quote by Guillaume Apollinaire, which invites us to overcome historical programming that has us falsely believe that we may "fall" if we actively seek change, that our vision for humanity is "too high," and that the evolutionary "push" for us to step off the edge of the old and into a new paradigm may not be supported by the evolutionary winds of change.

I invite you to follow the evolutionary impulse and step off the edge and into a new epoch for humanity:

Come to the edge, He said. They said, We are afraid. Come to the edge, He said. They came. He pushed them . . . and they flew.

GUILLAUME APOLLINAIRE

Afterword

Writing this book has been an entirely different experience from my previous one. Unlike *2012: A Clarion Call,* which I have always said wrote itself through me, this book was a different experience altogether, since I have written it! To have written both of these books has been fascinating and reassuring, too, for I have experienced both sides of the coin and have enjoyed them equally for very different reasons.

In this book, I have shared many unique evolutionary concepts and insights on personal and global evolution that were realized during my contemplations and meditations. There is so much within this book that can stand alone as teachings for psychological, conscious, and spiritual evolution. I really do feel that reading it could prove to be potentially life changing.

As you will have observed, this book includes many new evolutionary models, as well as an inspirational and unique map for evolving consciousness, which I wrote after encountering an ancient indigenous oral teaching many years ago. The Seven Dark, Seven Light, and Seven Rainbow Arrows stand as a complete model for psychological, conscious, and spiritual evolution.

In this book we have explored the true heart of religion, as well as a new approach to spirituality, which I term *Contemporary Spirituality for an Evolving World*. We have studied relationship and just what constitutes a higher love. We have looked at the reasons why the war with the ego has to stop and how we can literally love it into retirement. No more talk of "ego death"!

We have explored inner peace and how to embody this. We have realized that by cultivating peace in ourselves, we become co-creators of peace in the world. We have also established the necessity for new values and foundation stones, as reflected in the six core values for an evolving world and the twelve foundation stones for a new world paradigm, which I have written about in depth.

To further support psychological, conscious, and spiritual evolution are the three appendices. I specifically handpicked these for the transformational impact they can have on the evolving individual.

The focus of my work is to promote both personal and global evolution as crucial sides of the same coin. We could name this coin *peace,* which would be the main component in a currency of love. Throughout history the conscious human being has striven for a world in which peace and love prevail.

A new world needs to be built, one that reflects a new consciousness. It is those whose hearts and minds are awakened, and who have attained the required degree of evolutionary development, who will be the ones that evolve collective consciousness.

This book is for all those who are dedicated to consciously evolving and to those who feel they have a role in establishing new sociopolitical global systems that serve a new paradigm consciousness. What we can be sure of is that which we feel deep in our hearts, what we sense at a Soul level, and what becomes increasingly clear to us when we live a heart- and Soul-centered life.

And so my dear friends, I conclude with these final words:

> *I always wondered why somebody didn't do something about it, then I realized I am somebody.*
>
> (ANONYMOUS)

The Nature of an Evolved Planetary Consciousness

Sixteen Precepts

By Ervin Laszlo

1. I am part of the world. The world is not outside of me, and I am not outside of the world. The world is in me, and I am in the world.
2. I am part of nature, and nature is part of me. I am what I am in my communication and communion with all living things. I am an irreducible and coherent whole with the web of life on the planet.
3. I am part of society, and society is part of me. I am what I am in my communication and communion with my fellow humans. I am an irreducible and coherent whole with the community of humans on the planet.
4. I am more than a skin-and-bone material organism. My body and its cells and organs are manifestations of what is truly me: a self-sustaining, self-evolving dynamic system arising, persisting, and evolving in interaction with everything around me.
5. I am one of the highest, most evolved manifestations of the drive

toward coherence and wholeness in the universe. All systems drive toward coherence and wholeness in interaction with all other systems, and my essence is this cosmic drive. It is the same essence, the same spirit, that is inherent in all the things that arise and evolve in nature, whether on this planet or elsewhere in the infinite reaches of space and time.

6. There are no absolute boundaries and divisions in this world, only transition points where one set of relations yields prevalence to another. In me—in this self-maintaining and self-evolving, coherence- and wholeness-oriented system—the relations that integrate the cells and organs of my body are prevalent. Beyond my body other relations gain prevalence: those that drive toward coherence and wholeness in society and in nature.

7. The separate identity I attach to other humans and other things is but a convenient convention that facilitates my interaction with them. My family and my community are just as much "me" as the organs of my body. My body and mind, my family and my community, are interacting and interpenetrating—variously prevalent elements in the network of relations that encompasses all things in nature and the human world.

8. The whole gamut of concepts and ideas that separates my identity, or the identity of any person or community, from the identity of other persons and communities are manifestations of this convenient but arbitrary convention. There are only gradients distinguishing individuals from each other and from their environment and no real divisions and boundaries. There are no "others" in the world: we are all living systems and we are all part of each other.

9. Attempting to maintain the system I know as "me" through ruthless competition with the system I know as "you" is a grave mistake: it could damage the integrity of the embracing whole that frames both your life and mine. I cannot preserve my own life and wholeness by damaging that whole, even if damaging a part of it seems to bring me short-term advantage. When I harm you, or anyone else around me, I harm myself.

10. Collaboration, not competition, is the royal road to the wholeness that hallmarks healthy systems in the world. Collaboration calls for empathy and solidarity, and ultimately for love. I do not and cannot love myself if I do not love you and others around me: we are part of the same whole and so are part of each other.

11. The idea of "self-defense," even of "national defense," needs to be rethought. Patriotism, if it aims to eliminate adversaries by force, and heroism, even in the well-meaning execution of that aim, are mistaken aspirations. A patriot and a hero who brandishes a sword or a gun is an enemy also to himself. Every weapon intended to hurt or kill is a danger to all. Comprehension, conciliation, and forgiveness are not signs of weakness; they are signs of courage.

12. "The good" for me and for every person in the world is not the possession and accumulation of personal wealth. Wealth, in money or in any material resource, is but a means for maintaining myself in my environment. As exclusively mine, it commandeers part of the resources that all things need to share if they are to live and to thrive. Exclusive wealth is a threat to all people in the human community. And because I am a part of this community, in the final count it is a threat also to me, and to all who hold it.

13. Beyond the sacred whole we recognize as the world in its totality, only life and its development have what philosophers call intrinsic value; all other things have merely instrumental value: value insofar as they add to or enhance intrinsic value. Material things in the world, and the energies and substances they harbor or generate, have value only if and insofar as they contribute to life and well-being in the web of life on this Earth.

14. The true measure of my accomplishment and excellence is my readiness to give. The amount of what I give is not the measure of my accomplishment and excellence, but rather it is the relation between what I give, and what my family and I need to live and to thrive.

15. Every healthy person has pleasure in giving: it is a higher pleasure than having. I am healthy and whole when I value giving over having. A community that values giving over having is a community

of healthy people, oriented toward thriving through empathy, solidarity, and love among its members. Sharing enhances the community of life, while possessing and accumulating creates demarcation, invites competition, and fuels envy. The share-society is the norm for all the communities of life on the planet; the have-society is typical only of modern-day humanity, and it is an aberration.

16. I acknowledge my role and responsibility in evolving a planetary consciousness in me, and by example in others around me. I have been part of the aberration of human consciousness in the modern age, and now wish to become part of the evolution that overcomes the aberration and heals the wounds inflicted by it. This is my right as well as my duty, as a conscious member of a conscious species on a precious and now critically endangered planet.

Coming Home

Reweaving the Web of Life
By Wendy Webber

I offer this perspective into the conversation with a sense of gratitude at the opportunity to speak from a place of confluence and congruence. The confluence is of many tributaries that I have been following throughout my life, and the joy at finding them flowing together into a mighty river that I sense leads us back to the ocean of our belonging. The congruence is that I choose only to speak of those things that I have internalized experientially, or experienced while working with others, and while I will quote research at times and bring in various "authorities," the overall proposition comes from an inside place of *felt knowing*, not as "*the* truth," but as it currently lives in me.

I also want to say two things about myself: the first is that I have so far moved through life, now in my sixties, untouched by obvious trauma to me personally; the second is that I somehow came in with, and have maintained, an abiding sense of connection with Source. I don't say this is fortunate or unfortunate—it just is. Over the years, through my work

Originally published by the Association for the Advancement of Psychosynthesis in *Conversations in Psychosynthesis*.

as a core process psychotherapist in the '90s, and my work as a peace educator in the last decade, I have felt more and more drawn to working with people and systems where traumatization limits our capacity for choice and perpetuates suffering. In spite of the two things I wrote about myself, I have needed and continue to work diligently on freeing myself from the habitual patterns, individual and cultural, that keep us unconscious and in bondage to the myth of our separateness.

I chose the title "Coming Home" for two reasons: Firstly I propose a view that all trauma reflects the original trauma of our collective disconnection from Source, and the corresponding belief that we could be separate. It represents *fragmentation, disconnection,* and *disorientation* of our place in the scheme of things, and loss of our ability to navigate ourselves in the natural world of ebb and flow. Secondly, I propose the idea that a successful renegotiation of trauma calls us to "re-Source" ourselves in a way that gives us back our Self and our connection to Life.

One of the most important ingredients of successfully renegotiating trauma is to be able to stay connected to a felt experience of re-sourcing. As I use the word *re-source* I want us to picture it as a lifeline to Source—it is the way in which Source can inform us, a way in which we can be in presence to whatever else is arising in us. In that process I believe it brings us face to face with the unbroken wholeness which is our true identity of which Roberto Assagioli spoke.

My defining theme is that traumatization is not inherent in the natural order, even though it is "normal" and endemic in our human experience. Here I make the distinction between *trauma* as a physically or emotionally stressful experience that challenges the integrity of the person, and *traumatization* which occurs when the organism cannot process the energies of its shock response, so they remain in the system, cycling in what becomes the "trauma vortex," a tornado of trauma-bound energy.

John Firman and Ann Gila, in their book *The Primal Wound,* write about a widespread existential traumatization which they call *primal wounding,* and they say that "the ubiquity of primal wounding, its normalcy, must not be taken as a sign that it is necessarily innate or natural," or "that splitting is a natural phenomenon."* They use the term *splitting* to refer to a traumatized person's tendency to separate experience into two parts, one positive and one negative, in response to the trauma of disconnection.

This kind of splitting is only one of many self-separating or fragmenting responses that a person may use; therefore in this paper I am using the terms *splitting* and *fragmenting* interchangeably, using these terms to include the range of temporary defenses against the fear that we could be annihilated, based on the illusory belief of a separate existence.

In this context I come to Roberto Assagioli's approach to our relationship to Source, to Self: "There are not really two selves, two independent and separate entities. The Self is one: it manifests in different degrees of awareness and self-realization. The reflection (of Self, 'I') appears to be self-existent but has, in reality, no autonomous substantiality. It is, in other words, not a new and different light but a projection of its luminous source."† He also writes, "So complete is the giving of Self here that 'I' has even the freedom to disregard this relationship, and act in direct opposition to it."‡

The consequence of exercising that freedom to disregard this relationship results in a world where the belief that we are separate prevails, rather than an awareness of our existence as an integral and interconnected aspect of an unbroken whole. We have split ourselves off from the knowledge of who we truly are.

Faced with the consequences of this illusory belief, cut off from an experience of Source/Self, and our place in the natural order and scheme of things, we live as though our lifeline has been severed. It is as though we came through a doorway to see what separate looked like and we couldn't find the way back. The prevailing emotional background of this experience is fear.

We can see this fragmentation at work at the level of our biology.

---

*John Firman and Ann Gila, *The Primal Wound* (Albany: State University of New York Press, 1997), 100, 108.

†Roberto Assagioli, *Psychosynthesis: A Collection of Basic Writings* (New York: Viking Press, 1965), 20.

‡Roberto Assagioli, *The Act of Will* (New York: Viking Press, 1973).

In life-threatening situations or when we perceive ourselves to be threatened the psyche is *designed* to fragment. This is intended as a temporary defense, as a kind of shock absorber for the self; but when the natural reintegration is thwarted, parts of the consciousness may remain fixated in various places throughout space and time. Now we perceive ourselves and our world in terms of parts, and not as an interconnected whole. At the psychological level we start to perceive reality in terms of polarities—good and bad, right and wrong, either/or, me or you, my world view or yours. We become disconnected from our sensing, feeling organism that keeps us informed moment by moment of the flow of life, and rely on concepts and constructs based on the past.

The split in our sense of being becomes a fragmenting of our awareness. This in turn is reflected in our relationships with others and with the environment, which become characterized by attitudes of dominance or submission, violence and disregard for life—believing we can get our needs met at the expense of others. Thus inner fragmentation creates imbalance within the whole system of life on Earth.

The second part of my theme is built upon the proposition by Firman and Gila, that the cause of primal wounding (in the individual) is not specific events, but the absence of some empathic other and by a break in our connection to Self. In their view, splitting is caused essentially by a failure in the environment to mirror the wholeness of a person.*

They also say in their book *Psychosynthesis: A Psychology of the Spirit,* "We call the effects of these empathic failures primal wounding, not because this wounding is early or primitive, but because it breaks this primal—that is, fundamental or essential—connection to the ground of our being. . . . It was disruption in empathic connection that caused the splitting off of these layers, and thus it is only empathic connection that can heal them."†

They also say "It is crucial here to point out that this level of psychological trauma can occur with no conscious intention on the part of

---

*Firman and Gila, *Primal Wound*, 107.

†John Firman and Ann Gila, *Psychosynthesis: A Psychology of the Spirit* (Albany: State University of New York Press, 2002), 122, 128.

the ones who wound us . . . we can imagine a river of wounding flowing down to us through the generations, a river that takes on collective proportions."* I will return to this later.

Traumatization in essence is about broken connections. I contend that all individual traumatization responses are fractal expressions of the original one where the collective psyche fragmented, and our ability to reintegrate depends on the successful renegotiation of these fractal expressions. During the last few decades there have been enormous leaps in our understanding of the way trauma affects our biology and psychology.

There is also a growing inclusion of ancient Eastern understanding of our energy body through the meridian system, and also the shamanic understanding of the cause, effects, and treatment of traumatization. President Barack Obama has spoken of the importance of empathy and how we need to pay as much attention to the "empathy deficit" as to the federal deficit. As a collective, we are starting to wake up to this missing piece that will reweave the web of life.

For our purposes, relating to how to create empathic bridges that bring the fragmented parts of us back into wholeness, I will be referring to us *as* individuals, but as we do this, I suggest that we are also healing the original traumatization of our collective belief/illusion that we could actually separate from the One. As each of us awakens from the dream to embody our wholeness, so we can mirror that wholeness to others.

Based on this understanding of the cause of traumatization, I want to devote the rest of this paper to a number of modalities that I practice, ways that support the healing of traumatization with its concurrent broken connections, ways that enable a reintegration of the fragmented psyche and thus our return home.

I invite you to share an image to illustrate what I am presenting here: Picture three concentric circles. In the inner circle is Source (home) and included here is the word *presence,* as the mode of being that permeates us when we are in uninterrupted connection with Source. The outer or

---

*Firman and Gila, *Psychosynthesis,* 123.

third circle is how we live in this material world. The middle or second circle comprises the models, maps, understanding, and skill sets that help us bridge the gap between the inner and outer circles.

It also comprises the beliefs and concepts that distort—it is the realm of our psychology. When we are in uninterrupted connection with Source we don't need the second circle; however, most of us do. With a broken connection, we appear to live in a world characterized by fragmentation, relationship breakdown, polarization, good/bad, right/wrong, war, violence, winners and losers—and the river of wounding flows on, generation after generation.

Now picture the words *felt-sense* and *needs* right at the intersection of the inner circle with the middle circle. We have to use words, but in fact these are fundamental organic aspects of our "human beingness." This is how Source informs us of how to be in the world in life-serving ways, moment by moment.

Focusing and nonviolent communication (NVC), two modalities that have been most influential for me over many years, work through these fundamental aspects. Felt-sensing is at the heart of focusing, and an experience of universal human needs is at the heart of NVC. The developers of these two process models and skill sets, Eugene Gendlin and Marshall Rosenberg, did not create felt-sensing or identifying our needs as new activities, but they recognized them as integral aspects of our nature, and as ways to return to our nature. They developed and taught process steps that would enable those of us caught up in the outer circle, cut off from our nature, with distorted views about the nature of reality, to find our way back home.

Sometimes we can get lost in the method and miss the essence. So I'd like to speak to the essence of these two modalities, and leave my reader to learn of the specific skill sets through the references at the end of this article.

At the heart of both of these processes are empathic listening and generative listening, which then gives rise to life-serving actions and the restoration of right relationship. *Empathic listening* is simply being present to what is, with no attempt to "hide it, fix it, or fade it." In both focusing and NVC training and practice, most emphasis is placed on how to listen in these ways, and how to identify and undo the habits of our culture that take us away from this ability. "Empathy allows us to re-perceive our world in a new way and move on," as Marshall Rosenberg has said.* *Generative listening* enables us to hold a space for what wants to emerge, what wants to happen as we move on, after empathic listening has done its work.

In relation to traumatized energy it means we let our organism's knowing lead the way in releasing trauma-bound energy; this allows the completion of incomplete responses that restore our system to balance and dynamic equilibrium. In relation to the healthy organism, generative listening allows the creative mind full play.

Within the specific form that has been developed by Marshall Rosenberg in NVC, we find this principle at work when we refrain from finding or using specific strategies until the needs of those concerned are heard and held with care. In conflict situations, once there is trust among people that their voices will be heard and needs held with care, then it isn't long before creative solutions start to surface. Individually this process also applies to the inner relationship healing of all our "parts," resolving inner conflicts.

Firman and Gila say, "From the point of view of the individual, empathy is thus the force that *integrates* or *synthesizes* the personality. Through self-empathy we can hold all of the different parts of us, allowing a sense of inner multiplicity and unity at the same time. . . . At a social level, empathic connection functions much the same way; empathy is the source of a solidarity with others and the planet that can hold both unity and differences."†

Gendlin speaks to this in an oft-quoted piece from an article published in 1990 entitled "The Small Steps of the Therapy Process: How They Come and How to Help Them Come": "Focusing is this very deliberate thing where an *I* is attending to an *it*. . . . The client and I,

---

*Marshall Rosenberg, *Nonviolent Communication: A Language of Life,* 2nd ed. (Encinitas, Calif.: PuddleDancer Press, 2003).
†Firman and Gila, *Psychosynthesis, 146.*

we are going to keep it, in there, company. . . . What that edge needs to produce the steps is only some kind of unintrusive contact or company. If you will go there with your awareness, and stay there, or return there, that is all it needs; it will do all the rest for you."*

Peter Levine, in *Waking the Tiger,* writes of the felt sense as "a tool that can help you get to know yourself as a complex, biological and spiritual organism. The felt sense is simple and elegant. Yet, it is billions of times more sophisticated than the most powerful computers." He says, "As we begin the healing process we use what is known as the felt sense, or internal body sensations. These sensations serve as a portal through which we find the symptoms, or reflections of trauma. In directing our attention to these internal body sensations . . . we can unbind and free the energies that have been held in check."†

In my experience of it, the felt sense is the portal through which Source informs us, where the formless starts to take form; that's why it is close to awareness. It is subtle, and has not yet split into polarities. Being with the felt sense of any situation or experience, without conceptualizing it, takes us to the place where forward movement that is life serving is sensed and can unfold. We experience it through the holistic capacity of the heart and its neural connections to the whole-sensing right side of the brain. When we find just the right descriptive word, phrase, image, or gesture that resonates with the felt sense, the left side of the brain synchronizes with the right side. Our whole organism sighs with relief as we have a temporary experience of wholeness.

Ultimately I believe true healing is facilitated by supporting connection to the felt sense, in ourselves and others. Any content that is structured from the outside—guided imagery, guided meditations, and so forth—can lead us so far, but the guide that is the most resonant with our own moment-by-moment needs, and what needs to happen, is our internal experience through the felt sense.

---

*Eugene Gendlin, "The Small Steps of the Therapy Process: How They Come and How to Help Them Come," in *Client-Centered and Experiential Psychotherapy in the Nineties* (Leuven, Neth.:Leuven University Press, 1990), 205.
†Peter Levine, *Waking the Tiger* (Berkeley, Calif.: North Atlantic Books, 1997), 66.

This brings me to two other modalities that I use in conjunction with empathic and generative listening. These are EFT (emotional freedom technique) and "The Work" of Byron Katie. To introduce these I want to quote the simple question on the Work website: "Who would you be without your story?"

Our story can be as simple as "he's a liar," "I'm no good at singing," "all women are fickle," "my father never loved me," "I'll never get it right," "God will punish me," ad infinitum. There is no shortage of stories going round in our heads, triggering emotions, and interrupting the natural flow of energy through our body. Within the premise offered here that all wounding comes from breaks in empathic connection, we also understand that all stories get generated from those breaks, when we are in survival brain thinking.

We generate stories to create meaning and to try to feel safe in a world where separation seems to rule. When those stories have been in our neural circuitry for a long time, and particularly when they got imprinted in early experience in nonverbal ways, they form the "nearly unbreakable tape loop" that Joseph Chilton Pierce speaks of in his book *The Biology of Transcendence*. We can call this type of listening downloading—we are just listening to the same old stories (beliefs) time after time, and repeating the same old emotions, and eventually the body symptomizes that.

This is another way of describing Peter Levine's "trauma vortex," the cycling of undischarged energies that eventually results in psychological and physical symptoms.

A second loop, or neural pathway, can be established: a three-way connection between the emotional and the cognitive brain, the prefrontal lobes and the heart. We can think of this as the healing vortex, or the way home. This is the loop that empathic listening invites us into.

At the threshold to these two loops lies another form of listening: "factual" or observational listening. The NVC process starts with observation. It requires us to pause and notice. In focusing it's called the revolutionary pause, where we can start to notice inside ourselves what wants to be noticed. It is here at this threshold that the process of inquiry in the form of Katie's four questions can break the tape loop if we are willing to pause, notice, and identify/write down our story.

Byron Katie invites us to ask these four questions:

Is it true?
Can I absolutely know that it is true?
How do I react (feel), or what happens when I believe that thought?
Who would I be without that thought?

After experiencing the answer to these questions, we are invited to create turnarounds, statements that reflect alternatives, to the concept we are questioning.

Another modality that I use, the emotional freedom technique (a technique of energy tapping/meridian therapy), is also a great blessing for individuals and for our planet. EFT has been developed by Gary Craig as a self-help process that evolved from the discoveries of Dr. Roger Callaghan. It is a relatively new arrival on the scene, only developing in the 1990s, and it seems was forecast by Assagioli when he said, "But God is energy and the religion of the next century will be the study of energy."*

The radical discovery statement that energy psychology makes is, "The cause of all negative emotions is a disruption in the body's energy system."

It has been assumed previously (and still is in many circles) that the memory of past traumatic experience is the direct cause of the emotional upset in a person. The premise in EFT is that this is not so. There is an intermediate step—a missing piece—between the memory and the emotional upset. That intermediate step is the disruption in the body's energy system, in its flow through the meridians that are known to Chinese medical practice. It is this disruption that is the direct cause of the emotional upset. When the disruption is released, and the flow restored, the memory will remain, but without the traumatized emotional correlation.

This observation corresponds with Firman and Gila's proposition that it is not the event that causes wounding, but a break in the flow

---

*Assagioli, *Psychosynthesis.*

of connection. Empathy restores the flow and so, it seems, does energy tapping, judging by the amazing success stories and documented research with war veterans and others.

In my own work with this process with myself and clients over a period of nearly ten years, *I have found that the tapping process itself acts as an empathic connector.* There are many ways to explain the principle involved with the energy tapping techniques. Essentially what has been discovered is that stimulating the body in specific ways (for instance, tapping at key locations on the body, such as acupoints) while tuning in to a negative emotion, belief, physical symptom, or memory, changes the electrical flow in the meridians, and chemical processes within the body.

Acknowledgement of the current experience of reality is brought to focus by tapping at the meridian end points with a *reality statement* that acknowledges current feelings or other conditions. A beginning set-up process is used to correct psychological reversal, otherwise known as self-sabotage. This is brought about by tapping while stating first the current negative emotion (such as "even though I feel guilty about . . .") and then using a turnaround phrase or a self-acceptance phrase (such as "I deeply and completely accept myself, with all my problems and limitations").

I find this process to be very congruent with the main premise presented here, which is that we need to start with the current reality (not denial) and bring that to an empathic presence that can hold anything. It also presents a way to break that survival brain tape loop, and bring it into the heart brain loop, moving the client (or self) from the trauma vortex to the healing vortex.

Refinements and variations of EFT have been developed by many others, and I have found Dr. Pat Carrington's EFT choices method to be a simple and empowering way to actively use and continuously develop the Will in the terms Roberto Assagioli describes: "Its skillful and consequently successful use consists in regulating and directing all other functions toward a deliberately chosen and affirmed aim."*

The general protocol of the EFT choices method identifies the current reality while tapping on it, and then effects the turnaround by tap-

---

*Assagioli, *Psychosynthesis*, 8.

ping while using a choice phrase. While the default for the choice phrase is "I choose to feel calm and confident," the range of choices is nearly unlimited. A choice is made by the client in the present. This process is empowering, and is in many ways like a concrete doable request to ourselves if we are willing. It brings us into the present, not into an unrealistic future. (This also happens to be the fourth component of the nonviolent communication process.)

Before bringing these four methodologies alive with an experiential example, I want to make a few further comments regarding the journey of "coming home." A crucial factor here is *readiness*. No amount of self-help skills or therapeutic interventions are effective until the individual is ready.

Sometimes at a certain point in the evolution of our consciousness, a crisis or a traumatic event may open up the fault line that leads us to face those breaks in relationship and failures of empathic connection, reflections of the original separation from Self and Source. Something in us knows when we can call in the internal and external resources to help us navigate our way through. Firman and Gila speak of "a river of wounding flowing down to us through the generations, a river that takes on collective proportions,"* and a spiritual teacher of mine reminded us to say "let this end with me."

When we say, "let this end with me" we take on a massive work. It means we are taking on the responsibility of transforming (within our biology, our psychology, and our soul) the river of wounding, and of bringing it back into the river of life. It is here that I see the active use of and continuous development of the Will, as Assagioli describes it: "In times of silence and meditation, in the careful examination of our motives, or in the thoughtful pondering on decisions, there arises within us a voice, small but distinct, that urges us in a certain direction; a voice different from that of our ordinary motives and impulses. We feel that it comes from the real and central core of our being."†

I believe that Assagioli was describing here what we now call the felt

---

*Firman and Gila, *Psychosynthesis*, 123.
†Assagioli, *The Act of Will*.

sense: "However, the simplest and most frequent way in which we discover our will lies in determined action and struggle. When we make a physical or mental effort, when we are actively wrestling with some obstacle or opposing forces, we feel a specific power rising up within us; we become animated by an inner energy and experience a sense of *willing*."*

My experience is that "let this end with me" bubbles up at some point from the core of our being, and then there is the day-by-day use of *willing* to keep us true to that intent, or return to it when we falter or lose our way.

Finally, referencing the river of wounding flowing down to us through the generations leads me to include the work of Anngwyn St. Just, which she brings to us in her recent book, *A Question of Balance: A Systemic Approach to Understanding and Resolving Trauma*. A long-time colleague of Peter Levine, St. Just's current work has developed out of her connection with the work of Bert Hellinger and his "family constellations" work, and out of her own research.

To summarize it very simply, she makes the assertion that as we seek to heal traumatization and return a system to balance, it is not only the individual nervous system that develops symptoms with incomplete responses, but entire families and other systems (including national and racial groupings) also suffer from interrupted and incomplete responses. "In the study of trauma within a family, one often finds that traumas occur in relationship to current or previous imbalances in the system . . . if broken connections are not addressed, healing cannot happen."†

This brings me back full circle to recognition of the underlying cause of traumatization, which is broken connections in the web of life, with a belief in our separateness and all that follows from that belief. We are poised collectively at a threshold, where a realization is starting to dawn in the collective psyche that the answer lies within. This is a very significant time. Think how much of our collective world consciousness is currently focused outward—believing that "authority" is somewhere "out

---

*Assagioli, *The Act of Will*.

†Anngwyn St. Just, *A Question of Balance: A Systemic Approach to Understanding and Resolving Trauma* (Charleston, S.C.: BookSurge, 2008), 121–22.

there," that something outside of ourselves is responsible, and can fix us.

We must turn our direction from outward to inward to cross back over the threshold. I call it the eye of a needle. I believe it requires us to become present, unencumbered by baggage of the past, or fear of the future, in order to pass through. Through traumatization, aspects of our psyche have become frozen in space/time warps, and there is a massive work to be done, not only for individuals, but also for families, races, and nations. The wounds are many but the cause is only one.

The methodologies I have described here are invaluable when they are incorporated into the therapeutic process, but fundamentally they can be made available to all, and are all dedicated to moving us from pathology (disconnection) to coming home to our divine/human potential.

I rejoice in the fact that at this crucial time in our human evolution, we are being given tools and processes that can be made available to all, and that they are not dependent on external relationships, but rather support us as we reweave our own broken connection with Self and Source, through deep empathic relationship and through dissolving the mental and emotional obstacles to Love's expression. As we reweave our own broken connections, so we are reweaving the whole web of life.

IN PRACTICE

I have had the great privilege over the past year to be accompanying a woman on her journey of healing and awakening. I am in awe of her (and her husband's) courage, and single-minded commitment to halt the generational traumatization they came into, by their fundamental prayer, "Let this end with me," and their choice to remove all obstacles to Love's expression.

It is the most profound journey I have been blessed to participate in, and it is also enabling me to deepen my understanding of what I write about here. I will call her Grace, and I would like to share just a very small window into the work we have done together that I hope will illustrate both the premises of this paper, and some of the practices at work.

Grace was carried in a womb of fear, lived throughout her childhood with fear and terror, experienced abandonment at times, ongoing abuse from her father, and an almost complete lack of empathic other with whom any of her experiences could be heard or held. She made two attempts to end her life before she was twenty.

It is a testament to her spiritual strength and creative power that she created "sub-personalities" and a fantasy world that helped her to survive until the time she was able to begin her journey of healing and return. While that journey started many years ago, I was invited to come into her life about a year ago, at a time when they knew nowhere else to turn. We have met in person three times, and talk daily on the phone.

I see myself as a midwife to the Self coming into manifestation—to turn emergency into emergence. My role is to be that empathic other: holding the knowledge of her wholeness, unfazed by extremes of fear and anguish at times when her own knowing is temporarily overwhelmed or hidden, offering her reflection of her true identity and practices that gradually and gently dissolve the obstacles to Love's expression, which is her own fundamental choice.

Within that empathic holding, the work has been to build up felt experience of resourced states (rare moments when she experienced connection that was safe and loving, or when she finally found the power to stop her father's abuse) and her own deep connection to God and current loving relationships, using embodied practices like focusing to develop resilience.

The work has also involved cultivating her ability to just "be with" her arising experience of anxiety and to help her to acquire the skill to use energy tapping as a way to "depotentize" the intensity of negative emotions and old beliefs that no longer serve, and to clear the disruption of these old beliefs and emotions from her energy system. Sometimes we work together, but she has also learned to use the techniques on her own, and she has become skilled at detecting the specific aspects at work and at creating beautifully crafted, forward-moving choices for herself. Yet sometimes an unrecognized thought takes hold, the anxiety gets too high, and she needs to reach out for help.

Then it is important to detect the thoughts that create the suffering, and sometimes use Byron Katie's inquiry process of four questions. Interrupting the thoughts and the negative emotions that are part of the survival brain loop is a big piece of the work, and this allows her to shepherd the energy into the heart/brain loop.

Sometimes it is necessary to follow an incomplete response, something that was arrested, for example the expression of grief, or a physical shaking; sometimes what is needed is just being present to wordless raw experience that has been carried in the body cells since the womb, and learning to let the wave pass through.

Much of her work has been bringing her "girls," (the sub-personalities that developed along the way so she could survive) into the loving, safe reality of the present. Above all, working with this devoutly spiritual woman is to discover and celebrate with her how God, Spirit, and the Self have been there always.

Here is an excerpt from one of our sessions, at a time when she has committed herself to coming off the medications that she has been taking since she had a breakdown two years ago.

GRACE. There's such a lot for me to have to do. *[anxiety rising as she thinks of the many things she is doing—some medical and many holistic]* I tend to make everything a chore.

She expressed a worry that comes up a lot when she so longs for this ordeal to be over, and is discouraged by being told that withdrawing from medications is a slow process. So we put the Byron Katie questions to the thought she'd just declared, with rising anxiety, of "I'm in for a long haul, what am I going to do?"

Is that true?

Can I absolutely know that is true? "No."

How do I react/feel when I have that thought? "Discouraged, scared."

Who would I be without that thought? "I would be free each day to be who God wants me to be, where He wants me to be, peaceful."

Then we turn that into an energy tapping phrase, a choice phrase to be used while tapping on the EFT points. "Even though I have this long haul, discouraged and scared, I choose the joy of knowing I can be God's servant no matter what."

In effect, with the inquiry (always done within an empathic holding, never with judgment), and then the tapping, she navigated herself from the survival brain loop to the heart/brain loop, and returned to calm. After that we turned to the habitual pattern of making everything into a chore.

Nonviolent communication is very helpful in highlighting language that comes from black-and-white thinking (survival brain), such as using language like have to, should, or must. So we looked at the need underneath the feelings, which was to have choice and ease. After that, a strategy naturally presented itself, which was to create for herself a buffet of choices from the many strategies she uses daily (qigong, devotional reading, and many others activities—she found over twenty). She wrote and drew these choices in little circles within a big holding circle on a sheet of paper, and then it became more of an enjoyable experience to go to the circle and let her bodily felt knowing choose what was "right" in the moment (using her felt sense).

I'd like to finish this offering with a poem that came from the heart of Grace, a piece that she wrote following a really strong wave of clearing some deeply imprinted fear, and after her system had come back into balance.

The Promise

The wolf and the lamb shall feed together
And the lion shall eat straw like an ox
They shall not hurt or destroy in all my holy
mountain
For the earth shall be full of the knowledge of God.
[From Isaiah 65:25 and 11:9]
All that was created from Another, will come together
to be as one.
So they won't hurt each other anymore.
My heart beats out its silent, single note. . . . One, one,
Knowing that this is my part,
My duty to the All in All,
To answer all that hurts and is hurt
With the boundless, unstoppable, single note of LOVE.

◆

WENDY WEBBER is a United Kingdom-trained transpersonal psychotherapist who has worked with people suffering from traumatization for many years. She teaches NVC and focusing to individuals, parents, families, and organizations and maintains a private practice in Marlboro, Vermont.

◆

"COMING HOME" BIBLIOGRAPHY

Assagioli, Roberto. *The Act of Will.* New York: Viking Press, 1973.

———. *Psychosynthesis: A Collection of Basic Writings.* New York: Viking Press, 1965.

Firman, John, and Ann Gila. *The Primal Wound.* Albany: State University of New York Press, 1997.

———. *Psychosynthesis: A Psychology of the Spirit.* Albany: State University of New York Press, 2002.

Gendlin, Eugene. "The Small Steps of the Therapy Process: How They Come and How to Help Them Come," in *Client-Centered and Experiential*

Psychotherapy in the Nineties. Leuven, Neth.: Leuven University Press, 1990.

Levine, Peter. *Waking the Tiger.* Berkeley, Calif.: North Atlantic Books, 1997.

Pierce, Joseph Chilton. *The Biology of Transcendence.* Rochester, Vt.: Park Street Press, 2002.

Rosenberg, Marshall. *Nonviolent Communication: A Language of Life,* 2nd ed. Encinitas, Calif.: PuddleDancer Press, 2003.

St. Just, Anngwyn. *A Question of Balance: A Systemic Approach to Understanding and Resolving Trauma.* Charleston, S.C.: BookSurge, 2008.

ONLINE RESOURCES

Patricia Carrington's EFT Choices website. www.masteringeft.com

The Center for Nonviolent Communication website. www.cnvc.org

Gary Craig's Emotional Freedom Technique website. www.emofree.com

The Focusing Institute website. www.focusing.org

Byron Katie's The Work website. www.thework.com

APPENDIX THREE

Twin Flame Discourses

The following is taken from a set of discourses between myself and a heart brother, Padma Aon, author of *The Power of Shakti: 18 Pathways to Ignite the Energy of the Divine Woman* and coauthor of *Womb Wisdom: Awakening the Creative and Forgotten Powers of the Feminine*. It is a written conversation that took place over a number of days in February 2012, in which we explored varying aspects of the subject of twin flame love. I felt it to be an important addition to the discussion of twin flame love, as it delves deeply into and opens up the subtler layers of this subject, in a way that sometimes only a spontaneous conversation can. Padma has given his consent for me to do so.

Padma: Is it necessary to be with a partner, to enter sacred union with another human in order to become at one with God to enter into becoming this new human being of light? I have always felt this for me, but now I am not so sure. To trust, respect, and love another human being so deeply, intimately, and to let them fully in, to engage in Soul union, seems to be a very rare occurrence. What do you feel? I would appreciate your take on this.

Nicolya: Your inquiry is interesting in terms of my own thoughts as I have only just, yesterday, finished writing a piece on twin flames.

257

I feel Souls originally venture from Source in an "as one" state of Being and that descending into matter creates a split to occur. I believe that we become imprinted with a longing and unconsciously seek to return to the "as one" state. First we seek this with God/Source/Creator, but then we begin to "know" that we also long to become as one with another, as we recognize that this too is a pathway we can take to return to All that Is.

In essence, humans cannot fully comprehend the full Truth of existence, for our capacities within the human form limit us far too much. I do feel that all humans, the unawakened and more especially those who are consciously awake, understand by their gnosis that there is a fundamental Truth behind the phenomenon known as twin flames. For so long we have been at an evolutionary level of maturity that has dictated that the continuation of the species is what compels people into relationship. Yet, our deepest, deepest gnosis reveals that we are, indeed, continually searching and seeking our other half—and that we have been doing so ever since our perceived original separation from Source.

The extent to which we know this is entirely dependent upon the evolution of the individual Soul. The evolution of the Soul is mirrored in the type of relationship it finds itself in, especially love/romantic relationship. Very few are ready for total honesty, total surrender, total trust, absolute devotion, total transparency, complete merging, absolute respect, impeccability of conduct, conscious and nonviolent communication, harmony, or to lose oneself in love in order to find one's true self and experience oneness with their beloved.

For, at unconscious and conscious levels, humans are working through much process, history, karma, and in order to do this, seek drama to release, heal, and gain closure on that which stands in the way of the highest and most exalted level of human expression.

The highest evolved relationship seeks only harmony—and all that supports the experience of this—where the focus is not on the Self, but on the service that can be offered to the world, together, as one.

People speak of longing for a twin flame relationship, yet the reality is most are not ready for it. The cultivation, refinement, and self-mastery it requires are not present within most people. Self-love, self-awareness, self-realization, sacred inner union, and integration of all parts (shadow/ Light, ego/Self, Male/Female, personality/Soul, and more) are what is required.

I feel, when it comes to the examples of those such as Gandhi, the Dalai Lama, Amma, Thich Nhat Hanh, and many other beacons of light for humanity, that perhaps this process has already completed during former incarnations in this dimension. My sense is that these beings come to Earth as twin flames already embodied as one, or one incarnates on Earth with the other half remaining in the heavenly realms to support the other in service to humanity. It is also possible that both are incarnated at the same time, in different bodies here to fulfill a role for humanity, and that the place in which they meet in union is in their devotion to God/Source/Creator. Indeed, Thich Nhat Hanh has spoken of a great love he himself experienced.

With such high beings all their earthly needs are met so that they are free to do the work they have come to do. It is the wholeness of who they are that enables them to give themselves over entirely to a relationship with God/Source/Creator, an all encompassing connection that fully supports the chosen service they have come to offer to humanity. It's a long, long conversation, Padma, for as I write I am purposely not delving into deeper levels that would take me away from the main points I am trying to share.

And of course, this is all I am doing—sharing. For this is only my understanding and perception, so far.

Padma: Yes, I have written about much of what you say about twin flames, so yes I understand . . . and what to do if one of the flames is in a much worse soul condition and stage of evolution than the other? Yes, love can see no difference, but discernment also sees that the other may have many issues that may not mean one can trust that person, as they themselves are not trusting their own self, respecting their own self, honest with their own self, or loving one's own self, which is the foundation for any kind of love to be shared truly and unconditionally to another.

This is quite a common occurrence I have witnessed—that one is more evolved than the other, and has to be more of the guide and teacher, and it takes great patience and compassion to be with such a process. Maybe they are not twins, because twins surely have to be highly evolved and greatly healed in order to meet each other? What do you feel?

My desire and deep feeling for many years was always to be with an equal, a twin, in total mutuality, learning and sharing and helping each other to grow together in love, and giving to others in that mutual equality so the cycle is completed in truth. The respect and trust I would feel for this woman, and her own soul condition and loving truth she is holding by herself, would inspire me, the man, to surrender and open more to her, and vice versa. This has been my feeling.

I do love what you share here, always close to my heart, "The highest evolved relationship seeks only harmony—and all that supports the experience of such. Where the focus is not on the Self, but on the service that can be offered to the world, as one."

What about all the beings throughout history who have merged with God, without being with their twin? And of course there have been many who have also.

Nicolya: In response to the question in your first paragraph, Padma—this is an interesting point. Again, here is my own perception, which may not be the whole story but is how I understand the truth at this time.

I believe that when both twin flames are incarnate, that they only ever enter each other's lives when they are ready for an exalted level of human union and that they undergo all their healing while on their journey to meet each other in what we would term soul mate relationships. This completes upon meeting the twin soul. In terms of soul mate relationships there are many; for twin souls, there are a handful; yet for twin flame, there is only ever one.

My sense is that if anything other than the experience of what constitutes true twin flame love comes to us, then this is most likely to be a soul mate connection, although perhaps a highly advanced level of this. There are different levels of soul mate unions that are necessary to experience before we can encounter a twin soul. We either remain with a twin soul for life, or, as a result of the gentle clearing of the final residues of the healing and evolution of the human heart, we are led to our twin flame. Our twin soul could even transpire to be our twin flame, as we evolve to the level of self-actualization required to reunite with them.

So coming back to your question of "one being evolved more than the other," my sense is this is not the twin flame. I believe they evolve at the same level, simultaneously, reuniting in a single lifetime as twin flames, which can be defined by the quality of experience that they have of each other, and that others have of them.

In response to your final musing regarding the beings who have merged with God/Source, I can only go back to my thoughts shared yesterday—that I believe that they have already merged with the twin flame in previous incarnations, or never split in the first place and may be avatars who are incarnating for the first time on Earth and therefore arrive here as one, in one physical form, in devotional service to God/Source, humanity, all sentient beings, and the Earth.

There must be rare exceptions who incarnate as two beings to find each other and become as one, such as Yeshua and Magdalene, in order to mirror to the world that we have never been separated from Source, only from ourselves, and that such a union as twin flames brings us back to the truth of who we really are, and back into the center of the heart of God/Source.

Padma: There are many ideas about twins: yet the truth of love and humility and the actual twins I know is that they grow together despite the soul condition they are in. To not be in relationship and await a twin is a brave choice, and I appreciate that purity actually, and a certain degree of sexual mastery may be attained by this, but true mastery and total vulnerability will only happen with the twin while making love.

I can resonate with a lot of what you are sharing as deeply held beliefs of my own, which may or may not be absolutely True. One will only know when one is healed and with one's twin at the same time.

And yes, I have no memory either, so how is one to know such a love?

My life is full of Divine Love, and I am very blessed. Relatings help the healing into love for both souls has been my experience, and for that I am happy. There has been no drama involved in that either for me, in the last piece of time.

Nicolya: Here is a line I would like to share with you from something I have written, "Twin flame reunion requires the highest level of human and spiritual evolution on the part of the incarnated soul."

Here is what I believe at this point. We have to be at the highest level of human evolution to be in such a relationship. I believe that incarnated Souls at this level of evolution are rare; and yet, I am also aware that there are more on the planet now than at any other time in our known human history.

I feel that our evolution into Beings of Light does not require, nor is it dependent upon, such a union. However, my sense is that to become fully at one with God, or Source, does require the reunion of the two, who become one, whether this happens in this incarnation or a future one.

My perception informs me that for Souls who have attained an advanced level of conscious evolution, and even for those who have not, there are realities we become aware of by gnosis that are imprinted into our molecular and cellular memory, the biopsychospiritual blueprint, and the Divine genetic coding of the very essence of our Being.

Many people believe in past lives, most in a supreme divine force, call it God/Source/Creator, yet will not have had direct conscious experience of this, although we all energetically and superconsciously experience God/Source/Creator in every breath.

My gnosis and the guidance that comes through me from my own spiritual guides, inform me of this: that as we evolve toward human perfection, the energy bodies are released of all old imprints and memories and are cleared, cleansed, and purified. This increases the rate at which we vibrate and raises the energetic frequency of an individual. At this point, the truth of twin flame love downloads into the energetic fields, which in turn inform an aligned consciousness of such an evolutionary reality. At this stage, we come to use gnosis to understand the truth of twin flame love and, at this level of experiencing, we embody this as a living truth.

As it is revealed to me, the physical is the final body to be permeated by this experience and, when this occurs, all levels of our Being come to fully know this truth. Until this point, it remains exclusively a reality in the superconscious mind and in gnosis unconsciously, or consciously. My perception informs me that awakened and awakening incarnate souls understand by gnosis the truth of twin flame love at varying levels of awareness and consciousness depending on the degree of awakening.

Even Souls who remain asleep feel compelled toward romance, although this may be a momentary experience, which, like a match, burns out quickly. At this point, they seek another relationship to meet that compulsion, which science has categorized as stemming from a primal procreative drive. Yet true wisdom is only ever to be found within the heart, not the brain or lower mind. Even at these earlier levels of conscious awakening, the psyche senses something of the heart and is compelled toward romantic connection.

In the case of those who remain asleep, or are just stirring to an awakening consciousness, the light of revelation has too many psychological and karmic layers that are necessary to penetrate through in order to reveal the "more than," which they are compelled toward.

So, to conclude, my perception is that awakening and awakened souls recognize twin flame love through information the true Self receives through the energetic levels of the nonphysical bodies. In that, the physical experience is not the icing on the cake, for it is the anchoring of such a love, this ultimate reunion itself and how it serves as an evolutionary contribution to humanity and the Earth (twin flame love is also about two as one in service of bringing more Light to the planet and the collective consciousness), and this is what becomes the driving force that propels twin flames back together.

The physical embodiment of twin flame love marks the completion point of a journey of gnosis that began eons ago following the initial separation. The memory and reality of twin flames has emerged into our awareness as the Soul has become more and more awakened.

The greatest spiritual teachers and Lights to have walked this world were/are most likely two as one incarnate. If not, their twin flame walks with them in the higher realms, working with them to bridge heaven and Earth. Avatars, as Beings with no history of earthly lives who have spoken of twin flame love, know the truth of the existence of them. Their evolutionary advancement and capacity for higher-dimensional overview enables them to know things that are not fully revealed to humans.

All knowledge of the highest spiritual laws and realities are known by the few who have incarnated such as Buddha, Krishna, Jesus, Allah, and other Beings. Twin flame love is a spiritual love beyond anything else we experience and, as such, its basis in reality as a real phenomena is known by the rare handful of the highest evolved beings who have walked the Earth.

The pure truth of twin flame love is a reality that comes to all at some point in their existence as a human Soul, and especially to those who have achieved a certain level of evolutionary development who are experiencing a sequence of earthly lives.

It is a rare phenomenon to be reunited with our twin flame; yet the times we are living in now offer an unprecedented opportunity for the most awakened of us to do so, as an exception to the rule has been decreed by universal law.

Padma: To continue on the discourses: I feel that there will be a process between beloveds, and it will not be trying or a conflict, for sure; but there will be a process of opening, releasing, and heightening of emotions, pleasurable and painful, as between beloveds a great love is unleashed that brings up all that is not love within the souls involved.

[The experience of] life and love and creation is a process, so to not want this is going against what is. I too felt this is what I wanted, yet now I understand it is a process that can be graceful depending on the humility of both involved. The inevitable upheavals that will ensue can be surrendered into gracefully, and with this surrender things and emotions will also arise. It is inevitable.

To think otherwise is illusion, as without direct experience certain things can be known or intuited, and other things remain unknown until directly experienced.

It is like making love as an intuition, and actually engaging in it physically: one can imagine from past experience what it was like, but as you change and make love with the beloved, it will be a totally new experience, as all parts of you, many untouched and unknown before, become engaged and now known. This is the process and one never knows what will arise until it happens.

It's all learning in humility.

Nicolya: I have a different viewpoint to you regarding the nature of twin flames, which I really do feel can relate in harmony all of the time. I feel that when we have reached a high degree of integration within, and are operating on a different level of consciousness to most, then this is a place where true beloveds finally meet.

I have been giving a lot of thought to twin souls and meditating on the difference between twin souls and twin flames. My sense is that what you share describes twin souls, for twin flames are rare. I do not know if I shall encounter my own in this physical form.

For me, twin souls are the lower octave of twin flames, but beyond the highest level of soul mate relationships, and this is what I believe you are speaking of. I think what is coming to consciousness within me is the difference between twin flames and twin souls. The former are rare, the latter less so, but still far less common than any other form of relationship.

Something in my knowing, my gnosis, compels me to gain insight around twin flames. Yeshua and Magdalene were or are twin flames—both so finely developed that they will have transcended emotion and dwell within the kingdom of feeling—which is a very different expression.

This is my humble viewpoint, Padma.

Glossary

consciousness Awareness of one's present state of existence including the physical, emotional, mental, psychological, energetic, psychic, and spiritual levels of being as well as the outside conditions that affect and influence them.

core process psychotherapy A humanistic, transpersonal form of psychotherapy based upon the Buddhist principles of compassion and mindfulness.

enlightenment The state in which a human being is fully spiritually awakened and in harmony with the true nature of All that Is.

epoch A notable period of time distinguished by a remarkable event that triggers a shift in collective and cosmic consciousness and/or gives rise to a new era.

gnosis Knowledge of conscious or spiritual truths through intuitive cognition. To know, yet not know how we know. Knowing that arises from an inborn capacity to know the unknown as known.

mudra Spiritual/religious dance iconography that utilizes an arrangement of body positions and hand gestures to express, anchor, or integrate an attitude, thought, or feeling of a particular spiritual wisdom teaching or deity.

paradigm A model or standard ideology built, accepted, maintained, and agreed upon by a community. The framework in which a group perceives reality. A belief system accepted by the members of a community that forms the boundaries in terms of perception and behavior. An inner or external worldview.

phenomenological Perceptive reality experienced from the subjective view of phenomena occurring within the field of consciousness. An experience of all the senses (at the same time) experiencing a singular phenomenon.

psychosynthesis psychotherapy A transpersonal, humanistic psychotherapy founded by Roberto Assagioli.

psychological shadow The psychologically wounded self. The unhealed, unintegrated ego. Dysfunctional behaviors and patterns experienced unconsciously at a personality level.

psycho-spiritual An equal balance of psychological and spiritual. The conscious processing of life as an opportunity to integrate body, emotions, mind, Soul, and Spirit as well as cultivate psychological and spiritual integration.

projection Unhealed, unintegrated, unowned, unconscious (or in some cases conscious) psychological content projected onto others or the environment.

restorative circles A group formed with the intent to resolve conflict and restore relationships between individuals and their community. Each member of the circle is treated as an equal with a common vision, to provide a safe place to harmoniously resolve conflict, become empowered, experience mutual benefit, become self-responsible, and gain a deeper understanding of each other, and how the personal conduct of one impacts on another, and the environment/community.

self (small _s_) Adapted self, wounded inner child. A personality-centered ego state of consciousness that creates the illusion and belief in individual personalities separate and divisible from the whole. Living from _me_. A psychologically unintegrated individual.

Self (capital _S_) Authentic Self, Soul child. A Self-centered (as in centered in Authentic Self) level of consciousness. The consciousness of the whole that can consciously observe and experience itself both subjectively and objectively. Living from _I_. A psychologically integrated individual.

self-actualization   To realize, develop, or achieve one's full potential. In Maslow's hierarchy of needs, self-actualization precedes the ultimate human evolutionary level of development: self-transcendence.

transference   The process of transferring unintegrated historical/psychological issues and/or joyful or painful memories of someone or a place or situation onto someone else, or another place or situation.

zero-point field   The energy that remains when all other energy is removed from a system. In quantum field theory, the zero-point field is the lowest energy state of a field, which generally contains no physical particles.

Resource Directory

The resources listed below have been selected as those that provide important ideas, support, and inspiration for conscious evolution.

ONLINE RESOURCES

Astrology for Conscious Evolution

Cherry Williams

thirteenheavens@hotmail.co.uk

Cherry has been a transpersonal astrologer for many years and now works specifically with charts for those on an active spiritual path. She works with people at energetic and cellular levels acting as a catalyst to aid each individual on his or her evolutionary journey.

Julia Bondi

juliaabondi@gmail.com

Julia has been an accomplished counseling astrologer, intuitive, teacher, and writer for more than thirty years. With degrees in clinical psychology and esoteric philosophy, she brings insight, clarity, and caring to her work.

Stephanie Azaria

www.thecosmicpath.com/about-stephanie

Stephanie Azaria is one of the most well-respected rising stars in the world of astrology today. She hosts a number of workshops designed to educate people about astrology as it relates to their individual charts. Attendees have called her workshops a profound self-awareness experience.

Conscious Art

Luke Owen

www.lukeowen.com

Luke Owen's artwork lifts the viewer toward transcendence of the historical self and toward Self-realization.

Consciousness Evolution

Avaaz

www.avaaz.org

Avaaz, which means "voice" in several European, Middle Eastern, and Asian languages, is a global Web movement to bring people-powered politics to decision-making everywhere.

Barbara Marx Hubbard

http://barbaramarxhubbard.com

A prolific author, visionary, social innovator, evolutionary thinker, and educator, Barbara Marx Hubbard is the cofounder and president of the Foundation for Conscious Evolution.

Charles Eisenstein

http://charleseisenstein.net

Author and speaker Charles Eisenstein is the author of *Sacred Economics* and *The Ascent of Humanity*.

Ervin Laszlo

www.ervinlaszlo.com

Ervin Laszlo is generally recognized as the founder of systems philosophy and general evolution theory, serving as founder-director of the General Evolution Research Group and as past president of the International Society for the Systems Sciences. He is the author or editor of eighty-three books, translated into as many as twenty-one languages, and has over four hundred articles and research papers and six volumes of piano recordings to his credit. His current work focuses on prospects for Humanity's future and the interconnecting cosmic field that underlies all. Ervin Laszlo is Founder and President of the Club of Budapest (www.clubofbudapest.org).

Findhorn Foundation

www.findhorn.org

A spiritual community, ecovillage, and international center for holistic education, the Findhorn Foundation is helping to unfold a new human consciousness and create a positive and sustainable future.

Kingsley Dennis

www.kingsleydennis.com

Writer, researcher, and futurist Kingsley Dennis is the author of *New Consciousness for a New World* and *The Struggle for Your Mind: Conscious Evolution and the Battle to Control How We Think.*

The New Consciousness Academy (NCA)

www.nicolyachristi.com

NCA is an online learning institute for psychological, conscious, and spiritual evolution in service of personal and global transformation. It has been founded by Nicolya Christi to offer affordable introductory and advanced online courses, on a vast range of evolutionary and transformational subjects, to people all around the world.

Positive TV

www.positivetv.tv

Looks to reach across generations and energize us with positivity at a time when we may feel overwhelmed by the negative prognosis for the future of humanity and the planet. In covering all aspects of human activity Positive TV looks to broaden the global conversation and raise questions about the world we live in and what sort of future we want to create.

Resilience Circles

http://localcircles.org

A Resilience Circle is a small group of ten to twenty people that comes together to increase personal security during these challenging times. Circles have three purposes: learning, mutual aid, and social action.

WorldShift International (WSI)

www.worldshiftinternational.org

WSI is a conscious evolution initiative that promotes and supports a world shift both externally within our current global systems, as well as internally on a personal level. The WSI website was created to provide resources that will help to empower individuals in their own evolutionary process, as well as an awareness for the urgent need for global change.

WorldShift Movement

www.facebook.com/WorldShiftMovement

A Movement "for the people" to co-create a peaceful and sustainable world on behalf of all the people and the Earth. Calls forth humanity to unite in the co-creation of peace, compassionate justice, sustainability, social innovation, and conscious evolution.

Empowering Health Resources

Allicin

www.allicin.co.uk

AllicinMax is a scientifically proven preventative and cure for most viruses, from the common cold, to airborne/contact viruses, to infections. Importantly it is the *only* product scientifically proven to successfully prevent and cure MRSA. Featured on UK national television programs, including the BBC News, allicin is described as the "mother" substance of garlic, which is responsible for the majority of its remarkable properties. The patented process used to make AllicinMax is the first to provide biologically active stabilized allicin.

Essiac Treatment

www.essiacinfo.org

Essiac is an herbal concoction composed of burdock, Indian rhubarb, sorrel, slippery elm, and other ingredients. It was developed by a nurse in Canada, Rene Caisse (Essiac is Caisse spelled backward). Caisse gave the formula to a company in Canada who markets the product today.

Gerson Therapy

www.gerson.org

The Gerson Institute is a nonprofit organization in San Diego, California, dedicated to providing education and training in the Gerson Therapy, an alternative, nontoxic treatment for cancer and other chronic degenerative diseases.

Hemp Oil THC

www.phoenixtearsplus.com

Medical marijuana is becoming more and more associated with anti-carcinogenic effects, which may prevent or delay the development of cancer. This means that cannabinoids offer cancer patients a therapeutic option in the treatment of highly invasive cancers.

Hoxsey Therapy

www.cancure.org/hoxsey_clinic.htm

Since 1963, this clinic has provided Hoxsey therapy, an herbal remedy developed by Harry Hoxsey in the 1920s. It was one of the first alternative cancer facilities in Mexico. In addition to the Hoxsey treatment, comprised of a liquid elixir containing a mixture of herbs and several topical salves, the clinic may also use other supplements, diet, nutrition, and chelation therapy. They treat most types of malignancies, but it is said to be especially effective with skin cancer (including melanoma) and breast cancer, and has been successful with some recurrent cancers and even with patients who have had radiation and/or chemotherapy.

Tullio Simoncini

www.curenaturalicancro.com

Dr. Simoncini, an oncologist in Rome, Italy, has pioneered sodium bicarbonate (NaHCO3) therapy as a means to treat cancer. The fundamental theory behind this treatment lies in the fact that, despite a number of variable factors, the formation and spreading of tumors is simply the result of the presence of a fungus.

Genuine Oracles

Anna Kaye

http://annakayedestinydoctor.com

Anna Kaye is an international clairvoyant and psychic medium, soul mentor, Reiki master and teacher, metaphysical teacher, intuitive counselor, and life coach.

Donna Maxine White

www.donnamaxine.com

A professional reader for more than twenty years, Donna uses her psychic and clairsentient abilities in many ways. She offers past life tarot readings and in-depth karmic palmistry readings, which help the soul clear blockages and work through karmic patterns.

Psychological Evolution

A good place to begin your exploration of resources for psychological evolution is to perform an Internet search of the following practices:

Body Centered Therapy
Core Process Psychotherapy
EFT—Emotional Freedom Therapy
Gestalt Therapy
Humanistic Psychotherapy
Psychosynthesis
Restorative Justice
Transpersonal Psychotherapy

Byron Katie

www.thework.com

The Work of Byron Katie is a way of identifying and questioning the thoughts that cause all the fear and suffering in the world.

Center for Nonviolent Communication

www.cnvc.org

A global organization, founded by Marshall B. Rosenberg, that supports the learning and sharing of NVC and helps people peacefully and effectively resolve conflicts in personal, organizational, and political settings. The NVC community is active in more than sixty-five countries around the world.

The Focusing Institute

www.focusing.org

Focusing teaches how to pause and create space for new possibilities. It is supported by the research of Gene Gendlin and colleagues at the University of Chicago. The Focusing Institute offers resources for those new to the practice as well as for experienced Focusers.

John Bradshaw

www.johnbradshaw.com

In his role as counselor, author, management consultant, theologian, philosopher, and public speaker, John Bradshaw has become one of the leading figures in the fields of addiction/recovery, family systems, relationships, spiritual and emotional growth, and management training.

Spiritual Evolution

Lama Surya Das

www.surya.org

Lama Surya Das is one of the foremost Western Buddhist meditation teachers and scholars, one of the main interpreters of Tibetan Buddhism in the West, and a leading spokesperson for the emerging American Buddhism. He is the author of thirteen books, including the bestselling *Awakening the Buddha Within.*

Pema Chodron

http://pemachodronfoundation.org

Beloved Buddhist teacher, author, nun, and mother, Pema Chodron has inspired millions of people around the world by her example and message of practicing peace in these turbulent times.

Thich Nhat Hanh

www.plumvillage.org

One of the best known and most respected Zen masters in the world today, poet, and peace and human rights activist Thich Nhat Hanh lives in Plum Village, the meditation community he founded in France in 1982. He continues to teach, write, and lead retreats worldwide on the art of mindful living.

BOOKS

Bradshaw, John. *Healing the Shame That Binds You*. Deerfield Beach, Fla.: HCI, 2005.

———. *Homecoming: Reclaiming and Championing Your Inner Child*. New York: Bantam, 1992.

Christi, Nicolya. *The Diamond Heart Prayer Meditation and Affirmation*. Self-published, 2012.

———. *Ego/Self: A Fairytale*. Self-published, 2012.

———. *Meditation*. Self-published, 2013.

———. *New Human—New Earth: Living in the 5th Dimension*. Self-published, 2012.

———. *2012: A Clarion Call: Your Soul's Purpose in Conscious Evolution*. Rochester, Vt.: Bear & Company, 2011.

Chodron, Pema. *When Things Fall Apart: Heart Advice for Difficult Times*. Boston: Shambhala, 2000.

Cori, Jasmin Lee. *The Emotionally Absent Mother: A Guide to Self-Healing and Getting the Love You Missed*. New York: Experiment, 2010.

Dagher, Emmanuel. *Easy Breezy Miracle: A Fun, Exciting & Simple Guide to Creating a Miraculous Life*. Self-published, 2012.

Das, Lama Surya. *Awakening the Buddha Within: Tibetan Wisdom for the Western World*. New York: Broadway Books, 1998.

———. *Letting Go of the Person You Used to Be: Lessons on Change, Loss, and Spiritual Transformation.* New York: Three Rivers Press, 2004.

Dennis, Kingsley. *New Consciousness for a New World: How to Thrive in Transitional Times and Participate in the Coming Spiritual Renaissance.* Rochester, Vt.: Inner Traditions, 2011.

———. *The Struggle for Your Mind: Conscious Evolution and the Battle to Control How We Think.* Rochester, Vt.: Inner Traditions, 2012.

Eisenstein, Charles. *Sacred Economics: Money, Gift, and Society in the Age of Transition.* Berkeley, Calif.: Evolver Editions, 2011.

Gendlin, Eugene T. *Focusing.* New York: Bantam, 1982.

Hubbard, Barbara Marx. *Conscious Evolution: Awakening Our Social Potential.* Novato, Calif.: New World Library, 1998.

———. *Emergence: The Shift from Ego to Essence.* Charlottesville, Va.: Hampton Roads, 2012.

Katie, Byron. *Loving What Is: Four Questions That Can Change Your Life.* New York: Three Rivers Press, 2003.

Laszlo, Ervin. *Science and the Akashic Field: An Integral Theory of Everything.* Rochester, Vt.: Inner Traditions, 2007.

Laszlo, Ervin, and Kingsley Dennis. *Dawn of the Akashic Age: New Consciousness, Quantum Resonance, and the Future of the World.* Rochester, Vt.: Inner Traditions, 2013.

Levine, Peter. *In an Unspoken Voice: How the Body Releases Trauma.* Berkeley, Calif.: North Atlantic Books, 2013.

Nhat Hanh, Thich. *Reconciliation: Healing the Inner Child.* Berkeley, Calif.: Parallax Press, 2010.

Pradervand, Pierre. *The Gentle Art of Blessing: A Simple Practice That Will Transform You and Your World.* New York: Atria, 2009.

Rosenberg, Marshall. *Nonviolent Communication: A Language of Life.* Encinitas, Calif.: PuddleDancer Press, 2003.

About the Author

Nicolya Christi is an author, writer, and evolutionary guide. She is the founder of the New Consciousness Academy, the International Community of Light, and WorldShift Movement; cofounder of WorldShift International; and a coinitiator of WorldShift 2012. The author of *2012, A Clarion Call: Your Soul's Purpose in Conscious Evolution*, *2012, A Clarion Call: A Book of Meditations*, *Ego/Self: A Fairytale*, *New Human—New Earth: Living in the 5th Dimension*, *The Diamond Heart Prayer Meditation and Affirmation*, and *Meditation*, she lives in Rennes-le-Chateau, southern France.

For more information, visit www.nicolyachristi.com. Readers can also meet Nicolya on her Facebook page, which she utilizes as a teaching platform: www.facebook.com/nicolyac.

Index

Page numbers in *italics* represent illustrations.